Eclipse

www.**rbooks**.co.uk

Also by Nicholas Clee

DON'T SWEAT THE AUBERGINE

Eclipse

Nicholas Clee

BANTAM PRESS

LONDON · TORONTO · SYDNEY · AUCKLAND · JOHANNESBURG

TRANSWORLD PUBLISHERS
61–63 Uxbridge Road, London W5 5SA
A Random House Group Company
www.rbooks.co.uk

First published in Great Britain
in 2009 by Bantam Press
an imprint of Transworld Publishers

A CIP catalogue record for this book
is available from the British Library.

ISBN 9780593059838

Addresses for Random House Group Ltd companies outside
the UK can be found at: www.randomhouse.co.uk
The Random House Group Ltd Reg. No. 954009

The Random House Group Limited supports The Forest Stewardship Council (FSC),
the leading international forest-certification organization. All our titles that are printed
on Greenpeace-approved FSC-certified paper carry the FSC logo. Our paper procurement
policy can be found at www.rbooks.co.uk/environment

Typeset in 13.25/15pt Perpetua
by Falcon Oast Graphic Art Ltd.
Printed and bound in the UK by
CPI Mackays, Chatham ME5 8TD

2 4 6 8 10 9 7 5 3 1

Mixed Sources
Product group from well-managed
forests and other controlled sources
www.fsc.org Cert no. TT-COC-2139
© 1996 Forest Stewardship Council
FSC

For Nicolette, Rebecca and Laura

Contents

Prologue

GO TO THE RACES, anywhere in the world, and you'll be watching horses who are relatives of Eclipse. The vast majority of them are descended from Eclipse's male line; if you trace back their ancestry through their fathers, their fathers' fathers, and so on, you come, some twenty generations back, to him. He is the most influential stallion in the history of the Thoroughbred. Two and a half centuries after his imperious, undefeated career, he remains the undisputed paragon of his sport.

The story of this career begins on a spring morning in 1769, at a trial on Epsom Downs. Scorching across the turf towards a small group of spectators is a chestnut with a white blaze. Toiling in his wake is a single rival, who will never catch him – not if they race to the ends of the earth.

Among the witnesses at this awe-inspiring display are two men who, according to the tradition of the Sport of Kings, should not be associated with the horse who will become its greatest exponent. One, Eclipse's owner, is a meat salesman, William Wildman. The second, who wants to own Eclipse, is an Irish adventurer and gambler.

Dennis O'Kelly arrived in London some twenty years earlier, full of energy and optimism and ambition. He has had his ups and downs, including an affair with a titled lady and a spell in prison, but at last – thanks to his gambling abilities and to the remarkable success of his companion, the leading brothel madam of the day – he is starting to rise in the world.

What Dennis does not know is that certain sections of the establishment will never accept him. What he does know, as with quickening pulse he follows the progress of the speeding chestnut, is that this horse is his destiny.

1

The Chairman

L ONDON, 1748. The capital is home to some 650,000 inhabitants, more than 10 per cent of the population of England.
What image of Georgian metropolitan life comes to mind? You
may have a Canaletto-inspired view of an elegant square.
Bewigged men and women with hooped skirts are strolling; there
are a few carriages, and perhaps a wagon; the gardens are trim; the
houses are stately. Or you may be picturing the London of
Hogarth. The street is teeming, and riotous: drunks lie in the
gutter, spewing; dogs and pickpockets weave among the crowd;
through a window, you can see a prostitute entertaining her client;
from the window above, someone is tipping out the contents of a
chamber pot.

Both images are truthful.[1] London is a sophisticated city of
fashion, an anarchic city of vice, and other cities too. In the West
End are the titled, the wealthy, and the ton (the smart set); in the
City are the financiers, merchants and craftsmen; prostitutes and
theatre folk congregate in Covent Garden; north of Covent
Garden, in St Giles's, and in the East End and south of the Thames,

[1] Canaletto's version may be underpopulated, however, as a result of his use of
a camera obscura, which failed to capture many moving objects.

are the slums, where an entire family may inhabit one small room, and where disease, alcoholism and crime are rampant. 'If one considers the destruction of all morality, decency and modesty,' wrote Henry Fielding, the author of the exuberant comic novel *Tom Jones*, 'the swearing, whoredom and drunkenness which is eternally carrying on in these houses on the one hand, and the excessive poverty and misery of most of the inhabitants on the other, it seems doubtful whether they are most the objects of detestation or compassion.' Among the native populations of these districts is a substantial admixture of Irish immigrants. A new arrival, with some modest savings and a sunny determination to make a name for himself, is a young man called Dennis O'Kelly.

Dennis was born in about 1725. His father, Andrew, was a smallholder in Tullow, about fifty miles south-west of Dublin. Dennis and his brother, Philip, received little education, and were expected to start earning their livings almost as soon as they entered their teens. (There were also two sisters, who made good marriages.) Philip began a career as a shoemaker. Dennis had grander ambitions. Soon, finding Tullow too small to contain his optimistic energy, he set out for Dublin.

The discovery that Dubliners regarded him as an uneducated yokel barely dented his confidence. Charm, vigour and quick wits would see him through, he felt; and he was right, then and thereafter. A few days after his arrival in the city, he saw a well-dressed woman slip in the street, and rushed to her aid. There was no coach nearby, so Dennis offered his arm to support the woman's walk home, impressing her with his courtesy. She asked Dennis about his circumstances and background. Although he gave as much gloss to his answer as he could, he was heard with a concerned frown. You must be careful, the woman advised him: Dublin is a very wicked place, and a young man such as you might easily fall into bad company.

People who give such warnings are usually the ones you need to avoid. But this woman was to be one of several patronesses who would ease Dennis's passage through life. She was a widow in her thirties, and the owner of a coffee house, where she hired Dennis as a waiter. Under her tutelage he lost, or learned to disguise, his rough edges, grew accomplished in his job, and graduated to become her lover. There was supplementary income to be earned by defeating the customers at billiards. It was a pleasant arrangement. It could not satisfy Dennis, though. Once he had amassed a fortune of £50 (about £6,500 in today's money, but then a modest annual income for a middle-class provincial household), he said farewell to his mistress and made his way to London.

This account of Dennis O'Kelly's early progress comes from a sketch 'by our ingenious correspondent D.L.' that appeared in *Town & Country* magazine in 1770, just before the end of Eclipse's racing career. It offered the fullest portrait of Dennis until the publication in 1788, a year after his death, of a racy work entitled *The Genuine Memoirs of Dennis O'Kelly, Esq: Commonly Called Count O'Kelly*. The book belonged to a thriving genre of brief lives, hastily produced and written by hacks (the term 'memoirs' applied to biography as well as autobiography). Their tone was often cheerfully defamatory, and entirely suited to portraying the riotous, scandalous, vainglorious Dennis. But while no doubt legendary in spirit, and certainly unreliable in some details, the *Genuine Memoirs* do tell in outline a true story, verifiable from other sources, including primary ones. It must be admitted, however, that the anecdotes of Dennis's adventures in his younger days seem to be the ones for which 'D.L.' and the author of the *Genuine Memoirs* (who sometimes differ) allowed their imaginations the freest rein.

Dennis arrived in the capital with the qualification only of being able to write his own name. He spoke with a strong accent, which the *Genuine Memoirs* characterized as 'the broadest and the most offensive brogue that his nation, perhaps, ever produced', and 'the very reverse of melody'. (Various contemporary chroniclers of Dennis's exploits delighted in representing his speech,

THE
GENUINE MEMOIRS

OF

Dennis O'Kelly, Efq.

COMMOLNY CALLED

COUNT O'KELLY:

Containing many curious and interefting Anecdotes of that
CELEBRATED CHARACTER, and his COAD-
JUTORS on the TURF and in the FIELD, with
a Variety of authentic, fingular, and entertaining
MILITIA MANOEUVRES, never before publifhed.

LONDON:

Printed for C. STALKER, STATIONERS-COURT,
LUDGATE-HILL.

M DCC LXXXVIII.

With a typo ('commolny') indicating hasty production, The Genuine
Memoirs *appeared shortly after Dennis O'Kelly's death and offered a
racy portrait, uncompromised by notions of accuracy.*

peppering it with liberal exclamations of 'by Jasus'.) He was five feet eleven inches tall, and muscular, with a rough-hewn handsomeness. He was charming, confident and quick-witted. He believed that he could rise high, and mix with anyone; and, for the enterprising and lucky few, eighteenth-century society accommodated such aspirations. 'Men are every day starting up from obscurity to wealth,' Daniel Defoe wrote. London was a place where, in the opinion of Dr Johnson's biographer James Boswell, 'we may be in some degree whatever character we choose'. Dennis held also a native advantage, according to the coiner of a popular saying: 'Throw an Irishman into the Thames at London Bridge, naked at low-water, and he will come up at Westminster-Bridge, at high water, with a laced coat and a sword.'

In the *Town & Country* version of Dennis's early years in London, he relied immediately on his wits. Dennis, the ingenious D.L. reported, took lodgings on his arrival in London at a guinea a week (a guinea was £1 1s, or £1.05 in decimal coinage), and began to look around for a rich woman to marry. Needing to support himself until the provider of his financial requirements came along, he decided that gambling would earn him a living, and he frequented the tables at the Bedford Coffee House in Covent Garden and other smart venues. In the convivial company of fellow Irish expatriates, he played hazard – a dice game. Very soon, his new friends took all his money.

'By Jasus,' Dennis said to himself, 'this is t'other side of enough – and so poor Dennis must look out for a place again.' ('D.L.' had some fun with this story.) He got a position as captain's servant on a ship bound for Lisbon. Sea journeys were hazardous, but could be lucrative if they delivered their cargoes successfully. Dennis was lucky, and got back to London with sufficient funds to support a second stab at a gambling career. This time he avoided hazard, and his expatriate chums, and stuck to billiards.

Another new friend promoted his marital ambitions, suggesting that they form a partnership to court two sisters, each of whom had a fortune of £1,000 a year. It was the work of a week. The partners did not want their marriages to be legally binding, so they hired John Wilkinson, a clergyman who specialized in conducting illegal ceremonies at the Savoy Chapel (and who was later transported for the practice). Before the honeymoon was over, Dennis had managed to persuade his friend to entrust his new wealth to him. Then he absconded. He spent time in Scarborough, attended the races at York, and cut a figure in Bath and in other watering-places. It was some time before he returned to London, where he found, to his satisfaction, that his wife — with whom he had no legally binding contract — had become a servant, and that his former friend had emigrated to India. They could not touch him.

However, Dennis again struggled to earn his keep. The genteel façade that was necessary in the gambling profession was expensive to maintain. And he still had a lot to learn. In order to dupe 'pigeons', as suckers or marks were known, he employed a more experienced accomplice, with whom he had to share the proceeds. Before long, Dennis fell into debt again.

Version two of Dennis's story, from the *Genuine Memoirs*, has come to be the more widely accepted. In this one, he made use of his physical prowess. Leaving behind several creditors in Ireland, he made his way to London and found a position as a sedan chairman. Sedan chairs, single-seater carriages conveyed by horizontal poles at the front and back, were the taxis of the day. There were public, licensed ones, carried by the likes of Dennis and his (unnamed) partner; and there were private ones, often elaborately decorated and carried by men who were the antecedents of chauffeurs. The chairs had hinged roofs, allowing the passenger to walk in from the front, and they could be brought into houses, so that the passenger need not be exposed to the elements. Dennis, who was never shy or deferential, took advantage of the access to make himself known above and below stairs: 'Many and oftentimes,' the *Genuine Memoirs* reported, 'has he carried great personages, male

The Covent Garden Morning Frolick *by L. P. Boitard (1747). Betty
Careless, a bagnio proprietor (a bagnio was a bathing house, usually a
brothel too), travels to work in a sedan chair. Hitching a ride, without a
thought for the poor chairmen, is one of her lovers, Captain Montague.
Dennis O'Kelly was the 'front legs' of a chair.*

and female, whose secret histories have been familiar to his knowledge.'

The physical burdens were the least of the trials of the job. Chairmen carried their fares through London streets that were irregularly paved, and pockmarked with bumps and holes. There was dust when it was dry, and deep mud when it was wet. The ingredients of the mud included ash, straw, human and animal faeces, and dead cats and dogs. The winters were so fierce that the Thames, albeit a shallower river than it is now, sometimes froze over. Pipes burst, drenching the streets with water that turned rapidly to ice. Illumination was infrequent, as the duty of lighting thoroughfares lay in part with the inhabitants, who were not conscientious; people hired 'link-boys' to light their journeys with firebrands. In daylight, too, it was often hard to see far ahead: London smogs, even before the smoky Victorian era, could reduce visibility to a few feet. There was intense, cacophonous noise: carriages on cobbles; horses' hooves; animals being driven to market; musicians busking; street traders shouting.

The chairmen slalomed through this chaos with the ruthlessness of modern bike messengers. They yelled 'By your leave, sir!', but otherwise were uncompromising: a young French visitor to London, taking his first stroll, failed to respond to the yells quickly enough and was knocked over four times. Chairmen could set a fast pace because the distances were not huge. A slightly later view of the city from Highgate (the print is in the British Library) shows the built-up area extending only a short distance east of St Paul's (by far the most imposing landmark) and no further west than Westminster Abbey. To the north, London began at a line just above Oxford Street, and ended in the south just beyond the Thames. Outside these limits were fields and villages. The chairmen carried their customers mostly within the boundaries of the West End.

Dennis was in St James's when he met his second significant patroness (after the Dublin coffee house owner). Some three hundred chairs were in competition, but this November day offered plenty of custom: it was the birthday of George II. Horse-drawn coaches could make no progress through the gridlocked streets, and the chairmen were in demand. A lady's driver, frustrated on his journey to the palace (St James's Palace was then the principal royal residence), hailed Dennis from his stalled vehicle. Dennis leaped to the lady's assistance, accompanying her to his chair and scattering the onlookers who had jostled forward to view such a fine personage. He 'acted with such powers and magnanimity, that her ladyship conceived him to be a regeneration of Hercules or Hector, and her opinion was by no means altered when she beheld the powerful elasticity of his muscular motions on the way to the Royal residence. Dennis touched her ladyship's guinea, and bowed in return for a bewitching smile which accompanied it.'[2]

You may conclude that this mock-heroic description is an acknowledgement that the story is preposterous. But the eighteenth century was a period of great social, and sexual, intermingling. In some ways (ways that Dennis would learn about, but never respect), the class structure was rigid; in others, it mattered little. Important men conducted open affairs with prostitutes and other humble women, and from time to time married them. Not so many grand women took humble men as lovers, but a few did. Lady Henrietta Wentworth married her footman. Adventurous sex lives were common. 'Many feminine libertines may be found amongst young women of rank,' observed Lady Mary Wortley Montagu, the renowned letter writer. Lady Harley was said to have become pregnant by so many lovers that, the historian Roy Porter recorded, her children were known as the 'Harleian miscellany'.

The day following Dennis's encounter with Lady — (the

---

[2] From the *Genuine Memoirs*. I have amplified some of the details of the story of Dennis and Lady —.

Genuine Memoirs gives no name or initials), he was loitering outside White's Chocolate House, musing on her smile, when an elderly woman asked him the way to Bolton Row in Piccadilly. She offered him a shilling to escort her there. When they arrived, she invited him in from the cold to take a drink. The mistress of the house greeted Dennis and asked him whether he knew of any chairmen looking for a place. 'Yes, Madam,' Dennis answered, 'an' that I do: I should be very glad to be after recommending myself, because I know myself, and love myself better than any one else.' Well, then, the woman replied, he should go to the house of Lady — in Hanover Square, mention no name, but say that he had heard of the vacant position. 'God in heaven bless you,' Dennis exclaimed, draining his substantial glass of brandy.

The next morning, Dennis dressed himself as finely as he could, and presented himself in Hanover Square. He made the right impression, got the job, at a salary of £30 a year, and started work the next day. Standing in the hall, self-conscious in his new livery and excited at this access to grandeur, he looked up to see his mistress descending the staircase. She was of course the same Lady — whose teasing smile had occupied his thoughts since their journey to the palace. But she offered no hint of recognition. She hurried into her chair, making it known that she wished to be conveyed to the Opera House. Her expression on arrival was more encouraging; and when, at the end of her appointment, she came out of the theatre, she blessed Dennis with another smile, more provocative than before. Taking his hand, she squeezed it gently round a purse. He felt his strength liquefy; a tremendous effort of concentration was required to force his trembling limbs to carry the chair safely home. Alone, he opened the purse, to find that it contained five guineas.

The next day was busy. No sooner had Dennis returned from an errand to the mantua maker (a mantua was a skirt and bodice open in the front) than he was off again to the milliner, and then to the hairdresser, and then to the perfumer. Last, there was a parcel to deliver to Bolton Row – specifically, to the house where he had received the tip-off about his job.

Again, he was invited in, but this time ushered into a back parlour, where – as the *Genuine Memoirs* described the scene – a giant fire was roaring and where the only other illumination came from four candles. Dennis sat himself close to the blaze, the delicious heat dispersing the cold in his bones. A young woman, with shyly averted face, brought him a tankard of mulled wine. He drained half of it in a gulp. More warmth suffused him; he did not want to move from this room. He looked at the girl, who for some reason was loitering by the door, and got a general impression of comeliness. He asked her what she was called. She replied obliquely: she had been asked to entertain Mr Kelly[3] until her mistress should return, 'and indeed I am happy to be in your company, Sir, for I do not like to be alone'.

This was promising, Dennis thought. 'Upon my soul,' he asserted, 'I am equally happy, and wish to be more so. Come sit by me.'

The girl approached, sat, and turned towards him. She was Lady ——. They fell on each other; bodices, and other garments too, were ripped. As evening turned to night, and as the fire subsided, they enjoyed mutual happiness. At last, Lady —— said she must leave. Exchanging her servant's clothes for her usual ones, and leaving Dennis with another purse, she sought her coach, which had been waiting a few doors away.

Dennis, more dazedly, reassembled his attire. Returning to the workaday world was a wearying prospect. But there was another surprise, less welcome, in store. The door of the parlour opened, and the old woman whom he had conducted to the house three days earlier entered. You have done well for yourself, she observed; such fortune would never have befallen you had it not

---

[3] Dennis styled himself 'Kelly' – the anglicized version of his name – during his early years in London.

been for my assistance. No doubt you would want to reward me accordingly – my mistress and I depend on taking advantage of such eventualities. Your mistress gave you a purse earlier, and, as a man of honour, you should share it.

Dennis was nonplussed. Surely this woman had no claim on him? 'By Jasus,' he replied, 'but she never gave me a single guinea.'

The woman smiled complacently. 'Come, my dear creature,' she said (pronouncing it 'creter'), 'come along with me, and I'll show you the difference.'

She took him by the hand, and led him to the front parlour. On the wall was a small looking glass. She removed it, revealing an aperture, and invited Dennis to look through. He got a fine view of the back parlour, and particularly of the part of it near the fire. Resignedly, he reached for the purse, looked inside, and saw that it contained an enormous sum: twenty-five guineas. ''Tis only my right that I take ten,' the woman told him, 'as I must account for it to my mistress.' Dennis knew when he was cornered. He handed over the money.

This dampener did not submerge his enthusiasm for the affair, which continued happily for several months. It was both delightful and profitable. But Dennis was not Lady —'s only side-line. The *Genuine Memoirs* said that she took lovers among her own set, too; and, unfortunately, Lord — was not as liberal in his attitudes to such behaviour as were some eighteenth-century husbands. He threw her out of doors, and divorced her. With Dennis's mistress went Dennis's job.

After a taste of life in Hanover Square, Dennis was not inclined to return to hauling a licensed sedan chair. He might continue to enjoy the high life, he reasoned, if he lived by his wits. He frequented the Vauxhall pleasure gardens, where, for a shilling a ticket, people gathered to walk, eat, listen to music, and stare at one another. He spent many hours in coffee houses, at tennis courts, and at billiard tables, where he picked up some money as both marker (keeper of the score) and player. He made notable friends, among them the Duke of Richmond and Sir William Draper, the soldier. Everyone was clubbable — while he had money.

As the money ran out, Dennis continued to spend. He had discovered an addiction to extravagance, and he thought he could charm, or dupe, his creditors. But there was a way of taking revenge on people who did not honour the money they owed: you could get them jailed. Dennis's creditors sued, and saw him confined to the Fleet, the debtors' prison.

The year was 1756. Five years would pass before Dennis regained his freedom. It was the disaster of his life. But it led him to the woman who would be both his lifelong companion and his partner in making his fortune.

The Whore's last Shift.

The Whore's Last Shift. *A once-fashionable 'Cyprian lass' (one of the arch phrases by which Charlotte Hayes and her contemporaries were known) is down on her luck. On the table is* Harris's List of Covent Garden Ladies, *first compiled by Charlotte's sometime lover, Samuel Derrick.*

The Bawd

CHARLOTTE HAYES FLOURISHED in what one writer described as the 'golden age' of prostitution. It was golden for the clients, perhaps, particularly for the ones who could afford to frequent the splendid serails (harems – French terms and practices were fashionable in this world) that adorned eighteenth-century London. It was golden for a few, a very few, of the prostitutes. But there were ten thousand of them in the capital, according to Roy Porter; Johann Wilhelm von Archenholz, a contemporary visitor, put the figure at fifty thousand. For most of these women, beginning their careers in a kind of slavery and ending up in destitution and disease, gold was elusive.

You could not miss them. Von Archenholz wrote, 'At all seasons of the year, they sally out towards the dusk, arrayed in the most gaudy colours, and fill the principal streets. They accost the passengers, and offer to accompany them: they even surround them in crowds, stop and overwhelm them with caresses and entreaties. The better kind, however, content themselves with walking around till they themselves are addressed.' It was a happy hunting ground for James Boswell, who, like a bat or an owl, would set out as darkness fell. Sex in the open air gave him a particular frisson. He disported with a 'strong, plump, good-humoured girl called Nanny Baker' in St James's Park, and, armed with a condom, 'At the bottom of the Haymarket I picked up a strong, jolly young damsel, and taking her under the arm I conducted her to Westminster Bridge, and then in armour complete did I engage her upon this noble edifice. The whim of doing it there with the Thames rolling below amused me very much.'

What a rogue! We might regard Boswell's lusty antics indulgently, as mere boisterous transgression, from our vantage point two and a half centuries later. This was not a jolly industry, though. Von Archenholz saw the seamy side: 'I have beheld with a surprise, mingled with terror, girls from eight to nine years old make a proffer of their charms; and such is the corruption of the human heart, that even they have their lovers.' He also observed, without much sympathy, the fate of prostitutes later in life: 'Towards midnight, when the young women have disappeared, and the streets become deserted, then the old wretches, of 50 or 60 years of age, descend from their garrets, and attack the intoxicated passengers, who are often prevailed upon to satisfy their passions in the open street with these female monsters.'

In *A Harlot's Progress* (1732), William Hogarth depicted one method of recruitment to the profession. Moll Hackabout, young and fresh of face, arrives in London on the York wagon, to be met by an ingratiating woman. The woman offers lodging and a position; but in fact Moll's immediate future is to be raped by the leering man in the background.[4] The woman in Hogarth's print has been identified as the bawd Mother Needham (madams were often, ironically, 'mother'), and the leering man as Colonel Francis Charteris, who bore the unappetizing sobriquet Rape-Master of Great Britain. Both had died the year before the print appeared, Charteris of unknown causes and Needham following an appearance in the pillory, where she had received an enthusiastic pelting

---

[4] I am sorry to say that Charlotte Hayes, some years later, would not be above such stratagems.

by the mob. In Hogarth's subsequent prints, Moll Hackabout tastes a brief period of prosperity as the mistress of a rich Jewish merchant before declining into poverty, the workhouse and death.

Charlotte Hayes was (like Dennis O'Kelly) born in about 1725, possibly in Covent Garden – one historian has found a Joseph Hayes living in Tavistock Street at the time. She rose from obscurity alongside two other beauties, Nancy Jones and Lucy Cooper, whose fans congregated at venues including the Bedford Arms on the Strand and Ben Jonson's Head on Little Russell Street. Nancy's and Lucy's stories illustrate the precariousness of their calling. Nancy lost her looks, along with her ability to command admirers, to smallpox, and died of syphilis at the age of twenty-five. Lucy, 'lewder than all the whores in Charles's reign', found a rich protector in Sir Orlando Bridgeman, a wealthy baronet. Thanks to him, she was 'exalted from a basket to a coach' (a basket was a cheap seat on a stagecoach). But in 1765 Bridgeman died, leaving Lucy an annuity with the stipulation that she quit her profession. She ignored his wishes, with decreasing success. After several periods of imprisonment, she died impoverished in 1772.

The trick was to find a wealthy lover, be kept by him in style, but to hold other men in reserve should he go off you, or die. If you had the entrepreneurial skills, you could try setting up as a madam. Both routes offered golden rewards for the most skilful and the luckiest, in an era when keeping paid mistresses and visiting brothels were stylish activities, as long as they were conducted in the manner of a gentleman. Beautiful and charismatic courtesans such as Nancy Jones (briefly) and Lucy Cooper, as well as the likes of Fanny Murray, Kitty Fisher and Harriet Powell, were celebrated figures of the day, and had many aristocratic admirers. Nancy Parsons was the lover of the Duke of Grafton, Prime Minister during the 1760s – although the Duke went beyond the bounds of propriety by entertaining her in his box at the theatre, just a few seats away from his estranged wife. A few years later,

Mary Robinson and Elizabeth Armistead were lovers of the Prince of Wales, the future George IV. Sometimes these affairs ended in marriage. Elizabeth Armistead became the wife of Charles James Fox, the Whig politician, while Harriet Powell bagged the Earl of Seaforth.

Charlotte found no such happy outcome to her career as a courtesan, but, blessed with great entrepreneurial and marketing skills, she picked herself up, to go on to triumph as a madam.

She came of age as the protégée of one Mrs Ward, whose methods of keeping her girls subservient she would emulate. She received an education, because a patina of culture would be an asset in her destined career.[5] When Charlotte reached maturity, she came up for sale. Mrs Ward would have been able to charge up to £50, maybe even £100, for brokering a night with a beautiful young virgin; and she may have done it several times. Refreshing her charges' maidenhoods was another ploy that Charlotte would copy.

Although a young woman might claim to be deflowered more than once, she could not keep doing so indefinitely, and the time came when the ambitious and talented hoped to find wealthy lovers. A mistress could expect lavish apartments and the equivalent of a platinum credit card. She insisted on acquiring the finest clothes, jewels, hats, gloves and other accessories, and on mixing with people of fashion and position. But she maintained this lifestyle only for as long as she continued to bewitch her lover. Fortunately, Charlotte was bewitching. She had brown hair and grey eyes; her features were rounded and girlish, and at their most alluring with very little make-up. Hers was 'a countenance as open as her heart', and her deportment was dignified without affectation.

A bawd is necessarily a cold and sometimes a cruel person, but Charlotte earned indulgence even from chroniclers of the most scandalous episodes of her career. Looking back at the

---

[5] Charlotte did not sign her name with the éclat of Dennis O'Kelly, but she was more literate than he.

contemporary records, one wishes that they contained a little more venom, which might have drawn out more of her personality. Dennis O'Kelly leaps off the pages of those who describe him, while Charlotte – perhaps because she suppressed true feeling, or perhaps because she is portrayed only by men – is unfathomable.

Her greatest conquest was Robert Tracey, usually given the moniker 'Beau', applied to the most dashing bucks of the era. Tracey had accomplishments. 'Abstract him from women, and he was a man far above mediocrity'; he possessed a good library, and felt that reading was so important that he would always take a book to study while having his hair cut. He was also a libertine, and, from Charlotte's point of view, a delightful spendthrift. Still more delightful was his submission to her. Hitherto a man of fleeting affections, he found in Charlotte the love of his life. 'She had him so much at her command that she could fleece him at will' – in the words of the ribald chronicle *Nocturnal Revels*. Craving some extra cash, she would call on Tracey at his chambers in the Temple, tell him that she would not stay unless he play dice with her at a guinea a throw, take his money at each throw she won, and neglect to pay up at each throw she lost. After about a quarter of an hour, once she had amassed a reasonable sum, she would 'bounce away and laugh at him'.

Her other lovers included the poet Samuel Derrick, who offered no pecuniary attractions, as he never made a living from his verse. His most profitable venture, and his magnum opus, was *Harris's List of Covent Garden Ladies*, a publication with a distinctively eighteenth-century flavour. Appearing each year in a style we associate with more conventional guidebooks, it offered Derrick's intimate and witty pen-portraits of the finest prostitutes in London, along with warnings about ones to avoid.[6] But his

---

[6] Two examples: 'A smart little black gypsy [Miss Cross], with a very endearing symmetry of parts; has an odd way of wriggling herself about, and can communicate the most exquisite sensations when she is well paid'; 'She [Pol Forrester] has an entrance to the palace of pleasure as wide as a church door.'

involvement with the bestselling annual came after his affair with Charlotte had ended. While it was going on, he was simply a man 'of a diminutive size, with reddish hair and a vacant countenance', and with no funds. Perhaps Charlotte loved him. Certainly he was always fond of her, referring to her as 'my old friend and mistress Charlotte Hayes'. And no wonder he was grateful. In addition to enjoying her charms, he received entertainment from her 'in the most sumptuous manner' at the Shakespeare or Rose taverns, with Tracey picking up bills of up to £40.[7]

For unknown reasons, Charlotte and Tracey separated. Thanks to his own and Charlotte's efforts, Tracey's finances were in disarray; and then his health went. He died in 1756, leaving Charlotte merely £5 with which to buy a mourning ring. She was unable to find anyone to take his place, and soon she too fell into debt. On 14 June 1758, the Court of King's Bench sent her to the Marshalsea jail; three days later, she transferred to the Fleet. A Fleet record lists an outstanding sum of £45, and separate debts of five shillings (25p) and ten shillings, to a certain Jane Bateman.

Charlotte Hayes and Dennis O'Kelly took their reverses well, refusing to allow their circumstances to cramp their styles. While in the Fleet, Charlotte, in the words of *The Genuine Memoirs of Dennis O'Kelly*, 'did not forget to perform her midnight orgies, or sacrifice to the powers of love and wine'. Dennis was reduced to impoverishment, alleviated only slightly by a job in the tap room (bar), but he never lost his jovial manner. The Fleet was a place where, albeit in depressing and limited surroundings, you could try to lead some semblance of a normal life.

The prison had been built in 1197, near the Fleet river. It adjoined what is now Farringdon Street (to the north-east of Fleet Street). By the mid-eighteenth century it housed mostly debtors –

---

[7] As we have seen, that was £10 more than Dennis O'Kelly's annual salary as Lady —'s chairman.

about 110 of them in Charlotte's and Dennis's time, although sometimes there were up to three hundred, along with their families.

Again, Hogarth – whose father had a spell in the Fleet – gives us a flavour of the scene. Tom Rakewell, hero of *The Rake's Progress*, sits gloomily beneath a meagre grilled window, in a small room shared with two other debtors but containing, in the picture, ten people. One of them is Tom's wife, who is berating him; on his other side, a boy runner and a gaoler are demanding money. A note on the table is from the manager of Covent Garden Theatre, and says: 'Sir, I have read your play and find it will not do.' (For some writers, this print has particular power to chill.)

Tom is not a prisoner in the sense of one enduring punishment for crimes. Rather, he is in confinement until he settles his debts or reaches agreement with his creditors, and, in common with his fellow inmates, he has a key to his room. Some debtors went to the Fleet voluntarily: it offered a way of avoiding payment. Taking to the life there, they would remain inside to spite the people demanding money from them. A Mr Yardley, who had an income of £700 a year, spent ten years in the Fleet owing £100; on his death in 1735 he left in his room items valued at £5,000.

The Fleet boasted a number of distinguished inmates. John Donne, the poet, did time there, at the instigation of his father-in-law. William Wycherley, author of Restoration comedies, was in the Fleet for seven years. William Penn, the founder of Pennsylvania, got into financial trouble and lived for a while in the Rules of the Fleet – an area outside the walls. In fiction, the inmates included Tobias Smollett's Peregrine Pickle (1751), who was waited on by a former Guards officer, and, alliteratively, Charles Dickens's Mr Pickwick (1836–7).

One of the sadder declines of Dennis's and Charlotte's era was that of Mrs Cornelys, impresario of theatrically staged promenades at Carlisle House in Soho. They were, in the words of diarist and rake William Hickey,[8] 'quite the rage'. Each Sunday evening, an immense crowd, 'from the Duchess of Devonshire down to the little milliner's apprentice from Cranbourn Alley', would saunter through the Carlisle House rooms, meeting, greeting and ogling. The decorations might be in Indian, Persian and Chinese styles, with illumination from '9,000 candles', according to one account; the next week, there would be a different theme. 'The magnificence of the rooms, splendour of the illumination and embellishments, and the brilliant appearance of the company exceeded anything I ever saw,' the eighteen-year-old Fanny Burney wrote. But Mrs Cornelys faced competition from attractions such as Almack's Assembly Rooms in St James's and the Pantheon on Oxford Street. When these venues became quite the rage instead, she responded by increasing her expenditure. It did not work. She sank into obscurity, and died in the Fleet in 1797, dreaming of a comeback. Her 'melancholy end holds forth a warning to the imprudent', the *Gentleman's Magazine* observed.

The prison building had four storeys. In the cellar were a kitchen and a dining room, which was known as Bartholomew's Fair. (The original Bartholomew Fair was a summer jamboree at Smithfield.) On the ground floor were a hall and the tap room. The upper floors contained 110 rooms off central corridors. Most of the rooms were 14½ by 12½ feet, and 9½ feet high – the largest in any prison in Britain. A coffee room provided newspapers and journals; in the grounds, you could play games including skittles and tennis. There was a wine club on Mondays, and a beer club on Thursdays, often lasting into the early hours and prompting complaints from those trying to sleep.

On arrival, you paid a commitment fee of £1 6s. The Fleet staff commanded various other sums, and there was rent of 2s 6d (12½p) a week for the share of a furnished room. Hogarth's Tom

---

[8] From the 1930s to the 1980s, the pseudonym 'William Hickey' appeared under a diary column in the *Daily Express*.

Rakewell shares with two others; some rooms housed six, and dependants too. More prosperous inmates were able to live alone, and to decorate rooms according to their own tastes. One Elizabeth Berkley furnished her chamber with two cane and two stuffed leather chairs, an easy chair, a looking glass, elegant curtains, a chocolate mill and various items of silverware. This was the 'master's side'. The 'common side' was the southern wing, where prisoners slept in dormitories. No stuffed leather chairs and elegant curtains here, in what was probably Dennis's home. He did not earn enough in the tap room to afford better accommodation, but nevertheless became known for his 'jolly song'. And, as when he was a sedan chairman, he managed to insinuate himself into the company of his social superiors.

Delivering drinks for Charlotte's entertainments, he caught her eye; and so began a lifelong relationship, both affectionate and mutually profitable, and never compromised by Charlotte's way of life. 'Charlotte had many friends, it is true, but policy induced her to see them with complacency,' the *Genuine Memoirs* insisted. 'Her affections were still [always] centred in our Hero.' Dennis was both Charlotte's lover and the promoter of her professional affairs. In return, she paid him, financing a resumption of his former ostentation and swagger. He also earned a kind of honour in the jail. A man known as the Sovereign of the Fleet – the informal title belonged to a senior resident, and carried about as much authority as that of Father of the Marshalsea in Dickens's *Little Dorrit* – dubbed him 'Count' O'Kelly. Dennis flaunted the title, unwisely. It was to stick, as the symbol of his upstart status.

Charlotte also subsidized Dennis's transfer to the Rules of the Fleet, where debtors could lodge provided they compensated the prison staff for loss of earnings. During the day they could roam wherever they liked – a leniency that allowed Dennis to be 'as constantly seen in all public places, as if he had not owed a shilling', *Town & Country* magazine reported, with a hint of disapproval. He immediately returned to his old haunts – a potentially disastrous move. But, having endured a painful initiation as a gambler, Dennis was a master practitioner now.

Despite her lucrative enterprises during this period, Charlotte continued to get into trouble, as she would at various times during her long life. In January 1759, John Grinfield took her to court. On 13 April 1761, her accuser was Samuel Wilkinson; and four days later, Joseph Lessly claimed from her £15 10s in damages for her failure to fulfil 'certain promises and undertakings'. Charlotte may have enjoyed episodes of freedom, but in execution of the last debt the court sent her to the Fleet again.

This sentence did not last long. To advertise the generosity of George III, who had come to the throne the previous year, Parliament passed an act 'For the Relief of Insolvent Debtors'. In September 1761, Charlotte and Dennis each filled in and signed the appropriate form, headed 'A true schedule and account of all the real estate, either in possession, reversion, remainder, or expectancy'.[9]

They were free.

[9] Dennis's form claimed that several people owed *him* money.

3

The Gambler

ENGLAND IN THE mid-eighteenth century was mad about gambling, and had been for years. Charles II, brought back from exile to assume the throne on the collapse of the Commonwealth in 1660, set a very different tone from the Puritan one that had prevailed in the country under Oliver Cromwell. At Newmarket, where Charles established a court devoted to pleasure and high jinks, the fast set spent fortunes on horses, cock fights, dice and cards. In her history of Newmarket, Laura Thompson reported a story that Nell Gwynn, the King's mistress, once lost 1,400 guineas in an evening, and quoted Samuel Pepys's observation that Lady Castlemaine was 'so great a gamester as to have won £15,000 in one night, and lost £25,000 in another night, at play'.

The Merrie Monarch was succeeded by less breezy characters. But the kingdom of the Hanoverian Georges was no less playful than his. George II was himself the subject of wagering, when he led his troops at the Battle of Dettingen in 1743: you could get 4-1 against his being killed. A similarly ghoulish opportunity for the sporting arose when a man collapsed outside Brooks's club in London. The members staked money on whether he was dead. Perhaps, someone said, they should see if the man could be revived; that suggestion was bad form, the outraged members cried, because it might affect the bet. At another club, White's, the twenty-year-old Lord Stavordale lost £11,000 in an evening, then won it back in a single hand at hazard, exclaiming, 'Now, if I had been playing *deep*, I might have won millions!'

Stavordale's adventure was recorded by Horace Walpole, who was too fastidious to take part in such activities. Walpole's letters also featured another great gambler, the statesman Charles James Fox, characterized as 'dissipated, idle beyond measure'. Fox – at one time effectively the joint leader of the country – lost £140,000 at cards by the age of twenty-five. His escapades were careless and brilliant. Having entered into a wager about a waistcoat that was available only in Paris, he set off in the middle of the night to get hold of one. Mission accomplished, he returned to Calais, where he suddenly recalled that Pyrrhus and Trentham, horses owned by Lord Foley and himself, were carrying wagers to beat another horse at Newmarket; he commandeered a fishing smack, steered for East Anglia, and arrived at the races just in time. A witness reported: '[Fox] eyed the horses advancing with the most immovable look; he breathed quicker as they accelerated their pace, and when they came opposite to him he rode in at full speed, whipping, spurring, and blowing, as if he would have infused his whole soul into his favourite racer.' The instant the horses were past the post, Fox turned his attention elsewhere – a gentleman may sport full-bloodedly, but he is above showing exultancy in victory or dismay in defeat.[10]

Later, he set off with some companions for London, but on a whim stopped off at another friend's house. Dinner was served, the cards and the dice came out, and there was about £5,000 on the table by dawn, when there was a rapping on the door: it was a messenger, chasing Fox to remind him that he was due to speak in the House of Commons that afternoon. Fox swept away the empty

---

[10] He won the bet. Trentham was first, Pyrrhus second, and their rival, Pincher, third.

July 1782   J.ˢ Bretherton f

Charles James Fox, the brilliant Whig politician, whose girth and features at the age of thirty-three were evidence of his self-indulgence. A reckless gambler and womanizer, he ended up happily married to Elizabeth Armistead, a former 'nun' at the establishment of Charlotte Hayes's forerunner, Mrs Goadby.

bottles, threw the dice one last time, and rushed to the stables for his horse. Lacking sleep, underprepared, and with a good deal of alcohol still coursing through his system, he nevertheless 'answered both Lord North and Burke, ridiculed the arguments of the former, and confuted those of the latter', as Walpole reported.

This anecdote comes from Theodore Cook's *Eclipse and O'Kelly*, published in 1907, and the standard work on the great horse and his owner. Cook observed, 'Philosophic foreigners might well have imagined that England was little better than a vast casino from one end of the country to the other.' The Duke of Queensberry ('Old Q'), a notorious rake, once bet someone that he could convey a letter fifty miles in an hour. He won by inserting the letter into a cricket ball and hiring twenty-four men to throw it to one another around a measured circle.

Horsemen not only raced, they also contrived more exotic equestrian activities on which they and their circle could bet. On 29 April 1745, Mr Cooper Thornhill rode from Stilton in Cambridgeshire to London, from London back to Stilton, and from Stilton back to London again, covering the two hundred-plus miles in eleven hours, thirty-three minutes and fifty-two seconds. 'This match was made for a considerable sum of money,' reported William Pick in his *Authentic Historical Racing Calendar* (1785), 'and many hundred pounds, if not thousands, were depending on it.' More fancifully, Sir Charles Turner made a 'leaping match' with the Earl of March for 1,000 guineas: Sir Charles staked that he would ride ten miles within an hour, and that during the ride he would take forty leaps, each of more than a yard in height. He accomplished the feat 'with great ease'. At Newmarket in June 1759, Mr Jenison Shafto backed himself to ride fifty miles in under two hours, and came home in one hour, forty-nine minutes and seventeen seconds. 'To the great admiration of the Nobility and Gentry assembled, he went through the whole without the least fatigue,' Pick noted. For an even more gruelling challenge, Shafto commissioned a Mr Woodcock to do the riding on his behalf. He made a match with Mr Meynell for 2,000 guineas that Woodcock would ride a hundred miles a day for twenty-nine consecutive days, using no more than one horse a day. Woodcock started early each morning, his route illuminated by lamps fixed on posts. His only crisis came on the day when his horse, Quidnunc, broke down after sixty miles; he had to requisition a replacement and start again, and he did not cover the 160-mile total until eleven o'clock that night. But he went on to complete his schedule.

Gambling was not only a sport for grandees. The middle classes and the lower orders loved it too. Horse race meetings, cricket matches, boxing matches and cock fights all offered wagering opportunities, both at the main events and at various side shows – stalls and tables with dice, cards and roulette wheels. There was a national lottery, raising money for such causes as building bridges across the Thames, with a draw staged as a dramatic spectacle at Guildhall. You could – as you cannot today – place side bets on what numbers would appear, paying touts who were called 'Morocco Men' after the leather wallets they carried.

There were many gaming houses in London. Like brothels, they operated openly, but suffered occasional crackdowns. The *Gentleman's Magazine* reported one such incident: 'Justice Fielding [London magistrate, and half brother of novelist Henry], having received information of a rendezvous of gamesters in the Strand, procured a strong party of guards who seized forty five at the tables, which they broke to pieces, and carried the gamesters before the justice, who committed thirty nine of them to the gatehouse [overnight prison] and admitted the other three to bail. There were three tables broken to pieces . . . under each of them were observed two iron rollers and two private springs which those who were in the secret could touch and stop the turning whenever they had any youngsters to deal with and so cheated them of their money.'

These venues were both dodgy and the haunts of people of

Sir John Fielding, the 'Blind Beak of Bow Street', presiding at Bow Street Magistrates' Court. Dennis O'Kelly came before Sir John following a fight at the Bedford Arms; and escaped with a fine, thanks only to the intercession of a friend.

all classes. They were therefore ideal settings for Dennis O'Kelly, who was by now a master 'blackleg'. The origin of this term is obscure, although it may have come from the black boots that were the standard footwear of professional gamblers; or possibly the derivation was the black legs of the rook, a word that also meant sharpster. Another term was 'Greek', first used to indicate a wily character by Shakespeare. Whatever the derivation, Dennis personified the meaning: a person practised in the art of cheating others out of their money. His assiduous apprenticeship 'had reduced to a system of certainty with him, what was neither more or less than a matter of chance with his competitors'.[11]

Opportunities for making a profit were everywhere – even on his feet. Dennis, on achieving a level of affluence, wore gold buckles on his shoes, while also owning a pair of buckles made of pinchbeck, an alloy that resembles gold. If he wore the gold ones, he kept the pinchbeck buckles in his pocket, and vice versa. In company, one of his companions would strike up a discussion about whether the Count's buckles were gold, and encourage the pigeon (dupe) to bet on the question. Dennis would simply perform a bit of sleight of hand, no doubt during some distracting activity initiated by the companion, to produce the buckle that would take the bettor's money.

He continued to get into trouble. At the Bedford Arms, he won money from an American officer who, probably with good reason, suspected that chicanery had taken place, and refused to pay. There were scuffles, and eventually Dennis came before Sir John Fielding.[12] Sir John was inclined to be harsh, but Dennis was rescued by the actor, playwright and fellow Fleet graduate Sam

---

[11] From Pierce Egan's *Sporting Anecdotes* (1804).

[12] Knighted in 1761, Sir John was known as the Blind Beak of Bow Street. He had lost his sight in a naval accident, and was reputed to have been able to recognize three thousand criminals from the sounds of their voices. He had taken over as chief magistrate of London on the death in 1754 of his half brother Henry.

Foote, who persuaded the magistrate to accept a fine. Dennis's relief, according to *Nocturnal Revels*, was overwhelmed by his sense of ill treatment.

'By Jasus,' he exclaimed, licking his wounds at Tom's Coffee-House, 'he [the American officer] has ruined my character, and I will commence an action against him.'

'Poh, poh,' said Foote, 'be quiet. If he has ruined your character, so much the better; for it was a damn'd bad one, and the sooner it was destroyed, the more to your advantage.'

Mortifyingly, this riposte earned hearty laughter from Tom's clientele. Dennis had to prove that he was a sport by laughing too, especially as he was in Foote's debt.

At least he had the good spirits to rise to this challenge. His cohorts at the gambling centres of London included Dick England, in whom good spirits were entirely absent. England was a version of Dennis with the charm removed, and brutality added. Like Dennis, he was an Irish expatriate. Emerging from an 'obscure, vulgar and riotous' quarter of Dublin, he took an apprenticeship to a carpenter; but the only manual activity for which he showed an aptitude was fighting. Like Dennis, he became the protégé of a businesswoman – his was a bawd. England was rumoured to be involved in highway robbery, and when one of his companions was found shot at the scene of a crime he decided that it was time to decamp to London, setting himself up at a house of ill repute called the Golden Cross. He soon rose in the world, to an address in Piccadilly, where he acquired a manservant, a pair of horses and a smattering of French. There was an awkward moment when his former mistress, who 'could not boast of a single attribute of body or mind to attract any man who had the use of his eyes and ears',[13] turned up on his doorstep, but he got rid of her with a hefty pay-off. Back in Dublin, she used the money to drink herself to death.

[13] *The Sporting Magazine* (December 1795).

Contemporary magazines offer various dismal accounts of the outcomes of England's tricks. At the rackets courts, he cultivated the Hon. Mr Damer, a decent player, before going off to Paris in search of a better one, hiring him to play regularly against Damer, and instructing him to start off by losing. He pretended to back Damer; and Damer, encouraged by the support and by belief in his superiority, backed himself as well – thereby losing up to 500 guineas at a time. With debts of (according to *The Sporting Magazine*) 40,000 guineas, Damer threw himself upon the mercy of his father, but despaired of getting help. Even while his father's steward was on the way to town with the money, Damer was in Stacie's hotel, sending out for five prostitutes and a fiddler called Blind Burnett. He watched them cavort for a while, put a gun to his temple, and fired.

England's most notorious swindle, recounted in Seymour Harcourt's *The Gaming Calendar* (1820), was one of his rare failures. While passing some time in Scarborough, he got into company with Mr Da——n (hereafter called Dawson),[14] a man of property. At dinner, England refilled Dawson's glass assiduously, softening him up for the card game to follow, but he overdid it, causing Dawson to complain that he was too drunk to play. Sure enough, once the cards came out, he descended into a stupor. The conspirators, though, soon devised a fall-back plan to part him from his money. Two of them wrote notes, one recording 'Dawson owes me 80 guineas', the other 'Dawson owes me 100 guineas'; England wrote a note saying, 'I owe Dawson 30 guineas'. The next day, he met Dawson, apologized for his drunkenness and rough behaviour of the previous evening, said he hoped he had given no offence, and handed over thirty guineas.

'But we didn't play,' Dawson pointed out.

---

[14] Eighteenth-century reports often gave only initials, or initials with a few other letters. In formulas such as En——l——d, the attempt at concealment was feeble.

'Get away wit' ye,' England assured him. 'An' these be your fair winnings an' all.'

What an honest gentleman, Dawson reflected as the pair parted 'with gushing civilities'. Soon after, he bumped into England's companions. Further comparisons of sore heads ensued, and Dawson commented on the civility of their friend Mr England, who had honoured a bet that would otherwise have been forgotten.

'As you mention this bet, sir,' one of the companions said, 'and very properly observe that it is gentlemanly to honour debts incurred when intoxicated, I hope we may be forgiven for reminding you of your debts to us'; and the fictitious notes were flourished.

'This cannot be so,' Dawson protested. 'I have no recollection of these transactions.'

'Sir,' came the reply, 'you question our honour; and did not Mr England lately pay you for bets made at the same table?'

Defeated, Dawson promised to pay up the next day.

His own friends came to the rescue. With the help of a five-guinea gift, they encouraged the waiter at the inn to recall that Dawson had been paralysed by drink, and had not played cards. Dawson, with some contempt, returned England the thirty guineas, adding five guineas as his portion of the supper bill. England and his cronies left Scarborough the next day.

Dennis O'Kelly may have spent some time in Scarborough,[15] but there is no suggestion that he was involved in this attempted theft. He was, though, implicated with England – and fellow blacklegs Jack Tetherington, Bob Walker and Tom Hall – in the ruination of one Clutterbuck, a clerk at the Bank of England. Clutterbuck, as a result of playing with this crowd, fell heavily into debt, attempted to defraud the bank of the sum he needed, was caught, and hanged.

[15] See chapter 1.

Although the divisions between the classes in the Georgian era were as wide as they always have been, gambling threw together lords and commoners, politicians and tradesmen, the respectable and the disreputable. Some years later, eminent witnesses would testify on Dick England's behalf at his trial for murder. At the rackets courts, England's companion Mr Damer 'would not have walked round Ranelagh [the pleasure gardens in Chelsea] with him, or had him at his table, for a thousand pounds'.[16] One writer referred to 'Turf acquaintanceship', and offered the anecdote of the distinguished gentleman who failed to recognize someone greeting him in the street.

'Sir, you have the advantage of me,' the gentleman said.

The other man asked, 'Don't you remember we used to meet at certain parties at Bath many years ago?'

'Well, sir,' the gentleman told him, 'you may speak to me should you ever again meet me at certain parties at Bath, but nowhere else.'[17]

The fortunes of Charlotte Hayes, too, began to look up on her departure from the Fleet. Her newly won freedom from debtors' prison received ironic celebration in Edward Thompson's 1761 edition of *The Meretriciad*, as she took advantage of the new King's clemency to begin her ascent to the pinnacle of her profession:

> See Charlotte Hayes, as modest as a saint,
> And fair as 10 years past, with little paint;
> Blest in a taste which few below enjoy,
> Preferr'd a prison to a world of joy:
> With borrow'd charms, she culls th'unwary spark,
> And by th'Insolvent Act parades the Park.

[16] *The Sporting Magazine* (January 1796).
[17] From Seymour Harcourt's *The Gaming Calendar and Annals of Gaming* (1820).

Her opportunities in courtesanship may have closed – as Samuel Derrick gently put it in *Harris's List of Covent Garden Ladies*, 'Time was when this lady was a reigning toast . . . She has been, however, a good while in eclipse' – but other opportunities were opening. The brothel-keeping business, she saw, was going up-market, and was ready to boom.

Jane Goadby was showing the way. Back in the 1750s, Mrs Goadby had been on a fact-finding mission to Paris, touring the stylish brothels of the city. They were not known as brothels: they were 'nunneries', populated by 'nuns' under the charge of the 'Lady Abbess', or, in pagan terminology, the 'High Priestess of the Cyprian Deity' (a reference to Aphrodite, goddess of love). The abbess selected beautiful nuns from diverse backgrounds and faiths. They were required to submit entirely to her authority, and to behave in a demure manner, avoiding excesses of eating and drinking. But they were to show no such restraint in the bedroom, where their brief was to demonstrate 'le zèle le plus sincère pour les rites et les cérémonies de la déesse de Cypros' (the most devoted zeal in the rites and ceremonies of the Cyprian goddess). At a time when venereal diseases were widespread, the nunneries offered some degree of security to their patrons by ensuring that the nuns received weekly medicals. A gentleman, who was also expected to behave with decorum, could pass entire evenings there, eating a fine meal, enjoying musical performances, and at the end retiring with his chosen nun. As a bonus, it was all very reasonably priced.

On her return to London, Mrs Goadby set about reproducing these attractions, except the pricing. At her establishment in Great Marlborough Street, Soho, you could spend up to £50 – £20 more than Dennis's annual salary as Lady —'s chairman – for just the sex. But gentlemen who had been on the Grand Tour, and who had experienced the splendours of continental brothels, were delighted to find such services on their doorsteps. The *Covent Garden Magazine* announced excitedly: 'Mrs Goadby, that celebrated Lady Abbess, having fitted up an elegant nunnery in Marlborough Street, is now laying in a choice stock of virgins for the ensuing season. She has disposed her nunnery in such an uncommon taste, and prepared such an extraordinary accommodation for gentlemen of all ages, tastes and caprices, as it is judged will far surpass every seminary of the kind yet known in Europe.' Elizabeth Armistead (Charles James Fox's future wife) started her career as one of Mrs Goadby's nuns.

Charlotte Hayes saw this market as her opportunity too, and Dennis was able to help. Their relationship was one of true partners, sharing the rewards of their labours. In the Fleet, she had provided the funds to get him back into circulation; now he was in a position to reciprocate, and, through his sporting connections, to bring her a classy clientele. She opened a serail near Mrs Goadby's in Great Marlborough Street, and attracted regulars including the Duke of Richmond, the Earls of Egremont and Grosvenor, Lord Foley and Sir William Draper. Not only did these men bring prestige to Charlotte's establishment, they also – being gamblers as well as philanderers – offered synergy, as we say nowadays, with Dennis's business interests.

4

The Duke

POSTERITY HAS DECIDED that William Augustus, third son of George II, was on the whole a bad man. *BBC History Magazine* named him the Worst Briton of the 18th Century. He was cruel in battle, earning the nickname 'Butcher' for his conduct at the Battle of Culloden; he was physically unattractive; and he was self-indulgent. Nevertheless, the racing world, taking what may be a blinkered view, is inclined to view him generously. 'No man can fairly be said to have done more for English racing' is a typical verdict.[18] This was the man who created the finest stud farm of the eighteenth century. He bred Herod, one of the most influential of all Thoroughbred stallions. And he bred Eclipse.

He was born in 1721. His eldest brother, Frederick, Prince of Wales, was fourteen; another brother, George, had died three years earlier, aged only three months. It was William Augustus who became his parents' favourite, while George II and Queen Caroline grew actively to dislike Frederick, who was arty.[19] At four, William was made a Companion Knight of the Bath. That was

---

[18] From Theodore Cook's *Eclipse and O'Kelly* (1907).

[19] One report has Caroline on her deathbed reflecting unmaternally about Frederick: 'At least I shall have one comfort in having my eyes eternally closed. I shall never see that monster again.'

a mere taster for what was to come a year later: the five-year-old prince became Duke of Cumberland, a title that took in Marquess of Berkhamstead, Earl of Kennington, Viscount Trematon, and Baron of Alderney. Marked out for a career in the forces, he joined the navy, did not take to it, but showed precocious enthusiasm and aptitude in the army. By twenty-one, he was a major-general.

The War of the Austrian Succession, one of the immensely complex conflicts in which this period of history specialized, was in progress, and in 1743 Cumberland fought against the French at Dettingen, serving under his father. It was the last occasion on which a British monarch led his troops into battle. As noted in the previous chapter, there was betting that George II would not survive. He did; but Cumberland got a grapeshot wound below his knee, and would be plagued by the injury for the rest of his life. Nevertheless, the battle was a personal as well as a national triumph. Cumberland had given his orders 'with a great deal of calmness and seemed quite unwearied',[20] and was hailed as a hero.

His standing did not diminish two years later when, as captain-general and leader of the allied forces at Fontenoy in Flanders, he suffered defeat. It was a noble defeat, everyone thought, and the King was inclined to share Cumberland's view that the blame lay with the 'inexpressible cowardice' of their Dutch allies. 'Now he will be as popular with the lower class of men as he has been with the low women for the past three or four years,' Horace Walpole wrote. So, when danger arose at home, Cumberland was the obvious man to deal with it.

Ever since the Catholic James II had been ousted from the throne in 1688, he and his descendants had been trying to regain it. In 1689, James landed in Ireland, but was eventually defeated by the forces of William of Orange at the Battle of the Boyne (July 1690).[21]

---

[20] Quoted in *Bred for the Purple* (1969) by Michael Seth-Smith.
[21] We shall visit this scene again, because one of William's men, Colonel Robert Byerley, rode into battle on a horse who was to become one of the foundation sires of the Thoroughbred.

James's son, James Francis Edward, led a second rebellious invasion in 1715, and was also defeated. Thirty years later, the Jacobite
cause was in the hands of James's grandson, Charles Edward Stuart
– Bonnie Prince Charlie. He landed in Scotland in July 1745,
raised an army of supporters, but failed to increase his following
when he marched south, and retreated north of the border.

Cumberland caught up with him on 16 April 1746 at
Culloden Moor. The battle lasted only about an hour. When the
outnumbered Jacobites retreated, they left behind more than a
thousand dead, as many wounded, and some six hundred prisoners. This was when Cumberland earned his Worst Briton tag.
Ordering the wounded and the prisoners to be executed, he followed up the battle by hunting down the rest of the defeated army
and their sympathizers, jailing and deporting thousands of them,
and bayoneting and hanging more than a hundred. The policy was
'to pursue and hunt out these vermin from their lurking holes'[22]
– language that encouraged the English troops to go on a spree of
raping and pillaging. Bonnie Prince Charlie escaped, over the sea
to Skye ('Speed bonnie boat . . .', as the song has it) and then back
to France. He died, unfulfilled, in 1788.

Cumberland's destruction of the Jacobites got a mixed
press. For many, the bloody suppression of a threatened Catholic
coup was a glorious act. Parliament voted him an additional
income of £25,000 a year; Handel wrote the oratorio *Judas
Maccabaeus*, which included the march 'See, the Conquering Hero
Comes', in his honour; many English inns changed their names to
the Duke's Head; Tyburn Gate, in the area of London – now
Marble Arch – where executions took place, became Cumberland
Gate (the area now houses the Cumberland Hotel, on Great
Cumberland Place). For others, he was 'Butcher' Cumberland.
The nickname gained currency, with the encouragement, some
suspected, of the Prince of Wales, who had always been jealous

---

[22] Quoted in the *Dictionary of National Biography*.

of his brother's superior place in his parents' affections. In Scotland, the Duke is the Butcher irrevocably. The flower that the English call the Sweet William is, north of the border, the Stinking Billy.

Within a few years, the bad odour had spread. Cumberland did not confine inflexible brutality to his enemies: he also showed it, when they betrayed any hint of poor discipline, to his own troops. When, in 1751, Frederick, Prince of Wales died, leaving behind a son who was heir to the throne but only twelve years old, Cumberland wanted to be named Regent,[23] but Parliament refused. Then Cumberland's military fortunes reached their nadir in another highly complicated conflict, the Seven Years' War, which broke out in 1757. Leading a Hanoverian force, he was defeated at the Battle of Hastenback, and in September 1757 he signed the Convention of Klosterzeven, releasing Hanover to the French. He agreed to this settlement with the sanction, he believed, of George II; but he returned home to be informed by his father that 'he had ruined his country and his army, had spoilt everything and hurt or lost his own reputation'.[24]

Cumberland took the rebuke with dignity. He resigned his military posts, and retired to concentrate on the one pursuit in which he left an indisputably beneficial legacy: horseracing.

Cumberland may have been the first Hanoverian to take an interest in the Turf, but the status of racing as the Sport of Kings – a sport defined by royal patronage – had been embedded in British society since the Middle Ages. King John (reigned 1199 to 1216), who was 'not a good man' as A. A. Milne put it, was another controversial figure to benefit the sport, importing Eastern horses and setting up a royal stud at Eltham. Richard II (1377 to 1400)

[23] In the event of the King's death, the Regent would reign until the future George III came of age.

[24] Quoted in *Royal Thoroughbreds* (1990) by Arthur FitzGerald.

raced in a match against the Earl of Arundel; the outcome is not known, but some years later Arundel was beheaded. During the reign of Henry VIII (1509 to 1547), horses came to England from Spain, Morocco and Mantua, two of them as valuable gifts from Ferdinand of Aragon, whose generosity was ascribed to madness resulting from an aphrodisiac dinner fed him by his wife. Henry founded another royal stud, at Hampton Court, and kept an establishment exclusively for what were then known as 'running horses' at Greenwich, where there were a stable jockey and a trainer. He introduced a law designed to improve England's warhorses, also improving the racing stock: he outlawed the grazing of small horses, and he empowered rangers each Michaelmas to make a cull, including among their targets fillies and mares that 'shall not be thought able, nor likely to grow to be able, to bear foals of reasonable stature, or to do profitable labours'. It was the kind of ruthlessness he also applied to his marital affairs.

Elizabeth I (1558 to 1603) went to the races in Salisbury, and paid four visits to meetings in Croydon, where her host, the Archbishop of Canterbury, had great difficulty in finding suitable accommodation for the court. (The town would present him with a similar challenge today.) Elizabeth's successor, James I (1603 to 1625), was not a racing man, but he was a keen promoter of horsemanship, and very committed to hawking and hunting. 'The honourablest and most commendable Games that a King can use are on Horseback, for it becomes a Prince above all men to be a good Horseman,' he wrote. Alas, he lacked the skills to live up to these ideals. There is a story – probably exaggerated in order to emphasize his ineptness – that James once shot over his horse, falling head-first into a river through a sheet of ice, above which only his boots could be seen. His courtiers yanked on them and hauled him to the bank, where 'much water came out of his mouth and body'.

James's great contribution to the sport was to develop the place that was to become the headquarters of racing. Newmarket was a town of fewer than three hundred inhabitants when the King chanced upon it, realizing that it offered access to ideal sporting country. He built a palace there that collapsed, and then in 1613 commissioned Inigo Jones to design a second, where the court enhanced its reputation for profligacy. Some notables thought that the pleasures of Newmarket were a distraction, and Parliament dispatched twelve members to the town to call to the monarch's attention the affairs of state that required his gracious attention. He sent the delegation packing. Nor did he consider his queen's death in 1619 a sufficient reason to suspend the Newmarket sporting schedule.

The doomed Charles I (1625 to 1649) maintained these lavish standards. 'There were daily in his court 86 tables, well furnished [with 500 dishes] each meal,' an observer noted. Regular spring and autumn race meetings began at Newmarket in 1627. In 1647, Charles was held captive in the town before being moved to various other locations, and eventually to the scaffold.

Emphasizing the royalist nature of racing, Oliver Cromwell's republican government banned it. However, race meetings resumed, and flourished as never before, under Charles II (1660 to 1685). Or, as Alexander Pope put it,

> Then Peers grew proud in Horsemanship t'excell,
> Newmarket's Glory rose, as Britain's fell.[25]

Having established the Newmarket Town Plate, the new King first visited the town in 1666, bought a house there two years later, and, with the previous palace in disrepair, expanded his property to become a new home for himself and his court. His various

---

[25] Explaining these aberrant lines, the eighteenth-century racing writer B. Walker reassured his readers that Pope's jaundice stemmed from 'an infirm state of health, a figure he was not thoroughly satisfied with, and in consequence an unsocial tendency to lead a recluse life, detached from those splendid meetings instituted in almost every country'. It was certainly impossible to imagine a well-adjusted person frowning on the sport so.

mistresses, Nell Gwynn among them, lodged nearby. Charles conducted sporting, state and amorous affairs during two extended visits each year, coinciding with the spring and autumn meetings. Everyone had a gay time, as the diarist John Evelyn recorded: 'I found the jolly blades racing, dancing, feasting, and revelling, more resembling a luxurious and abandon'd rout, than a Christian court.' An accomplished horseman, Charles would sometimes ride races himself, and win – entirely on merit, according to the courtier Sir Robert Carr. 'I do assure you the King won by good horsemanship,' Sir Robert insisted. Charles rode about the town on his hack, Old Rowley. The name came to be applied to him, and later to the Rowley Mile course.

William III (1689 to 1702) owned a horse with the proud name of Stiff Dick. In a celebrated match in 1698, Stiff Dick defeated the Marquess of Wharton's Careless, hitherto considered invincible. William's sister-in-law and successor, Queen Anne (1702 to 1714), was one of the most enthusiastic of all racing monarchs, and founded the racecourse at Ascot. (The Queen Anne Stakes is run on the first day of the Royal Meeting.) Anne was pregnant eighteen times, suffered numerous miscarriages and stillbirths, and saw no child live beyond the age of eleven. She consoled herself with horses and food. The two pursuits proved incompatible: she grew too heavy for any horse to carry, but she continued to ride to hounds in a specially constructed horse-drawn carriage. Following her death, an ungallant vice-chamberlain noted that her coffin was 'almost square'.

George I (1714 to 1727) and George II (1727 to 1760) took little interest in the Turf. But Prince William Augustus, Duke of Cumberland, did. In addition to military affairs, Cumberland's great enthusiasms were gambling, hunting and racing. As a boy, he would play cards with the ladies of the bedchamber, winning or losing up to £100 in an evening. His appointment on returning from Culloden as Ranger of Windsor Great Park, where he employed demobilized soldiers to construct the lake known as

William Augustus, Duke of Cumberland *by George Townshend. Horses of this era had to put up with a number of notably fat men, among them Cumberland, Dennis O'Kelly and the future George IV.*

Virginia Water, gave him a base from which to develop all three pursuits. The park contained 1,200 red deer, which Cumberland and his guests would hunt on Tuesdays and Saturdays, those present at the kills qualifying for tickets that entitled them to enter their horses for certain races at Ascot (the fortunes of which, moribund since Anne's death, revived under his patronage). During lulls in the hunt, Cumberland and friends such as the Earl of Sandwich – he who liked to snack while working at the Admiralty on a piece of meat between two slices of bread – would get out their dice. Members of the public, who previously had entered the park to collect firewood, were barred, on the grounds that they would disturb the deer that the royal parties wished to pursue. It was an unpopular edict.

From his base at Cumberland Lodge, the Duke began to develop the Windsor Forest Stud, at nearby Cranbourne Lodge. In 1750, he acquired a brown horse from a Yorkshireman called John Hutton in exchange for a chestnut, and named the new arrival Marske.[26] It did not appear to be a momentous deal: Marske's sire, Squirt, had at one time been considered so worthless that he was saved from execution at Sir Harry Harpur's stable only as a result of a groom's pleading. Marske himself turned out to be a good, but not outstanding, racer. As a four-year-old he won a 100-guinea plate at Newmarket in the spring, and a 200-guinea match against Lord Trentham's Ginger in the autumn. He had just one race the following year, and came third. In 1756, he lost two expensive matches worth 1,000 guineas each to the Earl of Sandwich's Snap, one of the fastest horses of the day. He may have got injured after that, as in October he failed to keep a date to race against Thomas Panton's Spectator, with Cumberland paying a forfeit. Instead, Marske went to stud. This second career did not prove illustrious either, and by the time of Cumberland's death in 1765 Marske was commanding a covering fee – the fee that

[26] After the Yorkshire town where Hutton lived.

breeders would pay for their mares to mate with him – of only half a guinea.

Another purchase, from Sir Robert Eden in Durham, was a chestnut filly called Spilletta. She, too, saw the racecourse for the first time at the 1754 Newmarket spring meeting. Against three opponents, she finished last, and that was the end of her racing career. She retired to stud, where she also failed to shine. By 1763, she had produced only one foal.

Marske and Spilletta – not, from a breeder's point of view, a marriage made in heaven – mated in 1760, without issue. Three years later, they gave it another go. This time, Spilletta became pregnant.

Cumberland, meanwhile, was pursuing his own pleasures. Unlike current members of the royal family, he would travel about with substantial amounts of cash, a lot of which ended up in the pockets of Dennis O'Kelly, Dick England and their fellow gamblers. When someone came up to him with a pocket book he had lost at the races, he insisted that the finder keep it, even though it contained several hundred pounds. 'I am only glad that it has fallen into such good hands,' Cumberland said, 'for if I had not lost it as I did, its contents would now have been scattered among the blacklegs of Newmarket.' After his death, a soldier in his employment gained permission to wear one of his suits as mourning clothes, and found a concealed pocket containing banknotes to the value of £1,751. But Cumberland also gave away his money to more worthy recipients, donating £6,000 a year to charities.

His increasing disability as a result of the wound he had received at Dettingen, and his prodigious weight (thought to have been up to twenty stone), did not blunt his taste for high living.[27] But his health deteriorated. He required regular medical

---

[27] Horace Walpole observed him at a dinner party: 'He was playing at hazard with a great heap of gold before him. Somebody said he looked like the prodigal son and the fatted calf both.'

attention; during one operation, he held a candle to assist the surgeon hacking away at abscesses in the wounded leg. His father, George II, died in 1760 (he was on the lavatory at the time), repenting that he had treated Cumberland harshly and acknowledging him as 'the best son who ever lived'. At George's funeral, Cumberland, who had suffered a stroke, cut a sorry figure. According to the report of Horace Walpole, 'The real serious part was the figure of the Duke of Cumberland . . . his leg extremely bad, yet forced to stand upon it near two hours; his face bloated and distorted with his late paralytic stroke, which has affected, too, one of his eyes; and placed over the mouth of the vault into which in all probability he must himself so soon descend; think how unpleasant a situation! He bore it all with a firm and unaffected countenance . . . sinking with the heat, he felt himself weighed down, and turning round found it was the Duke of Newcastle standing on his train to avoid the chill of the marble.'

Cumberland was, however, enjoying some success on the Turf. In 1758, his mare Cypron had given birth to a foal named at first Dapper Tartar, later King Herod, and later still simply Herod. In a match at Newmarket in 1764, Herod met Antinous, owned by the Duke of Grafton. Both owners were formidable gamblers, and by the time the race got underway bets worth more than £100,000 were depending on the outcome. Herod won. He defeated the same opponent again the following year, this time in a match worth 1,000 guineas.

However, the thrill of betting huge sums of money at Newmarket on Herod's first match against Antinous may not have been what the doctor ordered. Cumberland suffered two fits, and was in such a bad way that the London papers announced his death. He recovered, but death was on his case. On 31 October 1765, he arrived home in Upper Grosvenor Street, London, and ordered coffee. When it arrived, he complained of a pain in his shoulder, and began shivering. The King's physician, Sir Charles Winteringham, was sent for. As physicians then were wont to do, he advised bleeding.[28] This treatment had no effect, of course, and Cumberland died soon after. He was forty-four.

'When the melancholy news of the Duke of Cumberland's death reached Windsor,' the *London Chronicle* reported, 'it was received with the utmost concern by all ranks of people, and especially by the labourers on His Royal Highness's works, who cried out they had lost their greatest benefactor.' One is inclined to soften a little towards Butcher on reading this account. But the historian Theodore Cook, writing 140 years later, was unmoved: 'To the common people he was invariably indifferent, and they were his sincerest mourners after he was dead.' Cumberland lay in state in the Painted Chamber at the Palace of Westminster, and on 10 November was buried, following a twenty-one-gun salute, in the royal vault at Westminster Abbey.

Cumberland left plate, pictures, furniture and other effects valued at £75,000, as well as the most significant collection of bloodstock ever to be assembled. There were private sales (among them one for Spilletta, to the Duke of Ancaster), and two auctions. On 19 December, at Hyde Park Corner, the racehorses came under the hammer of John Pond. Herod fetched the largest sum, going to Sir John Moore for 500 guineas. The lots included another horse who will re-enter our story: Milksop, so named by Cumberland because he was nursed by hand, his dam (mother) having refused to suckle him.

On 23 December, Pond supervised the sale of the Cranbourne Lodge stud. Marske was lot number 3, knocked down to Lord Bolingbroke for twenty-six guineas. Several of Marske's offspring were also in the sale. One of them was lot 29, a chestnut yearling. The colt had a white blaze on his face and a white 'stocking' – white colouring below the knee – on his off (right) hind leg. His name was Eclipse.

---

[28] Bleeding was based on the theory of the four humours: black bile, yellow bile, phlegm and blood. The aim was to restore the humours to their proper balance.

5

The Meat Salesman

Sunday, 1 April 1764 was a grey day in London. The cloudiness was disappointing, as it obscured a rare astronomical event that had not been visible from southern England for more than a hundred years: an annular eclipse of the sun. One amateur enthusiast rose early to get to a vantage point on Hampstead Heath, taking various smoked glasses with him, but soon realized that the phenomenon would fail to achieve its proper impact. He abandoned the glasses, and resorted to the homespun device of a wafer with a pinhole, sandwiched between two pieces of white paper. At 10.32 a.m., he observed despondently, the moon was at its central point in its path across the sun, but 'wanted many degrees of being annular'.[29] He looked with envy towards the north-west, where the land appeared to be in much greater shadow. Still, as he noted in his letter to the press, he did get the eerie thrill of experiencing a significant drop in temperature.

Unlike total eclipses, annular eclipses do not obscure the entire sun, but leave visible a ring of sunlight around the intervening moon.[30]

[29] From *Lloyd's Evening Post*, 30 March – 2 April 1764
[30] The last annular eclipse above Britain was visible from north Scotland, Orkney and Shetland in 2003. The next one will be in 2093. The last total eclipse in Britain took place in 1999, and the next one is due in 2090.

A correspondent for the *London Chronicle* in March 1764 had offered advance counsel for those suffering 'fears and apprehensions at so awful a sight. It will be very commendable in them to think at that time of the Almighty creator and Governor of the Universe.' There were no such fears for their royal highnesses Prince William Henry and Prince Henry Frederick (the sons of the Duke of Cumberland's late older brother; Henry Frederick was to inherit Cumberland's title, as well as his Turf enthusiasms) who were guests at the Royal Observatory at Greenwich and behaved 'with the most remarkable condescension and affability'. The princes concluded, perhaps on taking expert advice, that the predictions of the extent of the eclipse by the astronomer Mr Witchell had been only one tenth of a digit awry. They offered him 'their approbation'.

To the west, the paddock below the tower at Cranbourne Lodge in Berkshire lay in greater darkness. While the sun was obscured, did Spilletta give birth to a foal with a white blaze and a white off hind leg? So we like to believe. Or did the Duke of Cumberland, the foal's owner, simply appropriate the name of an event that had taken place during the same season? Or perhaps the birth was at the time of the lunar eclipse earlier that year, on 17 March? There is no contemporary record to tell us, although Cranbourne Lodge does have a later monument, commissioned by Cumberland's successor as Ranger of Windsor Great Park, Prince Christian of Schleswig-Holstein, stating that the paddock below the tower was Eclipse's birthplace. The horse was unlikely ever to have been stabled, as one story has it, in Newham in East London, although he is commemorated in the area with an Eclipse Road and a Cumberland Road. Still less likely is it that Eclipse entered the world at what the racing writer Sir Walter Gilbey described as 'the Duke of Cumberland's stud farm on the Isle of Dogs'.

The Royal Stud Book has no birth record, but it does contain a race entry for the new arrival. Following what was common practice at the time, when owners regularly offered such hostages to fortune, Cumberland paid 100 guineas to enter the son of Marske and Spilletta in a match to take place four years later at Newmarket, against horses owned by the Duke of Grafton, Lord Rockingham, Lord Bolingbroke, Lord Gower, Lord Orford and Mr Jenison Shafto. A note of the match also appeared in the 1764 *Racing Calendar*. The Stud Book record says that the colt is '[By] Mask [*sic* – spellings in the eighteenth century were erratic], out of Spilletta a chestnut colt, with a bald face, and the off hind leg, white up to the hock'.

These notes are the best evidence we have to solve one of the enduring mysteries in racing. When Eclipse became the most famous racehorse in the land, rumours began to circulate that his pedigree was fraudulent. His real father, some said, was not Marske but a stallion called Shakespeare. A painting by J. N. (John Nost) Sartorius showed Shakespeare and Eclipse together – though, to my inexpert eye at least, it is hard to spot the implied likeness between the bulky stallion and the fine-boned racehorse. John Lawrence, an equestrian writer who had seen Eclipse in the flesh, was told by Dennis O'Kelly's groom that Shakespeare, as well as Marske, had covered Spilletta in 1763; others told Lawrence that this double covering was 'well-known fact', and hinted that bribery had taken place to ensure that Shakespeare be expunged from the story. The connections of Marske, sceptics hinted, had a great deal to gain by promoting their horse as Eclipse's father. Lawrence himself observed that Eclipse 'strongly resembled' members of Shakespeare's family.

Shakespeare was a good horse, the winner of two King's Plates, and would certainly have been a worthy mate for a mare of Cumberland's. But in 1763 he was standing as a stallion in Catterick. Would Cumberland – or rather, his stable staff – have walked Spilletta from Windsor to North Yorkshire for an assignation?

The following year, Shakespeare moved to stables belonging to Josiah Cook at Epsom in Surrey, near to where Eclipse would be stabled; he was advertised as '15 hands 2 inches high, very strong, healthful, and as well as any horse in England; as to his performances tis needless to mention them here, he was so well known in his time of running to be the best running horse in England'. Perhaps the attempted deception was not by the connections of Marske, but by members of the Surrey racing fraternity? There was certainly no reason – unless he made a mistake – for the Duke of Cumberland, ignorant as he was of the astonishing potential of his colt, to enter a false parentage in his stud book. O'Kelly's groom told John Lawrence the Shakespeare version, but a certain Mr Sandiver of Newmarket, citing the authority of Cumberland's groom, assured him that it was nonsense.

The question, as Lawrence concluded, is of real significance only to those concerned with the accuracy of Thoroughbred records. Parentage by Shakespeare would not devalue Eclipse's pedigree. It is Eclipse, the supreme racer and progenitor, who defines the value of the pedigree.[31]

Just over a year after Eclipse's birth, Cumberland was dead. The royal racing stable and stud went to auction, and at the 23 December sale of the Cranbourne Lodge stud the chestnut colt (or chesnut, as was the usual spelling) was again ascribed to Marske (the description of lot 29 was 'A chesnut Colt, got by Mask . . .').[32] The bidder with the most determination to get him was William Wildman.

Described as a butcher in his marriage record of 1741, William Wildman (born in 1718) was not a retailer but a livestock middleman, operating as a grazier and as a salesman at Smithfield, the largest cattle market in the world. His business, which turned over

---

[31] There are further uncertainties in Eclipse's pedigree. See Appendix 2.
[32] The auctioneer went on to confuse Eclipse's pedigree with that of another horse. See Appendix 2.

between £40,000 and £70,000 a year, was solid, as was he: he sat on parish committees, and supported charities. And, thanks no doubt to his contacts with the sporting landowners whose cattle he sold, he became a man of the Turf. He leased a stud farm, Gibbons Grove,[33] at Mickleham, about ten miles from Epsom. A substantial place, it consisted of 220 acres, a farmhouse sporting a clock tower and parapet, and stabling for sixty horses.

This prosperity notwithstanding, Wildman was a lowlier person than was the norm among leading racehorse owners in the mid-eighteenth century. Yet he achieved a feat that almost all his illustrious competitors failed to match: he attained ownership of three outstanding Thoroughbreds. One gets the impression of a man who was decent, determined and energetic, but essentially cautious. Having acquired these horses, he sold them all.

The first of them was Gimcrack. Commemorated each August by the Gimcrack Stakes at York, Gimcrack was a grey horse no bigger than a pony. Wildman bought him in 1763, for about £35. At first he thought he had made a bad deal, and offered, unsuccessfully, to offload his acquisition for fifteen guineas (or £15 15s). But then Gimcrack started racing. He won seven times in 1764 (when the *Racing Calendar* placed him in the ownership of a Mr Green, who makes no further appearances in any volume). He also won his first race in 1765, a £50 plate at Newmarket, before Wildman, taking a course he was to repeat with Eclipse, sold him. Gimcrack went to Lord Bolingbroke, a prolific racehorse owner and ferocious gambler, for 800 guineas, and was to continue to shuttle between owners. He moved next to Sir Charles Bunbury, whose wife Sarah (née Lennox, and later to elope with Lord William Gordon, an army officer) described him (Gimcrack, not Bunbury) as 'the sweetest little horse that ever was'; then to the Comte de Lauraguais, for whom he won a wager by covering twenty-two miles in an hour; and then to Lord Grosvenor. He

---

[33] Now the Givons Grove estate.

retired to stud at the age of eleven in 1771, having won twenty-six of thirty-six races.

Another reward of Wildman's prosperity was his commissions from George Stubbs, Britain's greatest equestrian artist – and, you might argue, one of the greatest British artists in any genre. Stubbs painted *Gimcrack with John Pratt Up* for Wildman, showing Gimcrack on Newmarket Heath. Horse and jockey are next to the Beacon Course rubbing-house, where horses were saddled and otherwise groomed, and where Stubbs would later set his most celebrated painting of Eclipse. Gimcrack shows only a grey sheen on his coat, which whitened as he got older; he and his jockey are turning their heads in the same direction, with the lonely look that athletes assume on contemplating exertions to come. The picture hangs in the Fitzwilliam Museum, Cambridge. A subsequent Stubbs portrait of Gimcrack, one of the painter's best, has the narrative technique you sometimes see in early religious paintings, with different parts of the story appearing on different parts of the canvas: in the background, Gimcrack races several lengths clear of his rivals;[34] in the foreground, he is at the rubbing-house, with his jockey dismounted and two stable lads attending to him. (A version of *Gimcrack on Newmarket Heath, with a Trainer, Jockey and a Stable-Lad* is in the Jockey Club Rooms at Newmarket.)

Wildman, then, was well in profit on his recent racing transactions when he turned up at Cranbourne Lodge on 23 December 1765, looking to buy inmates of the late Duke of Cumberland's stud.

Eclipse's early life comes to us as legend. Accounts of his birth, his sale, his training, his first race – these, like a good many of the stories about Dennis O'Kelly and Charlotte Hayes, have the flavour of anecdotes that have gained embellishments with circulation. At some point, a historian has written them down. Subsequent

---

[34] There is no crowd and the stand is shuttered, indicating that the race is a trial.

historians have repeated them. We might be tempted to accuse eighteenth-century chroniclers of lax standards, had we reason to be complacent about our own regard for historical accuracy and truthfulness. Nevertheless, given the inclination, twenty-first-century reporters can try to gain access to people with memories of actual events, and they have a great deal more documentation to examine. Documentation on Eclipse's connections is sparse, and laconic. In only a few instances are there records to provide correctives to widely published accounts. One of these instances is the Cumberland dispersal sale.

The story goes that William Wildman arrived at Cranbourne Lodge late. Eclipse, his sole reason for attending, had gone through the ring and been claimed by someone else. Brandishing his watch ('of trusty workmanship'),[35] Wildman proclaimed to the auctioneer and assembled bidders that the sale had taken place before the advertised hour, and that every lot should be put up again. John Pond, who was in charge of proceedings, did not fancy doing this; so, to try to pacify the awkward customer, he offered him a lot of Wildman's choosing. This was exactly the compromise Wildman had been angling for. He chose the colt with the white blaze, and paid, according to the first published version of these events, seventy or seventy-five guineas.

It is a nice anecdote, but is it accurate? Wildman may well have missed the start of the auction: one advertisement stated that the proceedings would begin at 10 a.m., while another gave the starting time as 11 a.m. It is very likely that he was aiming particularly to buy the Marske yearling.[36] The advice to do so may have come from Lord Bolingbroke, to whom Wildman had sold

[35] From Bracy Clark's *A Short History of the Celebrated Race-horse Eclipse* (1835).
[36] Racing people use the name of the sire (father) as a kind of adjective. They might describe contemporary horses as a 'Kingmambo colt' or a 'Montjeu filly'. The sire, for reasons to do with how breeding operates rather than with the science of genetics, gets more credit for a racehorse's prowess than the dam (mother).

Gimcrack; the connection between the two is suggested by the Stubbs portrait, which shows Gimcrack in Wildman's ownership but with Bolingbroke's jockey, John Pratt, on his back. Bolingbroke was at the sale too, of course: he bought Marske, for twenty-six guineas. But Wildman made bids for other horses. He bought a nutmeg-grey colt by (sired by) Moro, for forty-five guineas, and a bay foal by Bazajet, for six. We know of these transactions because the sale document survives; it is in the possession of the Royal Veterinary College. It is that document that tells us Eclipse was the twenty-ninth lot to come under the hammer that day, and that his price was not seventy or seventy-five guineas, but forty-five. The sale raised 1,663½ guineas in total.

To recap: the legends we have questioned or dismissed so far in this chapter are that Eclipse was born on the day of the 1764 annular eclipse; that his father was Shakespeare, not Marske; that he was born or was stabled in East London; that William Wildman bought him alone at the Cumberland dispersal sale; and that Wildman paid seventy or seventy-five guineas for him. There is another to consider: that the auction was conducted by Richard Tattersall. Then a thrusting young man at the start of his career, Tattersall, who came from a modest background in Lancashire, went on to found, in 1766, the firm of Tattersalls (without an apostrophe), which soon became, and remains today, the largest bloodstock auctioneers in Europe. He also went on to buy, from Lord Bolingbroke, the champion racer Highflyer (a son of Cumberland's great horse Herod), and created numerous further champions by mating Highflyer with daughters of Eclipse. Reports cited Tattersall as one of the promoters of the rumour that Shakespeare was Eclipse's sire. His motive for doing so is obscure. One can see, though, why he was credited with involvement in what was, in hindsight, the most significant bloodstock sale of the era. But there is no evidence that he was anywhere near it. Certainly the advertisements for the sale mention only John Pond.

*

We have now met the four most important people in Eclipse's life: a gambler from a humble background in Ireland; a prostitute from Covent Garden; a royal prince; and a prosperous representative of the middle classes. The most famous of all Thoroughbreds is also the most representative of horseracing, the example of how a highly bred animal with a regal background can nevertheless bring into proximity disparate members of society. Racing is still thought of as a toffs' pursuit, yet it offers more varied material for the social historian than any other sport.

Look at the scene at Epsom on Derby day. The Queen surveys the Downs from her box in the Royal Enclosure. In a nearby box are the Dubai royal family, the Maktoums, who have significant racing interests. Their neighbours in the enclosure are grandees, trainers, racehorse owners, tycoons and celebrities; the men here are in top hats and tails, and the women are in designer dresses and hats. In the next enclosure, where lounge suits and high-street fashions are the order, congregate the professional classes, some of them enjoying corporate entertainment. On the other side of the course, packed into double decker buses, are rugby club members on a day out, and women on hen parties. Further away, in front of the cheaper stands, are families with picnics, and men and women who have come mostly to enjoy a sustained drinking session in the sun. Amid the funfair rides and market stalls on the Downs swarm gypsies and other travellers, touts and card sharps, bookmakers and hucksters.

There is proximity here, but very little interaction. Commingling across the social strata was greater in Dennis O'Kelly's day. Dennis and the Duke of Cumberland probably met on the racecourse, and in other gambling venues too; Dennis and Cumberland's great-nephew, the Prince of Wales (later George IV), were certainly racing acquaintances, and might almost be said to have been close, because 'Prinny' was a regular at gatherings at Dennis's Epsom home. Charlotte Hayes's business also brought her into contact with a great many esteemed clients,

and William Wildman came to racing through transactions with
Lord Bolingbroke and others.

Nevertheless, eighteenth-century Englanders needed to
have sharper antennae than the man in Seymour Harcourt's anecdote (chapter 3) who confused his Bath acquaintance with a social
equal. You did not presume that, because a gentleman or lady
might condescend to socialize with you on certain occasions, he or
she was your new best friend. Wildman shot game on the Duke of
Portland's estate, but he did not join the Duke's shooting parties:
he went at other times, with a companion from his own circle.[37]
We think of the memoirist and rake William Hickey as belonging
to the Georgian smart set, but Hickey, the son of a prosperous
lawyer, did not move in aristocratic company. Dennis O'Kelly
owned the greatest and most celebrated racehorse of the age, and
many other fine horses besides; he was a prominent personage at
the leading race meetings; and he was himself a celebrity, much
discussed in the public prints. But beyond certain portals he could
not go. Lacking the sense of deference that comes more naturally
to the English, he was enraged by the exclusion.

Relationships on the racecourse between owners, trainers,
jockeys, stable staff and members of the public give the most comprehensive picture of class relationships that a single location can
show. It is a picture that has changed only superficially since the
1760s. As the Queen, from her supreme vantage point at Epsom,
surveys the variegated scene, she can see too, through the woods
on the other side of the course, the house where Dennis O'Kelly
stabled his racers. The present merges with the past in this
panorama: with all the other Derby days she has witnessed; with
the Derby days before that, of Hyperion, Persimmon, Gladiateur
and Diomed; and before that, with a day in May 1769, when five
horses rode on to the Downs from nearby Banstead, and leading
them was a chestnut with a white blaze.

[37] The general point stands even if Wildman is not the figure in Stubbs's
portrait of the gentlemen's outing on the estate – see chapter 18.

6

The Young Thoroughbred

THE QUALITIES THAT William Wildman and Lord Bolingbroke saw in Eclipse were not obvious. He was leggy, and possessed, experts thought, an ugly head. His croup was as high as or higher than his withers,[38] a characteristic that was reckoned to be undesirable in a racer. He was 'thick-winded', breathing at disconcerting volume as he exercised. And his pedigree, on his sire's side, seemed to be no more distinguished than his appearance. Marske, his father, was worth only twenty-six guineas, and had been covering mares at the derisory fee of half a guinea.

Moreover, Eclipse was bad-tempered and unruly, so much so that his handlers at William Wildman's stables at Mickleham considered gelding him. Castration, a common procedure in the racing world, has a calming effect – but of course you avoid doing it to an animal who might become a valuable stallion. Fortunately for the history of horseracing, the Mickleham team entrusted Eclipse instead to a 'rough-rider', whose speciality was taking charge of untrained horses. George Elton, or 'Ellers', would don stout leathers to protect his legs and ride Eclipse into the woods

---

[38] The croup is the highest point of a horse's hind quarters. The withers are at the base of the neck above the shoulders.

on night-time poaching expeditions. It was good discipline for the horse, though a dangerous transgression for the rider. Later, Ellers was prosecuted for poaching, and transported.[39]

The Mickleham team had time on their side. Eclipse and his contemporaries belonged to the last generation of racers who were not expected to see a racecourse until they were four or five years old. (Many of their sons and daughters would begin racing at the age of two.) The tests they faced demanded physical maturity. Races were over two, three or more commonly four miles, and many events involved heats. Horses might have to run, in a single afternoon, four races of four miles each, with only half-hour intervals in which to get their breath back. To emerge triumphant at the end of that, they had to call on great reserves of courage and stamina – what the Georgians admiringly called 'bottom'.

During the winter and spring of 1768 and 1769, as Eclipse enters his fifth year, he begins to be subjected to an ever harsher training regime. As contemporary manuals show, he spends his nights, and the portions of each day when he is not at exercise, in an enclosed, windowless, heated stable. It is warm in winter and suffocating in summer, and he wears thick rugs. Sweating is good, believe the early trainers, who regularly turn up the heating and subject the horses, rugged and hooded, to saunas. As the racing season approaches, Eclipse is given purgatives, consisting of aloes or mercury.

Eclipse has his own 'boy', or groom, John Oakley, who sleeps in lodgings above the stable. Oakley gets up at about four each morning, sometimes earlier. After a breakfast of porridge, with perhaps cold meat from the previous day as well as cheese, bread and beer, he mucks out the stable, removes Eclipse's rugs and rubs him down, gives him a breakfast of oats, clothes him again, puts on his saddle and bridle, and mounts him. The pair then join the rest of the string for morning exercise on the Downs.

---

[39] Transportees at this time were usually sent to Maryland or Virginia.

They are under the supervision of the trainer, who is also commonly described as a groom.

Or perhaps Oakley was the trainer? It is a sign of the humble roles of trainers and jockeys at this time that we know so little about the handlers of even so famous a horse as Eclipse. By the end of the century, training was recognized as a specialist role, and trainers were ascending the social ladder. Men of the Turf in the eighteenth century would be surprised to discover that modern trainers, such as Sir Michael Stoute, are rather grand.

Once on the Downs, Oakley and Eclipse start off at an easy gallop.[40] After half a mile or so they come to an incline, and Oakley begins to urge Eclipse to go faster. They race uphill for another half mile before Oakley pulls on the reins. They walk back, and Eclipse gets a moderate drink of water – the Georgians do not believe that horses should be allowed very much refreshment. They gallop gently again, and then walk. Then they have another fast gallop, and then another walk. All this while, Eclipse has been burdened by heavy rugs. Every week or ten days, he wears this clothing on a 'sweat', a gallop of four miles or more. But even on less gruelling days he is sweaty enough.

At about nine o'clock, they return to the stables. Oakley leads him back to his stall, ties him up, rubs down his legs with straw, removes his rugs, and brushes and 'curries' him (with a metal currycomb). He clothes the horse again, and gives him some more oats or hay.[41] The stables are then shut up.

---

[40] Oakley has probably ignored the pre-exercise tip of Gervase Markham: 'Then do yourself piss in your horse's mouth, which will give him occasion to work and ride with pleasure.' (From *How to Choose, Ride, Train and Diet, Both Hunting-Horses and Running Horses*, 1599).

[41] The equestrian expert John Lawrence, writing in the early nineteenth century, thought that oats and hay were a sufficient diet for racehorses. Gervase Markham had recommended also bread, malt and water mash, and the occasional raw egg; and from time to time, Markham said, you should season the horse's meal with aniseed or mustard seed.

Jockeys, too, had to be hardy individuals. When Oakley joined the stable, and was about to ride his first race, he went through a fearful initiation. His colleagues told him that the best way to get his weight down to the eight and a half stone required was to borrow as many waistcoats as he could, go on a three-mile run, strip naked on his return, and immerse himself in the hot dung hill outside the stable boxes. He dutifully obeyed. As he emerged, caked with ordure, he heard a chorus of laughter. Suddenly he was surrounded by his gleeful fellow grooms, all carrying pails; they drenched him in freezing water.

Today, as Eclipse nears his racecourse debut, that episode is far enough in the past for Oakley to have had the fun of playing the same joke on several new recruits. He is an established member of the Mickleham team, and a valued rider of William Wildman's horses at race meetings. From now until mid-afternoon he and the other boys have time off. They play gambling games, many of them now obscure: fives, spell, null, marbles, chuck-farthing, spinning tops, and holes.[42] At four o'clock, they return to the stables and take the horses out for another round of exercise. Then there is more rubbing down, brushing and combing; feeding, of horses and boys; preparing the horse's bed. The stables are shut up again, with horses and boys inside, at nine.

Albeit physically demanding, lowly in status and derisorily paid, working in an eighteenth-century stable is not a bad job. In an enlightened establishment such as Wildman's, Oakley is well looked after, and enjoys the responsibility of being the most important person in the life of a horse he realizes may be special. Eclipse trusts him as he does no other human. Oakley knows that the horse requires special treatment: he will respond only to the most deferential of suggestions, and will rebel against the whippings and spurrings that are normal practice in race-riding.

---

[42] The temptation for present-day stable staff is to spend their free time in betting shops.

For the horses, however, the regime is brutal. It is not surprising that early racing paintings show animals that are etiolated and apparently long in the back: they are trained until every ounce of 'condition' – spare flesh – is sweated away. Twenty-five years after Eclipse was in training, a jockey called Samuel Chifney wrote a memoir with the modest title of *Genius Genuine*, and showed himself to be ahead of his time both in his attempt to market himself as a racing personality (while holding a job regarded as socially insignificant), and in his view that the accepted training practices of his era were 'ignorant cruelty'. Chifney described a horse returning from a sweating exercise: 'It so affects [the horse] at times, that he keeps breaking out in fresh sweats, that it pours from him when scraping, as if water had been thrown at him. Nature cannot bear this. The horses must dwindle.' In spite of his words, most racehorses continued to be trained in this way until well into the nineteenth century.[43]

Yet Eclipse thrives. He has an unusual way of galloping: he carries his head low, and he spreads out his hind legs to such an extent that, one observer said later, a wheelbarrow might have been driven through them. Even so, he eats up the ground. Oakley has never sat on a horse so fast. Eclipse is – though Oakley does not describe him in these terms – the most brilliant representative to date of a new type of running horse, the fastest the world has ever seen: the Thoroughbred.

During the previous half a century, some mysterious alchemy had been taking place in the breeding sheds of England. The horses that were emerging were blessed with an unprecedentedly potent combination of speed and stamina. How these qualities came

---

[43] Taking care not to 'overcook' a horse is one of the key skills of the modern trainer. In particular, the trainer does not put a horse through vigorous exercise too close to a race. As I write, one of the favourites for a sprint race at Royal Ascot, ten days away, has had his last serious gallop. He will gallop again in five days, but will not be asked to stretch himself.

about is the subject of much debate, hampered (though not dampened) by the haphazard standards of early record keeping. If you want to take a patriarchal view, you can give most of the credit to just three stallions. Their status has brought to their biographies various fanciful and romantic accretions; what is a matter of historical fact is that every contemporary Thoroughbred descends in the male line from the Byerley Turk, the Darley Arabian or the Godolphin Arabian.

The horse known as the Byerley Turk may not have been a spoil, as the early histories relate, of the Siege of Buda (1686), because recent research suggests that Colonel Robert Byerley of the Sixth Dragoon Guards was not there. The Turk may rather have been captured at the Siege of Vienna (1683) – the 'browne' horse, the least valuable among three Vienna captives, that John Evelyn saw parade in St James's Park in 1684: 'They trotted like does as if they did not feel the ground. Five hundred guineas was demanded for the first; 300 for the second and 200 for the third, which was browne. All of them were choicely shaped but the last two not altogether so perfect as the first. It was judged by the spectators among whom was the King, the Prince of Denmark, Duke of York and several of the Court . . . that there were never seen any horses in these parts to be compared with them.'

Colonel Byerley certainly owned the Turk by 1689, when he took him to Ireland. In spring 1690, they won a silver bell at a meeting held by the Down Royal Corporation of Horsebreeders. That July, Byerley fought at the Battle of the Boyne against the Jacobite forces of the deposed James II, riding the Turk on reconnaissance missions and narrowly escaping capture thanks to the horse's speed. After his side's victory, Byerley returned to England, retired from the army, married, sat as the MP for Knaresborough in Yorkshire, and put his horse to stud. Despite covering what historians consider to have been indifferent mares, the Byerley Turk established an enduring bloodline. He is the great-great-grandfather of the Duke of Cumberland's

Herod. And he appears three times in the pedigree of Eclipse.[44]

The second of the three lauded founding fathers of the new breed was by repute a pure-bred Arabian. He was descended on his mother's side – for Arabs, *this* is the important part of the pedigree – from a mare called the Mare of the Old Woman.[45] While few Englishmen at this time were bothering with the pedigrees of their horses, the Arabs had long been punctilious about them. The Duke of Newcastle wrote, 'The Arabs are as careful and diligent in keeping the genealogies of their horses, as any princes can be in keeping any of their own pedigrees.' Giving false testimony about a horse's background would bring ruin on oneself and one's family.

We have to assume, then, that the patter given to Thomas Darley, a merchant and British Consul in Aleppo, was genuine. Darley bought his Arabian from Sheikh Mirza II in 1702, and in a letter to his brother a year later described the horse's three white feet and emblazoned face, adding that he was 'of the most esteemed race among the Arabs both by sire and dam . . . I believe he will not be much disliked; for he is highly esteemed here, where I could have sold him at a very considerable price, if I had not designed him for England'. The problem was that the War of the Spanish Succession was raging, and Darley was having trouble securing a sea passage for his purchase, although he was hopeful that his friend Henry Brydges, son of Lord Chandos, would be able to take the horse with him on board a ship called the *Ipswich*. Then another problem emerged: the Sheikh changed his mind about the sale. Nevertheless, Brydges made off with the Arabian, who arrived in England at roughly the same time as a letter from the Sheikh to Queen Anne furiously alleging that his possession

---

[44] He appears once eight generations back in Eclipse's pedigree, and twice nine generations back. The formula to describe this inbreeding is $8 \times 9 \times 9$.
[45] Both sides of the family belonged to the valued strain called, in Darley's spelling, Manicha (also sometimes Managhi).

had been 'foully stolen'. The protests had no effect. The Darley Arabian stood at the family estate, Aldby Park near York, until his death in 1730.

Like the Byerley Turk, the Darley Arabian covered mostly unexceptional mares. One of the few good ones was called Betty Leedes, owned by Leonard Childers – pronounced with a short 'i', not as in 'child' – of Cantley Hall, Doncaster. Betty Leedes returned to her paddock in Doncaster, and eleven months later gave birth to 'the fleetest horse that ever ran at Newmarket, or, as generally believed, the world', Flying Childers. Here was the horse that demonstrated what this new breed, the descendants of Eastern stallions on British soil, could do. His portrait by James Seymour shows a prancing, compact, muscular colt, of a type we would assess as a sprinter. But Flying Childers had to race over long distances. In a match against two horses called Almanza and Brown Betty at Newmarket, he was reported to have completed the three-and-three-quarter-mile Round Course in six minutes and forty-eight seconds – about a minute faster than par. He later ran the four miles-plus Beacon Course at Newmarket in seven and a half minutes, 'covering 25 feet at every bound'. These reports come from the early 1720s, before the publication of John Cheny's first racing calendar (an authoritative record of race results), and may be exaggerated; but we do know that Flying Childers beat Fox, one of the best racers of the day and a winner of three King's Plates, by a quarter of a mile, despite carrying a stone more on his back than did his rival.

By this time, Flying Childers had passed from Leonard Childers's hands to the Duke of Devonshire, and he retired to the Duke's stud at Chatsworth. However, the best racehorses do not necessarily become the best stallions.[46] Flying Childers sired some

---

[46] For example, Brigadier Gerard, rated by John Randall and Tony Morris in *A Century of Champions* as the best British horse of the twentieth century, achieved little success at stud.

good horses, but his younger brother, who never raced, sired more, and continued the male line that dominates the bloodstock industry today. Bartlett's Childers, also known as Bleeding Childers because he would break blood vessels in hard exercise, sired Squirt, who sired Marske, who sired Eclipse.

On the maternal side of Eclipse's pedigree is the third of these famous stallions, the one with the most colourful story of all – although some of the colour may be the result of artful tinkering. The Godolphin Arabian was foaled in the Yemen in the mid-1720s, exported to Tunis, and given as a present by the Bey (Governor) of Tunis to Louis XV of France. The horse failed to please the King, and had been reduced (legend has it) to pulling a water-cart through the streets of Paris when he was spotted by a man called Edward Coke, who paid £3 for him. Coke returned to England, but did not enjoy the company of his acquisition for long, dying at the age of only thirty-two. The horse then passed to Francis, the second Earl of Godolphin. The Godolphins were a racing family. Of the first Earl, a prominent politician who died in 1732, it had been said, 'His passion for horse racing, cock-fighting, and card-playing, was, indeed, notorious, but it was equally notorious that he was seldom a loser by his betting transactions, which he conducted with all the cool calculation and wariness of a professional blackleg.'

The indignity of pulling a water-cart may have been in his past, but there were further indignities for the Arabian at the Godolphin stud at Gog Magog in Cambridgeshire. He was employed as a 'teaser', the horse with the job – it remains an important though unglamorous role in the breeding industry today – of perking up a mare before the main man, the stallion, came along. The main man at Gog Magog was Hobgoblin, a grandson of the Darley Arabian. But when Hobgoblin met a mare called Roxana, he decided that he did not fancy her. So the Godolphin Arabian, no doubt gratefully, covered her instead, and Roxana duly gave birth to Lath, the best racehorse since Flying Childers.

The parents, having hit it off, met again, this time producing Cade – not as good a racehorse, but the sire of the outstanding Matchem, through whom the Godolphin Arabian male line continues to the present. The Godolphin Arabian also got (sired), this time with a mare called Grey Robinson, Regulus, who won eight royal plates and retired undefeated to stud. There, with a mare called Mother Western, he sired Spilletta – Eclipse's mother.[47]

Later, in about 1793, George Stubbs painted the Godolphin Arabian, working from an original by David Morier. In the background, next to the barn, is the Godolphin Arabian's friend, Grimalkin the cat. There are various stories about Grimalkin; again, you can take your pick. One is that when the Godolphin Arabian died, in 1753, Grimalkin placed herself on his carcass, followed the body to the burial ground, and after the interment crawled miserably away, never to reappear until found dead in the hay loft. Another version, even sadder, is that the Godolphin Arabian accidentally crushed Grimalkin; furious with grief, the horse would attempt to savage any other cat that came across his path.

The horse in Stubbs's portrait has the thick neck characteristic of a horse at stud, to an exaggerated extent: his crest – the top of his neck – is so high and convex that his back appears to begin halfway between his legs. What kind of horse is he? Some equestrian writers think that he resembles a Barb, a breed of horse from North Africa, and indeed he has been known as the Godolphin Barb.

Is every contemporary racehorse descended, in male line, from a stallion of one of three different breeds, or were the Byerley Turk, the Darley Arabian and the Godolphin Arabian all in fact, as some historians have argued, Arabs? We cannot be sure. The early owners applied the terms 'Turk', 'Arab' and 'Barb' with

[47] But see Appendix 2.

71

little concern for breeding; they meant only a horse of Eastern blood.

Eastern horses were not renowned racers, and of these three, only the Byerley Turk, with his cup at Down Royal, saw a racecourse. Why, then, did the early breeders – grandees and substantial landowners, largely based in Yorkshire – import them? They did so because they esteemed Eastern horses for a quality known as 'prepotency': the ability to breed true to type, and to maximize in their offspring the attributes of the mares with whom they mated. The theory worked too, getting its most spectacular early demonstration in the career of the Darley Arabian's son Flying Childers.

In the years following the Restoration and in the early years of the eighteenth century, these breeders imported some two hundred stallions who were to appear in the first *General Stud Book* of 1791. Examination of pedigrees shows that the Byerley Turk, the Darley Arabian and the Godolphin Arabian should not get all the credit, and that many others made significant contributions, even though their male lines expired. You can easily see, for example, the influence of Alcock's Arabian: he was grey, and appears in the pedigrees of every grey Thoroughbred.[48] And of course half of the credit is due to the early mares, although, as is so often the case with females in history, they are obscure figures, many of them nameless. It seems that they, too, had a good deal of Eastern blood; how high a proportion is a contentious matter. At the end of the bottom, maternal line of Eclipse's pedigree is a mysterious 'Royal mare'.[49]

What we do know is that the Thoroughbred, this cross of

---

[48] A grey horse must have a grey parent, of either sex.

[49] Only about twenty foundation mares feature widely in contemporary Thoroughbred pedigrees. At one time, it was said that the 'royal mares' were imported during the reign of Charles II. Now it is thought more likely that most of them lived at the Sedbury stud of James Darcy, who employed them to breed '12 extraordinary good colts' each year for the King.

Eastern stallions with English mares, transcended its parentage. In the century when the English refined the rules of cricket, and a century before they compiled the rules of football and rugby, they created a new breed of sporting horse, a racer that was bigger, more powerful, and faster.[50] Soon after, Thoroughbreds emigrated and founded dynasties in every horseracing country.

Flying Childers had shown what this new breed could do. But Eclipse became the horse who, in his own time and ever since, represented the Thoroughbred's abilities *in excelsis*.

---

[50] I am told that Arabs are gentle creatures. Thoroughbreds tend to be less amiable, and more highly strung.

Coup de Foudre

WILLIAM WILDMAN DID NOT get where he was in business without the talent of foresight. If, he reasoned, Eclipse turned out to be the superstar that the Mickleham team thought he was, the horse's unfashionable sire, Marske, would suddenly become a valuable property. Breeders would pay good money to send their mares to Marske, hoping to produce Eclipse mark two. So Wildman travelled down to a farm near Ringwood in Hampshire, where Marske's progenitive worth had risen to three guineas a covering, and offered to buy the stallion for twenty guineas. At eighteen, Marske was getting on a bit and might not have many fertile years left; his owner accepted Wildman's offer. Wildman returned to Mickleham with his purchase, and advertised him in the 1768 *Racing Calendar* at five guineas – a fee that would soon rise.

The window of opportunity for taking advantage of such inside information was not open for long. Others saw the chestnut with the white blaze speeding over the Downs. It is likely that these observers included Dennis O'Kelly.

Dennis by this time had graduated from blackleg to racehorse owner. In 1768, he entered his horse Whitenose in a £50 plate at Abingdon, and there he met Wildman, who had a chestnut filly in the same race. In spring 1769, Dennis owned four horses in training at Epsom, and made regular visits to the town to check on their progress. As he watched them go through their paces, he spotted another horse, head held low, galloping with awesome power.

It was as momentous an occasion in Dennis's life as his first meeting with Charlotte Hayes, and probably more romantic. For an owner or trainer, the first sight of a young and exceptionally talented horse is very like falling in love. You know that this is the real thing; you know, too, that what you recognize is potential, and that much can go wrong. Adrenalin courses through your system; you are exhilarated, insanely hopeful, and scared. 'He really filled my eye,' trainer Vincent O'Brien said of the yearling Nijinsky, who two years later, in 1970, would win the 2,000 Guineas, Derby and St Leger.[51] 'When he was working, you would just see that he would devour the ground,' Simon Crisford of Godolphin said of the two-year-old Dubai Millennium, who went on to win the 2000 Dubai World Cup. This is what Dennis saw on the Epsom Downs. A recently established owner, ambitious to acquire champion racers, he had found the embodiment of his hopes.

He learned that the chestnut belonged to William Wildman. Dennis, the boisterous adventurer, and Wildman, the solid member of the middle classes, became friendly. Wildman outlined Eclipse's history: how the horse had been bred by the late Duke of Cumberland, had got his name because a solar eclipse had taken place at the time of his birth, had come up for sale following Cumberland's death. Dennis congratulated his neighbour on such a splendid acquisition, and offered to help prepare Eclipse for his first race: he would lend a competitor for a trial.

William Wildman and Dennis O'Kelly were interlopers in the upper levels of horseracing. The men who bred the Thoroughbred

[51] The English Triple Crown. Nijinsky was the last horse to achieve this feat.

in the late seventeenth and early eighteenth centuries, and whose names were to be immortalized in racing bloodlines, were the likes of the Lords Darley and Godolphin; the distinguished soldier and MP Byerley; the royal stud master Darcy (the Darcy Yellow Turk, the Darcy White Turk); and the landowner Leedes (the Leedes Arabian). All these stallions appear in the pedigree of Eclipse; and Eclipse was bred, as was fitting, by a royal duke. He was not, in the normal scheme of things, the kind of possession suited to a commoner. But society was changing. As the eighteenth century wore on, humbly born, entrepreneurial tradesmen were acquiring the means to take part in pursuits that had belonged exclusively to the gentry. When Eclipse came up for sale, Wildman had the contacts and the money to take advantage. His ownership of a horse who was to win five King's Plates in his first racing season was curious enough; what really astonished the Turf establishment was the champion horse's connection with an Irish adventurer whose companion was a brothel madam.

Dennis's progress to Epsom Downs would have seemed even more improbable eight years earlier, when he and Charlotte Hayes emerged from the Fleet prison. Yet by spring 1769 they had reportedly amassed £40,000 – a colossal sum, worth, if the website Measuring Worth is a guide, nearly £4.5 million in today's money. You have to back an awful lot of winners, and sleep with an awful lot of men, to earn that sort of cash. Still, there is no doubt that the couple did extraordinarily well. Charlotte set up a brothel in Soho, and moved on to the fashionable environs of St James's. Dennis hit the coffee houses and the racecourses.

There were – historians' figures vary – between five hundred and two thousand coffee houses in London, and men spent substantial portions of their days in them. The rudimentary spaces, murky with pipe smoke, contained communal benches and tables, counters, and fires above which coffee bubbled in giant pots; the overbrewed beverage must have tasted disgusting. Some had booths, as well as private rooms upstairs. Coffee houses offered

The Coffee-house Politicians *by an anonymous artist (1772). This is an elegant establishment. Dennis O'Kelly's favourite haunt, Munday's, was probably more rough-and-ready.*

newspapers to their customers, and so contributed to the rise of the press. They had particular clienteles: marine insurers met at Lloyd's, the clergy at Child's, authors at Button's, actors and rakes at the Bedford. And blacklegs congregated at Munday's.

Munday's was at New Round Court, near the Strand, until in the late 1760s or early 1770s it moved nearby to number 30, Maiden Lane. It became notorious briefly in the mid-1760s as a source of sedition, when a writer styling himself 'Junius' left at the counter the latest instalments in a series of letters satirizing George III and members of the Grafton administration. But it was more lastingly notorious for its association with Dennis O'Kelly, Dick England, Jack Tetherington, and their gang. Anyone inexperienced in gambling was advised to stay clear of Munday's. One day, a butcher at the table made the mistake of accusing England of thievery, and the even bigger mistake of referring disparagingly to the blackleg's background. England, who was as prone to violent rages as a psychopathic Mafioso in a Martin Scorsese film, beat him up until he recanted.

In spite of this edgy atmosphere, professional men and 'persons of quality' would also drop in, knowing that they would be able to find sportsmen willing to bet to hundreds of pounds. The equestrian writer John Lawrence was, some years later, among these more refined regulars. He found the proprietor, Jack Medley, an amusing fund of sporting anecdotes, though he sensed that Medley's knowledge of racing was not deep. The proprietor was popular with his customers, providing a four-shilling dinner each Sunday at 4 p.m., after some of them had been for their ride in Rotten Row. On Munday's closure, Medley lived on a retirement income of £50 a year provided by, according to Lawrence, the coffee house regulars.[52]

Medley's general line, that his customers' racing conduct

---

[52] Medley's obituary in the *Gentleman's Magazine* in 1798 stated that the sum had come from the Jockey Club.

was not entirely scrupulous, was well informed enough. When he heard that O'Kelly's horse Dungannon had been well beaten in a race, after starting at odds of 7-4 and 6-4 on, he exclaimed, 'Pshaw, tis false it was *not three*, the horse has only *two pails of water* before starting!' This anecdote, which appeared in *The Times*, is not entirely transparent (what has 'three' got to do with it?), but in general alleges that the water was meant to hinder Dungannon's progress. Dennis, Medley is implying, wanted either to bet against Dungannon, or to ensure that the horse would, on the back of a loss, start at longer odds next time.

That was in the future. Meanwhile, Dennis was growing wealthy from gambling, on horses and on cards. We can be sure that his sportsmanship was often dubious, but also that mostly he made money from horses because he understood them. He could spot the good ones to back, and he could spot ones that were not ready to run their best – ones that he could lay (a layer takes others' bets). Once he and Charlotte had started to make money, he was confident that he could use his knowledge to get wealthier still, and to acquire social status. He determined to become a race-horse owner, and not in a small way: he wanted to own the stables and the stud too.

Dennis's aim was not simply to acquire a few racehorses and to land prizes and betting coups with them. The real money, he saw, was in breeding. He would send his best racers to stud, hype up their achievements, and promise owners of mares the prospect of breeding offspring of similar ability. A fashionable stallion might cover forty mares or more in a season, at fees for his owner of upwards of twenty-five guineas a time. The owner might also mate his own mares with the stallion, and then sell the offspring, or – with a view to finding further stallions and mares for the stud – race them. In pursuing this ambition with dedicated profession-alism, Dennis was ahead of his time. His methods anticipated the business philosophy of Coolmore, the Irish bloodstock empire that is the most powerful force in the racing world today. Coolmore has a training centre, Ballydoyle, run by Aidan O'Brien; but the real money rolls in when O'Brien's champions (and other horses in Coolmore ownership), such as Galileo and Montjeu, transfer to the firm's stud farms. Winning races is merely the means to an end, as it was for Dennis.[53]

The base Dennis was considering for his stud was in Epsom, Surrey – then, as now, one of the racing centres of the south of England. Like Newmarket, Epsom is a racecourse with a raw quality. It does not belong to a park, an area of regulated space; it is a route through a landscape. The horses gallop over downs that, beyond the course, roll into the distance. The running rails describe a horseshoe: one tip is past the finishing post below the grandstand; the other, opposite, is where the runners set off at the start of the Derby, the most famous horse race in the world.

The starting stalls clang open, and the Derby runners begin their mile-and-a-half journey with a steep uphill climb. There are thick canopies of trees on their right until, after two furlongs, a gap reveals Downs House, once Dennis O'Kelly's stables. The course continues to climb until beyond the mile marker; then it curves left and descends towards Tattenham Corner, where during the 1913 Derby the suffragette Emily Davison stepped in front of King George V's horse Anmer, with fatal consequences. Some horses hate this bend. The 1986 Derby favourite Dancing Brave, later to prove himself one of the greats, raced downhill so awkwardly that by the time he had entered the finishing straight he was at the back of the field and many lengths behind the leaders. He came storming down the outside, but just failed to catch the winner, Shahrastani. Five years earlier, Shergar had put up a similar performance in the straight, but with the advantage of starting his

[53] Dennis would covet today's stud earnings. Fifty guineas, Eclipse's initial fee, is the equivalent of about £6,000 today. Montjeu's covering fee is 125,000 euros – and he covers a hundred mares in a season.

acceleration from near the front of the field: he won by ten lengths, the biggest margin in Derby history. The ground here has a camber, sloping down to the far rail, and, with just over a furlong to go, it begins a final ascent. Only at this point, having coolly delayed, did Lester Piggott urge his mount Sir Ivor to chase and overtake Connaught to win the Derby of 1968.

There is grandeur about a classic race in such a setting. History is a presence here. The horses racing for the Derby join that history, and indeed represent bloodlines tracing back through Sir Ivor and other great winners to Diomed, who won the first Derby, in 1780, and further back still, to a time before the Derby course was laid out, when Eclipse galloped to the Epsom finishing post from nearby Banstead, with his rivals a distance behind.

In the dry summer of 1618, a herdsman called Henry Wickes, or Wicker – those unreliable early spellings again – stopped with his cattle at a spring on Epsom Common, but found that the animals would not drink. The water was loaded with magnesium sulphate. Wickes and the cows had chanced upon Epsom Salts.[54] Soon, Epsom was famed as a spa town, and visitors were swarming in to take the waters, experiencing the natural distaste that Wickes's cows had shown but suppressing it in the name of health. Samuel Pepys managed to force down four pints of the stuff when he stayed in 1667. He had returned to Epsom despite having found the society there rather vulgar four years earlier, and enjoyed himself a lot more this time: there was 'much company', and next door to his lodgings at the King's Head a party including Nell Gwynn – soon to be Charles II's mistress – kept a 'merry house'.

The patronage of the smart set was fickle. In the early eighteenth century, a man called Livingstone damaged the town's reputation by setting up his own well as a rival to the original,

[54] One local history spoils the story by telling us that Dr Nehemiah Grew of the Royal Society had made the discovery some thirty years earlier.

which he managed to close; visitors decided that Livingstone's water was less invigorating, and they began to stay away. There was hope of a revival of fortunes when Mrs Mapp, also known as Crazy Sally but nevertheless in strong demand for her marvellous powers as a bone-setter, lodged in the town. But Epsom's worthies could not persuade her against moving to London, and when, in the 1750s, Dr Richard Russell promoted the benefits of bathing in the sea, he put an end to the career of Epsom as a resort, inspiring health-conscious pleasure-seekers to head for Brighton instead. Epsom Salts endure of course, even though ingesting them has unsurprisingly gone out of fashion, and even though the name no longer indicates provenance. The Epsom Salt Council, an American organization, recommends dissolving the crystals in your bath, with advertised benefits including an improvement in heart and circulatory health, and a flushing away of toxins.

While visitors were arriving in large numbers, Epsom needed to provide more than salty water to keep them amused. It staged athletics competitions, in which the grand folk watched their footmen race. There were concerts and balls, hunting and gambling; and there was horseracing. The first mention of the sport in the local archives is a sad one: the burial notices for 1625 include the name of William Stanley, 'who in running the race fell from the horse and brake his neck'. The next record helps to explain why Oliver Cromwell banned horseracing: in 1648, during the English Civil War, a group of Royalists met on the Downs 'under the pretence of a horse race . . . intending to cause a diversion on the King's behalf'. The sport got going again immediately after the Restoration, and Charles came, with mistresses, before transferring his sporting activities to Newmarket. A poet called Baskerville recalled a visit by Charles, in lines worthy of the master of bathos William McGonagall:

Next, for the glory of the place,
Here has been rode many a race —

King Charles the Second I saw here;
But I've forgotten in what year.

By the early eighteenth century there were regular spring
and autumn race meetings at Epsom. Another piece of doggerel
portrays the scene:

On Epsom Downs, when racing does begin,
Large companies from every part come in.
Tag-rag and Bob-tail, Lords and Ladies meet,
And Squires without Estates, each other greet.
Bets upon bets; this man says, 'Ten to one.'
Another pointing cries, 'Good sir, tis done.'

Less polite in tone was this reflection on Epsom and its neigh-
bouring towns:

Sutton for mutton, Carshalton for beeves [cattle],
Epsom for whores, Ewell for thieves.

A rather better writer, Daniel Defoe, also observed the scene:
'When on the public race days they [the Downs] are covered with
coaches and ladies, and an innumerable company of horsemen, as
well gentlemen as citizens, attending the sport: and then adding to
the beauty of the sight, the racers flying over the course, as if they
either touched not or felt the ground they run upon; I think no
sight, except that of a victorious army, under the command of a
Protestant King of Great Britain, could exceed it.'[55]
Epsom had horseracing, gambling and whoring, as well as
incursions during race meetings by pleasure-seeking Londoners;

[55] Defoe's lines give you an idea of the atmosphere in which, a few years later,
the Protestant Prince William Augustus, Duke of Cumberland, would be
greeted as a hero for destroying the Catholic Jacobites.

what, Dennis might have reflected if he had used twenty-first-century idioms, was not to like? He took lodgings in the town, and looked round for a house to buy.

It would not be his first property. For unclear motives, in 1766 Dennis had bought a house about six miles from the centre of London, in the village of Willesden, paying £110 to a Mr Benjamin Browne. He found his Epsom house, on Clay Hill,[56] some time in 1769, and that year he borrowed £1,500 against three properties: Clay Hill; a house in Clarges Street, Mayfair, where a Mr Robert Tilson Jean was living; and a house in Marlborough Street, Soho, where Dennis was living, conveniently next door to Charlotte's brothel. Dennis arranged this loan from Mr John Shadwell, giving him in return an annuity of £100; he repaid the sum in 1775. The evidence suggests that he was constantly exposing himself, financially, and that bloodstock purchases and gambling setbacks would occasionally leave him naked. Charlotte, too, was apt throughout her life to get into financial difficulty, although by the end of the 1760s her affairs were thriving. She had opened up a new establishment at a prestigious address off Pall Mall, and she was turning it into the most celebrated serail in London.

Dennis was buying horses as well as property. His name appeared for the first time, as subscriber and owner (and as 'Dennis Kelly'), in the 1768 *Racing Calendar*, the book recording the Turf results of that year. The entry gave no hint of the triumphs to come. Dennis owned a single horse, Whitenose, who ran in a single race (the previously mentioned one at Abingdon), and came last. The winner of the £50 prize was Goldfinder, later to play a small role at the end of Eclipse's career; third was the chestnut filly belonging to William Wildman.

By the time of publication of the 1769 *Calendar*, however, Dennis, now sporting his 'O', owned Whitenose, Caliban,

---

[56] Now West Hill.

Moynealta and Milksop – the horse rejected by her mother and nurtured by hand at Cumberland's stud. Milksop, formerly owned by a Mr Payne, was little, and specialized in 'give-and-take' races, in which weight was allocated on the basis of height. He proved to be a money-spinning purchase. In 1769, he won £50 races at Brentwood, Maidenhead and Abingdon, meeting his only defeat on his home turf at Epsom. He won at Epsom in 1770, and also at Ascot, Wantage and Egham. But by then Dennis owned another horse, who, living up to his name, put the others in the shade.

Eclipse ran his trial against the opponent supplied by Dennis a few days before he was due to contest his first public race. Such trials were common, as a means of getting horses fit and of assessing their abilities. They were popular with the touts – gamblers and their associates who would invade gallops and racecourses in search of intelligence. Sir Charles Bunbury, first head of the Jockey Club and owner of horses who competed against Eclipse, disliked the practice. 'I have no notion of trying my horses for other people's information,' he grumbled.

Trials have gone out of fashion, but the acquisition of inside information never has. Nowadays, journalists and other 'work-watchers' scrutinize horses on the gallops, and stable staff earn a few bob to add to their ungenerous incomes by disclosing news about their charges. This horse is so speedy that he is catching pigeons in exercise, they might report; this one has suffered a set-back and will not be fully fit on the day; this one will not be 'off' (primed to do his best) for his next race, but is being laid out for a later contest. By the time horses get to the racecourse, the betting market is well primed, and offers a fair reflection of their chances of success.

One would assume that Dennis, with his gambling interests, wanted to keep this trial quiet. If so, he failed: Eclipse's early biographers report that touts, no doubt members of Dennis's circle, travelled down from London to see Eclipse in action. But, like

Wildman (reputedly) at the Cranbourne Lodge auction, they arrived too late. Scanning the Downs for a chestnut with a white blaze, and unable to spot one, they asked an elderly woman, who was out walking, whether she had seen a race. The woman replied that 'she could not tell whether it were a race or not, but that she had just seen a horse with white legs, running away at a monstrous rate, and another horse a great way behind, trying to run after him; but she was sure he would never catch the white-legged horse, if they ran to the world's end'. The touts returned to the capital. By that evening, the prowess of Eclipse was the talk of Munday's coffee house.

8

The Rest Nowhere

O N WEDNESDAY, 3 MAY 1769, Dennis O'Kelly set out on horseback for the two-mile journey from Epsom to the race-course on the Downs. An imposing man in his mid-forties, Dennis wore a thick overcoat, which emphasized his increasing bulk; perched on his bewigged head, above blunt features tending to fleshiness, was a battered tricorn hat. Observers would have sympathized with the beast of burden beneath him. Dennis was on his way to watch the Noblemen and Gentlemen's Plate, a good but not top-class contest open to horses who had not previously won £30, and carrying a £50 prize. He may already have backed Mr Wildman's Eclipse; he certainly fancied that the afternoon would offer further betting opportunities. But his interest in Eclipse would not be satisfied by betting alone.

The racecourse was roughly at the site it occupies today, with a finishing straight running from near Tattenham Corner – the downhill bend on the Derby course – and stretching towards the rubbing-house, now the site of the Rubbing House pub. At about this time, a Frenchman called Pierre-Jean Grosley visited Epsom while researching a book called *A Tour to London* (1772), in which he described the scene: 'Several of the spectators come in coaches, which, without the least bustle or dispute about precedency, were

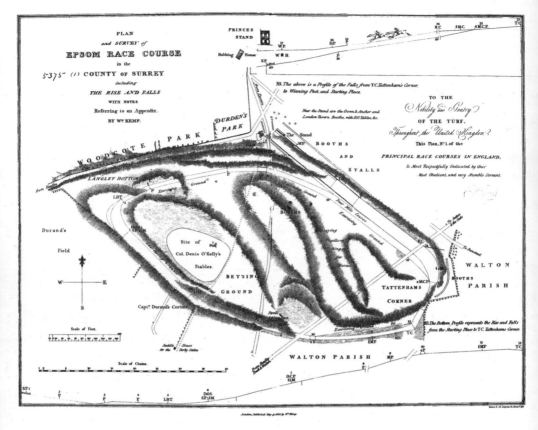

This map of Epsom racecourse shows Dennis O'Kelly's stables inside the course. The course now runs inside the site, and Downs House. Eclipse's first race may have started from near Banstead, off the map to the right.

arranged in three or four lines, on the first of those hills; and, on the top of all, was a scaffolding for the judges, who were to decree the prize.' Some courses, such as Newmarket, were marked by posts. When Charles I visited Lincoln races in 1617, he ordered that rails be set up a quarter of a mile from the finish, 'whereby the people were kept out, and the horses that runned were seen faire'.[57] At Epsom, there were no barriers. The crowd towards the finishing post pressed forward from either side, allowing only a slender passage for the racers. There was no betting ring either, on this or on any other course; gamblers congregated at betting posts, shouting out the prices of horses they were prepared to back or lay. The betting post was Dennis's first port of call.

When he arrived, he realized that the blacklegs from Munday's coffee house had got wind of Eclipse's ability, as Eclipse was the only horse in the race that anyone wanted to back. In response, his odds had contracted severely, and no layer was prepared to take bets on him at longer than 4-1 on. In other words, you would have to bet £4 to win £1; or, to put it another way again, if a horse trading at that price were to compete in five races, the betting says that he would win four times and lose only once. Eclipse had, the betting said, an 80 per cent chance of victory. Those are extraordinary odds for a debutant, and they did not interest Dennis. He had another idea for making money on the race.

Meanwhile, Eclipse's groom, John Oakley, was walking his horse to the start, four miles away in Banstead. The field were due off at 1 p.m., and Oakley was to ride. This doubling up as groom and jockey was normal. Until the early eighteenth century, owners – from Charles II, winning by 'good horsemanship', down – often rode their own horses in matches. Otherwise, they employed stable staff, who were not yet recognized as 'trainers' or 'jockeys' (the latter term might mean, as it did in the context of the Jockey Club, anyone associated with the Turf).

---

[57] Charles, in an ironic prefiguring of his fate, viewed the action from a specially erected scaffold.

The riding groom was a humble figure. But a groom from Oakley's era who managed to transcend the role was John Singleton, who worked for the Marquis of Rockingham. After Singleton had ridden the Marquis's Bay Malton to victory at Newmarket over a field including Herod, Rockingham commissioned for him an engraved gold cup, gave him several paintings showing him mounted on the stable's best horses, and generally treated him 'more as a humble friend than as a servant'. Singleton went on to acquire several farms and stables – a rare ascent. But it was not until the next generation, when the roles of trainer and rider split into specialities, that jockeys became noted figures, and even so they remained lower in social rank than training grooms had been. It is a class structure that persists. Jockeys such as Frankie Dettori in Britain and Garrett Gomez in the US may be jet-setting millionaires, but they are nearer in status to stable lads and lasses than they are to the leading trainers.

All we hear of Oakley (c.1736–1793) is that he was 'a very celebrated rider, in great repute'; we cannot even be sure, because the racing calendars do not tell us,[58] that he was Eclipse's regular partner. John Lawrence, who saw Eclipse at stud, stated, 'We believe, Oakley, a powerful man on horseback, generally, or always rode Eclipse', and there is a J. N. Sartorius painting entitled *Eclipse with Oakley Up*. But a catalogue entry for George Stubbs's portrait of Eclipse at Newmarket identifies the jockey as 'Samuel Merrit, who generally rode him'. This was written more than twenty years later, when Stubbs made a copy of his original work, but it presumably reflects an accurate memory for such details. Merriott (as he is more usually spelled), who has in the painting the long, lugubrious face of the comic actor and writer Eric Sykes, is also associated with Eclipse's two 1770 races at York. Nevertheless, the earliest report we have asserts that Oakley was Eclipse's jockey on 3 May 1769.[59]

[58] They did not list jockeys' names until 1823.
[59] For further discussion of Eclipse and his jockeys, see Appendix 1.

Jockeyship required nervelessness and aggression. Some contests permitted 'cross and jostle', meaning you could hamper your opponents. At a race at York, 'Mr Welburn's Button and Mr Walker's Milkmaid, in running the last heat, came in so near together, that it could not be decided by the Tryers [stewards]; and the riders showing foul play in running, and afterwards fighting on horseback, the plate was given to [the owner of the third horse] Mr Graham.' Jockeys wore spurs, and used them; in the days before whip rules, they beat their mounts without restraint. But no jockey ever spurred or whipped Eclipse.

There were four rivals for the Epsom Noblemen and Gentlemen's Plate: Mr Castle's Chance and Mr Quick's Plume, both six-year-olds; and the five-year-olds Gower (Mr Fortescue) and Trial (Mr Jennings). There was no starting tape, or even a flag; there was simply a starter, who shouted 'Go!'

The five set off, well out of the viewing range of the Epsom crowd, and with only a gathering of local spectators lining their route, as at an early section of a stage of the Tour de France. Oakley and Eclipse took the lead, galloping easily and waiting until they approached the Epsom Downs, with about a mile to go, to pick up the pace. From their perspective, the banks of people swelling forward on either side of the course ahead formed converging lines, narrowing at the finishing post almost to a point.

While his rival jockeys began to wield their spurs and whips, Oakley, who wore no spurs, sat motionless in the saddle. He knew that his mount would rebel against any urging. The racers sped through the banks of spectators, and Eclipse, seemingly cantering, eased further ahead. As the field went by, local gentlemen on horseback peeled away from the crowd and galloped behind, braying encouragement.[60] Eclipse passed the post first without having

[60] Early representations of horse races are confusing at first sight. The course is not clearly delineated; various horses and riders are in motion, and it is not obvious whether all or some of them are racing. Gradually, you realize that the posse behind the leading horses consists of sporting gentlemen, not contestants.

at any point stepped up from a low gear; Gower, Chance, Trial and Plume followed, in that order. Oakley offered his mount a tactful hint that they should pull up. But this was not the end of the contest. It was only the end of the first heat.

Plate races – the most important contests – were staged in heats, and if three different horses won three heats, they would meet again in a decider. The way to settle the matter earlier was to do what Eclipse did several times, and win two heats; or to take advantage of another rule, centring on the distance post, 240 yards from the finish: as the winner passed the finish, horses that had not reached the distance post were declared to have been 'distanced', and were eliminated. Adding to the ordeal of up to four races in an afternoon, each was a marathon by modern standards, two, three and more commonly four miles in length, and had been so ever since medieval times.[61] Most Flat races in Britain today are contested at distances between five furlongs (five-eighths of a mile) and twelve furlongs (the Derby distance). The Ascot Gold Cup distance of two and a half miles is unusual. The Queen Alexandra Stakes, which also takes place at Royal Ascot, is the longest race in the Flat calendar, at two miles and six furlongs. In the US, the emphasis on speed is greater still. The twelve-furlong Belmont Stakes, the third leg of the Triple Crown,[62] is regarded as a stamina-sapping anomaly.

Why did the Georgians subject their horses to these gruelling tests? The answer is their admiration for 'bottom'. If men

---

[61] There is a reference to a three-mile race in the medieval romance of Bevis of Hampton. The earliest chronicler of British horseracing is Fitzstephen, who during the reign of Henry II described a contest at Smithfield market: 'The horses on their part are not without emulation; they tremble and are impatient and are continually in motion. At last, the signal once given, they strike, devour the course, hurrying along with unremitting velocity. The jockeys, inspired with the thought of applause and the hopes of victory, clap spurs to their willing horses, brandish their whips, and cheer them with their cries.'
[62] Following the Kentucky Derby and the Preakness Stakes.

had bottom, they were sound fellows; if horses had bottom, they were sound horses. Dennis O'Kelly was remarkable, in the fond words of John Lawrence in *The Sporting Magazine* in 1793, 'for his attachment to horses of bottom'. In other words, Dennis valued staying power; and, Lawrence may also have meant, he profited in his betting from horses with the ability to cope with racing in heats. If they lost one heat, by design or otherwise, they could win the next. Eclipse had superlative bottom, and never lost either a heat or a race.

However, within ten years of his racing career – and thanks in part to his siring of speedier, more precocious racers – the priorities of men of the Turf started to change, and heat racing died out. New types of races, run over shorter distances, were introduced, the most prestigious ones acquiring the status of 'Classics'. Breeders aimed to produce horses that might win these races, and no longer wanted stout stayers, unless they were breeding for the emerging sport of steeplechasing.

Eclipse was speedy, and would have excelled, as his sons and daughters were to do, at these new contests. But on 3 May 1769, and throughout his career, he needed stoutness too. After heat one, he and John Oakley retired to the rubbing-house for a break of just half an hour. Perhaps William Wildman joined them there, to check on the well-being of his horse. Oakley got on the scales, with his saddle, to assure the stewards that he had ridden with the required weight, while another 'boy' tended to Eclipse with a special sponge or cloth – special in that it had been soaked in urine and saltpetre, and then dried in the sun. At some meetings, but probably not at a reputable one such as Epsom, the horses enjoyed tots of alcoholic refreshment, as long as no one in authority was about. The rules from 1666 at the Duke of Newcastle's course at Worksop stated, 'If any other relieve their horses with any thing but faire water . . . the offender shall lose the Cup.' The five horses were then walked back to Banstead. This retracing of a four-mile course seems an odd arrangement, and one would be inclined to suspect that the plate was run over a different, circular Epsom course were it not for the fact that local historians imply that the Banstead one was in more common use.[63]

Meanwhile, the Epsom crowd may have been entertained by boxing matches. There were probably cock fights, the enjoyment of which by people 'of all ranks' bemused Monsieur Grosley, who considered them to be 'after all, no more than children's play'. Gypsies, who had set up an encampment on the Downs for race week, offered to tell your fortune. Other attractions at the course included food and drink stalls, and gambling booths at which you could play EO, an early form of roulette (the wheel consisted of compartments marked 'E' and 'O'), as well as card and dice games, which the inexperienced were well advised to avoid. At Doncaster in 1793, the EO tables, which had been producing results suspiciously biased towards the operators, were seized and burned in front of the Mansion House. Six years later, at Ascot, a gentleman's servant who had lost all his money, as well as his watch, denounced those who had got the better of him as rogues and thieves; a brawl ensued, and then a riot, which was quelled only by the arrival from Windsor of a party of the Light Horse Brigade. Racegoers also had to keep their eyes open for pick-pockets, who themselves had to take care that they were not caught: they risked summary judgment by the crowd, who would cut off their pigtails, duck and beat them. A report from 1791 described a pickpocket's death 'from the severe whipping the jockey boys gave him'.

Dennis O'Kelly thought that there was more gambling to be done on the Noblemen and Gentlemen's Plate, in spite of the apparently foregone conclusion of the contest, and returned to the betting post. You get a flavour of the scene from a caricature by Thomas Rowlandson featuring Dennis as well as his later

[63] At Newmarket, matches were run over the dog-legged Beacon Course, but races run in heats were staged on the Round Course.

acquaintance the Prince of Wales. Mounted men crowded round. They roared, pointed and waved their arms, somehow in the confusion hoping to find layers or backers at their chosen prices.[64] Dennis, who knew how to make himself heard, got the assembly's attention when he put in his bid: he would name, he shouted in his rough Irish accent, the finishing positions of the horses in the second heat. He tempted three layers, who offered him even money, 5-4 and 6-4. Then he made his prediction: 'Eclipse first, and the rest nowhere.'

It is the most famous quotation in racing, the line that summarizes Eclipse's transcendent ability. It was not a simple piece of hyperbole, of the 'the other horses won't know which way he went' or 'they'll have to send out a search party for the others' kind: it had a precise meaning. Dennis was predicting that Eclipse would pass the post before any of his rivals had reached the distance marker; they would not receive placings from the judge, who would make the bare announcement 'Eclipse first.' Gower, Chance, Trial and Plume would be, in the context of the official result, 'nowhere'.

Dennis's words have proved telling in other contexts too. Reviewing a new (1831) edition of James Boswell's *Life of Johnson*, the historian Thomas Macaulay wrote, 'He [Boswell] has distanced all his competitors so decidedly that it is not worth while to place them. Eclipse is first, and the rest nowhere.' As ever in our story, however, there are alternative versions. One has Dennis saying, 'Eclipse first, and the rest in no place'; another, 'Eclipse, and nothing else.' There are also reports that he made the bet before a race at Newmarket. It was a neat piece of blackleg's trickery: an interpretation of the letter, if not the spirit, of the bet. At the later, Newmarket race, Eclipse faced only one rival after the first heat,

[64] You cannot lay horses in a modern betting ring unless you are a licensed bookmaker, and you are supposed to offer prices about an entire field. But the internet has revived the Georgian way of gambling: customers of betting exchanges such as Betfair can back or lay individual horses.

and was backed heavily to win heat two by a distance. Dennis is certain to have been among the backers. He would not have referred to 'the rest' then, but he may have predicted something along the lines of 'Eclipse first, the other nowhere'.

Over at the Banstead start, Eclipse, Chance, Plume, Gower and Trial set off in the second heat. Once again Eclipse set a steady gallop, and after three miles, as the horses came into distant view, the layers may have been feeling confident: the field was tightly grouped. Then Eclipse began to draw clear. Reports say that Oakley was pulling back the reins 'with all the strength [he] was master of'. Dennis, who needed Eclipse to put more than an eighth of a mile of daylight between himself and his rivals within the next mile, cannot have been pleased at these efforts at restraint. But he had no cause for concern. Eclipse continued to extend his lead. He raced through aisles of bellowing spectators, head low, his long stride devouring the ground. When he passed the post, his nearest pursuer was more than a distance away.

The judge's summary was terse: 'Eclipse first!' A mass of people surged towards horse and jockey, cheering. 'The victor,' Pierre-Jean Grosley wrote, 'finds it a difficult matter to disengage himself from the crowd, who congratulate, caress, and embrace him, with an effusion of heart, which it is not easy to form an idea of, without having seen it.' (How the temperamental Eclipse responded to this adulation, we do not hear.) It is like this today at the Cheltenham Festival, particularly when there is an Irish winner. The 'effusion of heart' unites the racegoers: owners, trainers, jockeys, gamblers; royalty, grandees, middle classes, working classes. William Wildman felt it. Dennis O'Kelly felt it too. In the latter's case, there were unsentimental reasons for the excitement: he had just won a good deal of money. And he had set his sights on the means of making a good deal more.

9

1-100 Eclipse

A T EPSOM ON THAT early May day, William Wildman and his team at Mickleham saw for certain that they had a potential superstar in their stable. Their tasks now were to maintain his form, to keep him sound, and to plan a programme of races that would prove his greatness.

Modern trainers would have let Eclipse take it easy for a while. Following the race, they would have given him no more than gentle exercise, only by gradations building up to a stiff gallop or two; finely tuned, he would have returned to modest workouts in the days before his next race. It is a regime that would have struck Georgian trainers as namby-pamby. At Mickleham, Eclipse was back to the uphill gallops and 'sweats' right away.

Getting to race meetings was tougher then as well. There were no horseboxes: you had to walk. Setting off, with his groom beside him, in the small hours of the morning, a horse could cover about twenty miles in a day. So Eclipse and Oakley probably made their journey from Mickleham to their next race, thirty miles away at Ascot, in two stages, with an overnight stop at an inn. They would have arrived about five days before the race, and continued training on the racecourse, where they may have run a trial against their prospective opponents. Perhaps Eclipse's performance at the trial explains why just one other horse braved turning up for the race itself.

Eclipse's rival at Ascot on 29 May 1769, for another £50 Noblemen and Gentlemen's Plate, was called Cream de Barbade. Eclipse was quoted at 8-1 on. He won the first heat as easily as the betting had suggested he would. But Cream de Barbade was not a distance behind him, so they raced again. It seemed an unnecessary exercise, and it was: Eclipse won again.

This was when Dennis O'Kelly stepped in to make William Wildman an offer. He asked for a share in Eclipse, and Wildman accepted. Why did Wildman give up any portion of this exciting horse to a man such as Dennis? No doubt Dennis was very charismatic and persuasive, and he certainly offered a generous sum, 650 guineas, for a share that was, according to *The Genuine Memoirs of Dennis O'Kelly*, 'half a leg'. Six hundred and fifty guineas (assuming the sum was reported correctly) must have been worth more than that, even in a horse of Eclipse's potential: Herod, a proven champion, had cost 500 guineas at the Cumberland dispersal sale, and his buyer got all of him. Whether Dennis's share was half a leg or a whole one or even two or three, his intention was clear: having bought property in Epsom, with land for racehorse stabling, he wanted the star inmate to be Eclipse. The horse would make his name and his fortune — he knew it. With hindsight, one is tempted to describe Wildman's decision to take the money as one of the biggest mistakes in the history of horseracing, but one can see why the price at that time, for a horse with victories in just two moderately significant races, was irresistible.

Eclipse's next race was a greater challenge. King's Plates, instituted by Charles II, were the most prestigious contests in the racing calendar, worth 100 guineas. To add to the test of 'bottom' that heat racing set, they usually stipulated that horses should carry twelve stone.[65] For the King's Plate at Winchester on 13

[65] Horses are rarely asked to carry more than ten stone in modern British Flat races. In the championship National Hunt races at the Cheltenham Festival, the horses carry 11st 10lb.

June, Eclipse faced five opponents, including Slouch, who already had a King's Plate under his belt, and a decent horse called Caliban, who belonged to Dennis. Caliban was 2-1 in the betting, one report stated. The short price is a mystery, because Dennis, knowing Eclipse, cannot have fancied Caliban's chances. One possible explanation suggests itself: Dennis and his associates backed Caliban in order to lengthen Eclipse's odds. Eclipse was available to back for the plate at even money – the longest price at which he would ever start a race.[66]

The backers of Caliban knew by the end of the first heat that they had, as the punters say, done their money: the horse trailed in a distance behind, and was eliminated. Did Dennis bet on this result? Did he instruct Caliban's jockey not to offer serious opposition? One can get carried away with conspiracy theories, particularly when someone such as Dennis is involved. In any event, Eclipse needed no help from him. He won the first heat, and the second too, this time at odds of 1-10. Even less effort was required two days later, when he turned out for the £50 Winchester City Plate. There were no opponents. It was a walkover, literally: Oakley mounted Eclipse, and they walked over the course to collect the prize.

Rivals were either scared off by Eclipse's growing reputation, or by his performances against them in pre-race trials. At his next engagement, the King's Plate at Salisbury on 28 June, he walked over again. At the same course the following day, Eclipse started at 1-8 for a thirty-guinea City Plate, and won after two heats. He journeyed down to Canterbury on 25 July for the King's Plate there – another walkover. A painting by Francis Sartorius (father of J. N.) commissioned by Dennis a few years later shows the Salisbury or the Canterbury King's

---

[66] The rules of the race put Eclipse at an apparent disadvantage. The contest was for six-year-olds; younger horses did not get the weight concessions available in other types of contest. Eclipse, who was five, carried the same weight – twelve stone – as his older rivals.

Plate:[67] Eclipse and Oakley, in isolation, are walking over a sloping cross-country course marked with white posts.

A new jockey, John Whiting, enters reports of the King's Plate at Lewes in Sussex on 27 July. Whiting was 'up' (in the saddle) when Eclipse defeated a sole rival, Kingston, over two four-mile heats. (The next day, Kingston won a race worth £50.)

Eclipse had one more race in 1769, meeting another of his several opponents with jocular names. 'Eclipse' is itself a fine name for a racehorse, suggesting how he overshadowed his contemporaries. 'Milksop', also one of Cumberland's choices, is less glamorous. We have already met Stiff Dick – it is not clear whether his owner, William III, first called him that. Queen Anne suffered the indignity of seeing her horse Pepper finish behind an opponent called Sturdy Lump. The names of foundation sires and mares were often strikingly descriptive: Old Bald Peg, in reference to white markings; and, indicating reddish tints, the Bloody-Shouldered Arabian and the Bloody Buttocks Arabian. Some owners and breeders went for irony, choosing names that they hoped their horses would belie in performance. There was Slouch, among the runners-up at Winchester; later, Eclipse would compete against Tortoise. At Lichfield on 19 September, he faced Tardy. The result: Eclipse's fifth King's Plate of the season; odds: 1-7. He was undefeated in nine races, and it was time for his winter break. At last, he was allowed to rest from daily gallops, and to enjoy the freedom of a paddock. He would pick up the routine again the following February.

Some time over the winter, or possibly after Eclipse's first race in the spring of 1770, Dennis O'Kelly fulfilled the ambition he had cherished since first catching sight of the chestnut with a white blaze scorching

---

[67] The title is *Eclipse with Jockey up Walking the Course for the King's Plate*. The identification of Eclipse as a five-year-old is the clue pointing towards one of his two 1769 walkovers.

across the Epsom Downs: he bought Eclipse outright, taking ownership of the three and a half legs still in Wildman's possession – or
whatever Wildman's outstanding share was – for a sum generally
agreed to have been 1,100 guineas; he also appropriated Wildman's
racing colours of red with black cap. Eclipse moved the seven miles
from Mickleham to Dennis's new Epsom stables in Clay Hill.

Another story, plausible in its portrayal of Dennis but hard
to believe in this context, is that Wildman and Dennis gambled
over the share. Dennis put two £1,000 notes in one pocket, and
one £1,000 note in another, and invited Wildman to choose.
Wildman plumped for the pocket with the single £1,000. Would
Dennis have risked arousing ill feeling over this important transaction? Perhaps. A less hypothetical question is this: why did
Wildman sell a horse who was clearly a superstar? One theory is
that there may have been threats to 'nobble' Eclipse. In fact,
Wildman would not have had to receive specific threats to be
aware that his champion was at risk: villains were known to break
into stables and dose horses with opium; one poor horse died after
being fed balls consisting of duck shot. You can see why Wildman
may have decided that Dennis and his associates were the men to
handle such difficulties.

But there is a pattern to Wildman's bloodstock transactions.
His ambition and astuteness led him to acquire fine horses, and his
caution prompted him to offload them as soon as they showed
their worth. He might have earned a lot more money if he had
held on to Gimcrack, his first outstanding racer. He was starting
to earn good money from Marske, Eclipse's sire; but a few years
later, before Marske's market value had reached its peak, Wildman
would sell him too. And he might have earned a small fortune, as
well as a more prominent role in racing history, if he had not sold
Eclipse to Dennis O'Kelly.

After his legendary debut at the 3 May 1769 Noblemen and
Gentlemen's Plate at Epsom, Eclipse never raced again at his home

course. In April 1770, at the beginning of his second season,[68] he had more prestigious dates on his schedule. Newmarket, ninety miles to the north-east in East Anglia, hosted a spring meeting that occupied the sporting set, as well as those who visited the town merely for the society, for a week at the end of April. You needed to be there, even if you did not care for racing. Horace Walpole, with magnificently languid insouciance, declared, 'Though . . . [I] have been 50 times in my life at Newmarket, and have passed through it at the time of the races, I never before saw a complete one. I once went from Cambridge on purpose, saw the beginning, was tired and went away.'

Eclipse made the five-day journey to the Suffolk town to face his sternest test yet. He was to race in a match against Bucephalus, the finest horse in the stables of Peregrine Wentworth, a Yorkshire MP and landowner with substantial racing interests and a reputation for sartorial elegance. Bucephalus was another five-year-old chestnut, and he came to the match unbeaten; his prizes included the 1769 York Great Subscription, which was among Eclipse's future engagements. He had the same parentage as Spilletta, Eclipse's mother,[69] and thus was Eclipse's uncle.[70] Wentworth had made the match with William Wildman, contributing 600 guineas to Wildman's 400 – another way of expressing odds about Eclipse of 4–6.

The prelude to this famous race, which took place on 17 April 1770, is the subject of George Stubbs's *Eclipse at Newmarket, with a Groom and Jockey*. Eclipse and his human companions are at the rubbing-house at the start of the Beacon Course, four miles

---

[68] He was still, officially, a five-year-old. Racehorses in this era celebrated their birthdays on 1 May. Now, they all become a year older on 1 January.

[69] By Regulus, out of Mother Western – but see Appendix 2.

[70] Horses are described as related if they have ancestors in common on their dams' sides. Horses are half brothers or sisters if they have the same mother; but they are not described as such if they have the same sire, perhaps because sires are so prolific.

away from the Newmarket stands. The groom looks apprehensive; the jockey is purposeful and confident; the horse is fit and alert. The scene is quiet, but pregnant with the implication of the superlative performance to come.[71]

Eclipse and Bucephalus, nephew and uncle, set off from the Beacon Course start, Eclipse assuming the lead as usual. They galloped for more than two miles before taking a dog-leg right turn and heading towards the finish. As they came within sight of the stands, Bucephalus moved up on Eclipse's flank to challenge, goading Eclipse into the most determined gallop of his career. Eclipse surged ahead. Bucephalus strained to keep in touch until, broken, he fell away, leaving Eclipse to arrive at the line well in front. Bucephalus never raced again. Eclipse, by contrast, shrugged off his exertions to race again two days later.

The records of the match in the racing calendars list Eclipse as Mr Wildman's. But Dennis commissioned the Stubbs painting to mark the victory. And the horse was certainly in Dennis's ownership on 19 April, the date of the Newmarket King's Plate. The race was in four-mile heats over the Round Course (a vanished feature of the Newmarket landscape adjoining what is now the July Course), and Eclipse's opponents were a fellow five-year-old, Pensioner, and two six-year-olds, Diana and Chigger. Diana was the winner of previous King's Plates at Newmarket, York and Lincoln. Chigger had already lost once to Eclipse, at the 1769 King's Plate at Winchester. He was owned by the Duke of Grafton, who had resigned recently as Prime Minister and who a few years earlier had scandalized certain sections of society by flaunting his mistress, the courtesan Nancy Parsons. Grafton, later to own three Derby winners, once skipped a Cabinet meeting because it

---

[71] For a fuller discussion of Stubbs's painting, see chapter 18. Stubbs later identified the jockey as Samuel Merriott. Perhaps John Oakley, if Eclipse's ownership had already changed, was no longer involved. One report describes Oakley as Eclipse's 'constant groom'; another asserts that he was a jockey riding for various owners. It is hard to know what to conclude. See Appendix 1.

clashed with a match involving one of his horses. In common with the sport he patronized, he was despised by Horace Walpole (he who had got 'tired' halfway through watching a race), with the result that his reputation is locked to Walpole's description of him as 'like an apprentice, thinking the world should be postponed to a whore and a horserace'.

Chigger got no closer to Eclipse at Newmarket than he had at Winchester, and was withdrawn after Eclipse won the first heat. Mr Fenwick, owner of Diana, decided that his mare had no chance of adding another King's Plate to her tally. Only Pensioner maintained a challenge to Dennis's horse. Dennis made his way to the betting post, where he found Eclipse quoted at 7-4 and 6-4 to distance his single rival. This is the moment, in some accounts, when he announced, 'Eclipse first, and the rest nowhere', or, 'Eclipse, and nothing else.' But if the Newmarket race is the source of the legendary prediction, the phrasing must have been tampered with, because 'the rest' was a single horse. So it seems more likely that he uttered the words at Eclipse's Epsom debut. Nevertheless, Dennis, and no doubt his cohorts too, backed Eclipse to distance Pensioner, placing 'large sums' at 7-4 and 6-4. Eclipse landed the gamble.

As noted earlier, King's Plates were the most valuable races in the Turf calendar, private matches apart. Even so, owners were starting to see little point in challenging for them if it meant racing against Eclipse. He walked over the course for the 100-guinea prize at Guildford (5 June); he journeyed north, to Nottingham, and walked over there (3 July); then he headed further north, to York, for the hat-trick (20 August). We can picture him on his journey, perhaps with two grooms by his side. He is a national celebrity, and as he and his companions pass by inns on the route, proprietors and their customers come out to see him. At the inns where they stop each night, the senior groom gets a bed while the junior sleeps with the horse, to keep him safe.

At last, at York on 23 August, Eclipse met some competition, and recorded his most impressive victory. It should have been one of Dennis's finest hours. Instead, he was in disgrace.

Late one night at Blewitt's Inn in York, Dennis was apprehended after disturbing in her bed a certain Miss Swinburne, whose screaming had wakened the house. Miss Swinburne was the daughter of a distinguished local citizen, a Catholic baronet. To compromise her honour was a serious affront.

The August issue of *Town & Country* magazine carried the titillating news, dating it 27 July: 'A certain nominal Irish count, it is said, forced himself into a young lady's bedchamber in the night, at York, in the race-week, for which offence he has been apprehended and committed to York castle.' In its next issue, *Town & Country* amplified the story. 'The renowned Count K', owner of 'the celebrated Eclipse', had passed the evening, and early hours of the morning too, at the coffee house, playing the dice game hazard. Returning tipsily to his hotel, he found his room locked. His solution to this problem was to barge the door open, only to discover, in what he had expected to be an empty bed, Miss Swinburne, terrified out of sleep by his crashing entrance. Typically, Dennis saw this as a delightful opportunity, and made a soothing overture.

'Tis all one to me, my dear,' he gallantly averred. 'Sure we may lie here very cosily till morning.'

This proposal was the opposite of soothing for Miss Swinburne, who leaped out of bed and fled into the corridor, 'naked as she was', yelling in horror. Fellow lodgers came to her aid. Realizing at last that to salvage this situation was beyond his powers of charm, Dennis retreated to his room, where he constructed a makeshift barricade. Miss Swinburne's rescuers gathered outside the door, broke through his defences, and seized him.

The author of *The Genuine Memoirs of Dennis O'Kelly* enjoyed himself when he got to this episode. His account had Dennis, on

A Late Unfortunate Adventure at York. *Dennis O'Kelly (centre — note the portrait of Eclipse above the bed) tries to get out of trouble with both bluster and cash, while Miss Swinburne swoons.* 'Honi soit qui mal y pense' *says the motto — rough translation:* 'Shame be on him who makes a scandalous interpretation of this.'

arriving in his room, drawing back the silken curtain of his bed, finding Miss Swinburne there, and gazing 'with astonishment and delight' on her countenance. 'The chisel of Bonerotto! [*sic*] The pencil of Corregio! [*sic*] Never formed more captivating charms. For some time our hero stood, like Cymon, the celebrated clown, when he first beheld the beauties of the sleeping Ephigenia.' Dennis looked around for some means of identifying the intruder, but found only 'a fashionable riding-dress, a watch, without any particular mark of distinction, and the other common accommodations of women'. Then, in what is one of the less credible passages of a generally unreliable book, Dennis became suspicious: what if this woman had heard about his vast winnings at the meeting and was out to use her feminine wiles to rob him? Drink exacerbated the dark thoughts typical of the late hour, and Dennis began shouting accusations at Miss Swinburne. When she shouted in return, Dennis immediately sobered up. He tried to calm her, but a crowd had already gathered at the door. He escaped out of the window. No dishonour was done to Miss Swinburne, 'who was altogether as chaste as she was charming'.

The fact that the York meeting had not yet started and Dennis's winnings were still to arrive dents the credibility of this account of his behaviour. The *Town & Country* version rings truer: you can picture the ever-bullish and well-oiled Dennis hoping to seduce the terrified young woman, still trying to win her round as she flees into the corridor, and conceding defeat only when rescuers appear on the scene.

How extraordinary it was, the *Memoirs* added, that Miss Swinburne should have been given Dennis's room. 'The cause of the young lady's nocturnal invasion could never be rightly accounted for. Beds were, no doubt, scarcely to be obtained by fair means . . .' Yes; or Dennis's avowal that it was his room was a desperate attempt to soften the offence.

Anyway, there was a stink. A prosecution was mooted. But Dennis, thanks to representations by influential friends, escaped with a payment of £500 to local charities and an advertisement in the press. On 2 October, the *York Courant* ran the following notice on its front page:

> I do hereby acknowledge that I was (when in liquor) lately guilty of a very gross affront and rudeness to a young lady of a very respectable family, which I am now very much concerned at, and humbly beg pardon of that lady and her friends for my behaviour to her, being very sensible of her lenity and theirs in receiving this my public submission and acknowledgement; and, as a further atonement for my offence, I have also paid the sum of five hundred pounds to be disposed of for such charitable purposes as that lady directs; and am content that this may be inserted in any of the public newspapers. Witness my hand this 25th day of August 1770. D. O'Kelly

Dennis may have had to prostrate himself before another. *Town & Country* amused itself in this respect, inventing a letter to Dennis from Charlotte Hayes:

> Sir,
> Your behaviour at York, which is in every body's mouth, strongly merits my resentment, that the condescension of writing to you is more than you ought to expect. After the many repeated vows you have made, and oaths you have sworn, that I, and I alone, was the idol of your heart, could so short an absence entirely efface me from your remembrance? And was I to be abandoned for the accidental rencounter of a new face? Had she yielded to your embraces, your amour would probably have remained a secret to the world, and I only from your behaviour might have made the discovery. But you are justly punished, did I not share in the loss.
> Oh! Dennis, are my charms so faded, my beauty so decayed, my understanding so impaired, which you have so often and so highly praised, as to destroy all the impressions you pretended they had

made upon you! But if love has entirely subsided, surely gratitude might have pleaded so strongly in my behalf as to have excluded all other females from your affections. Remember when in the Fleet, when famine stared you in the face, and wretched tatters scarce covered your nakedness – I fed, clothed, and made a gentleman of you. Remember the day-rules I obtained for you – remember the sums you won through that means – then remember me.

But why do I talk of love or gratitude! Let interest plead the most powerful reason that will operate on you. What a wretch! To fling away in a drunken frolic – in the ridiculous attempt of an amour – more money, aye far more money,[72] than I have cleared by my honest industry for a month – or even your horse Eclipse, with all his superior agility, has run away with in a whole season.

This last reflexion racks my soul. Write to me, however, and tell me of some capital stroke you have made to comfort me, for I am at present,

Your most disconsolate
Charlotte Hayes
Marlborough Street
September 4th

A print appeared, with the title *A Late Unfortunate Adventure at York*. It shows a crowded bedroom, with a portrait of Eclipse above the bed; in the centre of the room Dennis is making emollient gestures, holding out notes marked '500' and '1000', while a man threatens him with a pikestaff. An angry woman is holding a swooning Miss Swinburne, beneath a sign reading 'The Chaste Susanna'. From behind a door peeks another woman, barebreasted.

[72] An amusing rhetorical emphasis. In fact, Eclipse earned £2,157 that year. Charlotte's monthly turnover – if not her profit – from her 'honest industry' was probably greater than that.

Nearly twenty years later, following Dennis's death, *The World* reminded its readers of the adventure, alleging that Dennis had commented bitterly – and untruly – that he would never donate another penny to charity. It was also said that he gave an undertaking never again to set foot in Yorkshire. The 1770 York meeting (if he was there) was the last he attended in the county – where, the *Genuine Memoirs* related, 'he was considered, by the ladies, as satyr; and by the gentlemen, who very laudably entertained a proper sense of female protection, a ruffian'. This was Dennis's reputation outside Yorkshire too, and the 'unfortunate adventure' helped to cement it. Miss Swinburne recovered her good name; Dennis, among the people who mattered, did not.

One of the people who was to matter most was the owner of a rival to Eclipse for the York Great Subscription (worth £319 10s to the winner). Sir Charles Bunbury, single again after his wife Lady Sarah (née Lennox) had eloped the previous year, was the steward of the Jockey Club, and was on his way to establishing himself as 'The First Dictator of the Turf'. His entry for the York race was called Bellario. A second rival, Tortoise, came from the stables of Peregrine Wentworth, winner in 1769 with Bucephalus (defeated by Eclipse at Newmarket in April). Bellario and Tortoise had fine reputations, which counted for little in the betting: Eclipse's starting price was 1-20.

The race was run over four miles on the Knavesmire, a stretch of common land that was once the site for executions. York racing week was the north's answer to the big meetings at Newmarket, and the huge crowd at the course included the Duke of Cumberland (nephew of the Cumberland who bred Eclipse), the Duke of Devonshire, the Dukes and Duchesses of Kingston and Northumberland, and the Earl and Countess of Carlisle. One would like to know whether the disgraced Dennis O'Kelly had the brass neck to join them. It would have been a shame to miss this race.

Eclipse set off in his customary position at the front of the field, and this time never allowed his rivals, as he had done briefly at Epsom and Newmarket, to get close to him. Head low, raking stride relentless, he powered further and further clear. At the betting post, a layer shouted that he would take 100-1 *on* Eclipse.[73] After two of the four miles, Eclipse was already a distance (240 yards) ahead of the others, and he maintained the gap, coming to the line 'with uncommon ease'. In one account, Dennis gave a group of men the scary task of standing to form a wall beyond the finishing line to encourage Eclipse to pull up.

Sir Charles Bunbury took the defeat with the lack of grace of a modern football manager. Jibbing at the loss to the upstart O'Kelly, he never accepted that Eclipse was his horse Bellario's superior. And he seems never to have been willing to accept Dennis as his equal – an attitude that was to blight Dennis's Turf ambitions.

Eclipse's 1770 schedule included four further engagements. But he raced only once. At Lincoln on 3 September, he walked over for his tenth King's Plate. Then he returned to Newmarket, where on 3 October he met another of Sir Charles Bunbury's horses, Corsican, in competition for a 150-guinea plate. In the view of the betting market, there was no competition: Eclipse was 1-70. You might have offered those odds about his getting from one end of the Beacon Course to another. He managed it, as did Corsican – only somewhat more slowly. On 4 October, Eclipse yet again scared off the opposition for a King's Plate, and walked over the Newmarket Round Course.

He was due to meet Jenison Shafto's unbeaten Goldfinder

---

[73] Betting in running is another feature of the eighteenth-century betting market that has made a comeback in the internet era. The same odds with a betting exchange such as Betfair would be 1.01. A winning bet would return a one penny profit on a £1 stake.

(son of Shafto's Snap, who had twice defeated Eclipse's sire Marske), prompting jokes from O'Kelly about how the rival connections would be 'gold losers'. But Goldfinder broke down at exercise, and the match did not take place.[74]

That was the anti-climactic end of Eclipse's career as a racer. He had won eighteen races, including eleven King's Plates. His prize money totalled £2,863.50 – the equivalent of about £304,000 today. It is a relatively modest sum: for winning the 2008 Epsom Derby, New Approach won for his owner, Princess Haya of Jordan, more than £800,000.

However, Eclipse's money-making days were far from over.

He had defeated all the best horses of his day. 'He was never beaten, never had a whip flourished over him, or felt the tickling of a spur, or was ever, for a moment, distressed by the speed of a competitor; out-footing, out-striding, and out-lasting, every horse which started against him,' the equestrian writer John Lawrence said. John Orton, in his *Turf Annals*, wrote, 'The performances of Eclipse . . . have always been considered to exhibit a degree of superiority unparalleled by any horse ever known.' The racing historian James Rice put it more fancifully: Eclipse 'never failed in a single instance to *give them all their gruel*, and the need of a spyglass to see which way he went, and how far he was off'. Eclipse was without dispute – except possibly by Sir Charles Bunbury – the champion of his era. Horsemen agreed that he was 'the fleetest horse that ever ran in England, since the time of [Flying] Childers'.

It was time to set about transmitting that ability to future generations.

[74] Jenison Shafto, overburdened with gambling debts, shot himself in 1771.

The First Lady Abbess

SEX FOR A LIVING IS a pursuit that Eclipse and Charlotte Hayes had in common. As Eclipse embarked on his remunerative second career as a stallion, Charlotte was already the undisputed 'first lady abbess of the town'. Her Marlborough Street establishment in Soho, though thriving, had not satisfied her ambition, which was to set up a brothel that was still more lavish, and that would adorn the most prestigious district of London. So, in the late 1760s, she set up in a street in St James's called King's Place,[75] a narrow thoroughfare within sight of the royal residence St James's Palace. Fashionable clubs such as White's and Boodle's were nearby. The grandest members of society had their homes in the parish, and were all – including a few of the women – potential customers, who might visit a brothel as they would a gambling club, as part of an evening's entertainment.

Number 2, King's Place was a smart town house of four floors. You could pass a complete evening there: listening to musicians and watching dancers, conversing with the delightful residents, gambling, dining and drinking, before repairing upstairs. A night with one of the 'nuns' might set you back £50,

---

[75] The road is now Pall Mall Place.

sometimes more; if you had enjoyed all the extra amenities as well, you were looking next morning at a bill of at least £100. That kept out the riff-raff. It was at least a third of what many professional London men, such as lawyers and civil servants, earned in a year.

Cheaper options were available, however. A 'bill of fare' for an evening at Charlotte's – as reported in *Nocturnal Revels*, a scandalous account of the lives of Charlotte and her contemporaries – included the hiring of 'Poll Nimblewrist' or 'Jenny Speedyhand' for 'Doctor Frettext, after church is over' (the doctor's fee for this brief business was a modest two guineas). 'Sir Harry Flagellum' was down to pay ten guineas for the severe attentions of 'Nell Handy', 'Bet Flourish' or 'Mrs Birch herself': it was gruelling work, as the woman eventually entrusted with it complained. 'Two long hours,' she groaned, 'have I been with this old curmudgeon; and I have had as much labour to rouse the Venus lurking in his veins, as if I had been whipping the most obstinate of all mules over the Alps.'

Nocturnal Revels alleged that the most valuable customer of the evening was 'Lady Loveit, just come from Bath, much disappointed in her amour with Lord Atall'. Keen to be 'well mounted', her ladyship was assigned a fee of 50 guineas for the services of 'Captain O'Thunder, or Sawney Rawbone'. For the evening dramatized in the book, O'Thunder got the job. He and his lady neglected to lock their door, and were interrupted *in flagrante* by one Captain Toper, who was reluctant to leave. 'By Jasus,' O'Thunder exclaimed, 'this is very rude and impartinent to interrupt a Gomman and a Lady in their private amusements!' He set about the interloper, but when the question of a duel came up, declined to test his honour. Lady Loveit, dismayed by his lack of gallantry, favoured Sawney Rawbone thereafter.

According to E. J. Burford, author of several books set in this milieu, Lady Loveit was Lady Sarah Lennox, and Lord Atall was Lord William Gordon, for whom Lady Sarah had abandoned her marriage to Sir Charles Bunbury. It is tempting to imagine that Captain O'Thunder was Dennis O'Kelly (who was a captain in the Middlesex Militia by this time), performing stud duties for Charlotte and relishing a liaison with the former wife of the first Dictator of the Turf, the man who was to be responsible for excluding him from the inner circle of horseracing. But the author of *Nocturnal Revels* seems not to have been making this connection, and later introduced 'the Count', a new figure, to the scene.

Nocturnal Revels portrayed Dennis as a general man about the house, and credited him with dreaming up 'elastic beds', specially designed for the delight of Charlotte's customers, who experienced on them 'the finest movements in the most ecstatic moments'. When Charlotte retired, a bawd called Mrs Weston bought these beds, winning for her house great popularity among 'peers and peeresses, wanton wives, and more wanton widows', for whose satisfaction she provided 'some of the most capital riding masters in the three kingdoms'. Charlotte employed males in various capacities too. A satirical sketch in the *London Magazine* reported an auction for 'Cream-coloured Tommy – In plain English, a pimp deep in the science of fornication and intrigue . . . He will cringe, fawn and flatter like a Parisian. A guinea for him! Well spoke Charlotte! A true whore's price! Charlotte Hayes has got him, to be chaplain at her nunnery.'

Charlotte's name appeared in the public prints, in memoirs, and in topical verses – a level of fame that her modern counterparts would prefer to avoid. Cynthia Payne, who held 'parties' at her house in Streatham, and Heidi Fleiss, 'the Hollywood madam', became celebrities who appeared on chat shows, but they did so after scandals and court cases had ended their sex industry careers. Charlotte was a celebrity when she was in her prime. As would be the case in our own age, her status quelled moral considerations; that she provided titillating copy was the main thing. But, entertaining as her story is, it cannot be dissociated from its basis in exploitation and its association with misery.

Consider Charlotte's employees. Although well-known molls catered to Doctor Frettext and Sir Harry Flagellum,[76] the chief attractions of Charlotte's establishment were her own protégées, whose recruitment often involved distressingly underhand methods. One, tried and tested in the business, was to lurk at register offices, dressed modestly and purporting to be in search of a young woman to attend to a lady. On snaring an appropriate candidate, Charlotte would take her to a house that, under a false name, she had rented specially, and wine and dine her. The young woman, perhaps up from the country, would retire to bed, only to find her sleep interrupted by one of Charlotte's customers. 'In vain she laments the fraud that has been played upon her,' *Nocturnal Revels* explained, with a mixture of prurience and compassion. 'Her outcries bring no one to her relief, and probably she yields to her fate, finding it inevitable; and solaces herself in the morning with a few guineas, and the perspective view of having a new gown, a pair of silver buckles, and a black silk cloak. Being once broke in, there is no greater difficulty in persuading her to remove [from] her quarters, and repair to the nunnery in King's Place, in order to make room for another victim, who is to be sacrificed in the like manner.'

For the privilege of raping this virgin, 'Lord C-N, Lord B—ke, or Colonel L—e' would have paid a handsome sum. Deflowerment was a highly prized pleasure, and was the subject of a certain amount of fraud. 'A Kitty Young or a Nancy Feathers . . . could easily be passed off for vestals, with a little skilful preparation.' Charlotte seemed to be happy to convince herself that she was operating with essential honesty, arguing that, 'As to maidenheads, it was her opinion, that a woman might lose her maidenhead 500 times, and be as good a virgin as ever. Dr O'Patrick had assured her, that a maidenhead was as easily made

---

[76] Burford was unable to identify Frettext, but claimed that Flagellum was the Earl of Uxbridge.

as a pudding; that she had tried herself, and though she had lost hers a thousand times, she believed she had as good a one as ever . . . She had one girl, Miss Shirley, just come from the play with Counsellor Pliant, who had gone through 23 editions of vestality in one week; and being a bookseller's daughter, she knew the value of repeated and fresh editions.'

Charlotte would also place advertisements in the press, seeking young women to go into service, and would meet the applicants herself at the specially rented house. Sometimes, the nuns would come, or be brought, to her. Betsy Green arrived in the care of a Captain Fox, who clearly thought that he was doing his charge a favour. A sickly girl in her early teens, Betsy had been soliciting on the street when Fox found her, and had been placed by him in the care of his friend Lord Lyttelton. Since Lyttelton was later to earn the title 'The Wicked Lord Lyttelton', Fox's arrangement showed a lack of insight. However, when he learned of Betsy's mistreatment at Lyttelton's hands, he rescued her and entrusted her to Charlotte. 'Under [Charlotte's] care and tuition her wonderful beauty was brought out,' Burford quoted. 'No age or clime has ever produced such a perfect model of voluptuous beauty.' Betsy became the mistress of Colonel John Coxe, who doted on her. When Coxe (whose name Betsy assumed) was away, though, she regularly summoned 'all her most abandoned companions of either sex and converted his house into a temple of debauchery'. Reports of these orgies got back to Coxe, who threw Betsy out. Later, she acted in Drury Lane, and boasted lovers including Lord Falkirk, the Earl of Craven and the Earl of Effingham. But the relationships did not endure, and she eventually returned to brothel life.

Betsy's decline was the fate of most prostitutes, even when they had the contacts that employment by Charlotte afforded them. Nevertheless, some had the beauty, charm and determination to make good lives for themselves, above all enjoying the luck to find men who did not suddenly abandon them to poverty. A gentleman of means might take one of the 'nuns' as his mistress, setting her up (after compensating the madam) in fine apartments, with servants and a carriage. As long as he did not vulgarly flaunt her, as the Duke of Grafton did Nancy Parsons, it was a dashing way to behave. In that respect, Captain Fox had taken Betsy Green to a woman who offered her better prospects of advancement than almost any other employer in London.

A 'shaggy-tail'd uncomb'd unwash'd filly of 14 . . . bought from her industrious painstaking mechanick of a father for a song' blossomed, under Charlotte's care, to become Kitty Fredericks, 'the veritable Thais[77] amongst the *haut ton*, the veritable flora of all London'. Harriet Lamb, seduced by an aristocrat and abandoned at Charlotte's, became another favourite: 'Kind Charlotte Hayes,' wrote the poet Edward Thompson, 'who entertains the ram / With such delicious, tender, nice house-lamb!' Though well trained in how to behave in society, these women were usually bereft of education. A possibly apocryphal story about Polly Vernon, who adorned the parties that Captain Richard Vernon ('Old fox Vernon') held for his racing chums, told how she reacted to Wicked Lord Lyttelton's enquiry about whether she knew Jesus Christ: indignantly, she protested that 'she wondered at his Lordship's imperence [*sic*] . . . she never had no acquaintance with foreigners'.

In the modern era, prominent mistresses such as Antonia de Sancha (who had an affair with the Conservative minister David Mellor) and Bienvenida Buck (whose lover was the Chief of the Defence Staff, Sir Peter Harding) achieve tabloid celebrity. In the eighteenth century, you could be a courtesan (the paid mistress of a grand figure) and former prostitute, and become a subject for the most prominent artist of the day. Emily Warren was walking the streets with her father, a blind beggar, when she met Charlotte; she was then twelve years old, and illiterate. Charlotte

[77] The courtesan who travelled with the army of Alexander the Great.

did not correct that deficiency, but taught Emily deportment and manners that 'attracted universal admiration wherever she appeared abroad'. Emily modelled for the painter Sir Joshua Reynolds, who portrayed her as Thais and declared that 'he had never seen so faultless and finely formed a human figure'.[78]

It was 'to the great astonishment of all beholders', *Town & Country* magazine reported in an archly ironic tribute to the 'Monastery of Santa Charlotta', that Charlotte was able to transmute 'the basest brass into the purest gold, by a process as quick as it is unaccountable'. Charlotte provided her nuns not only with tutoring in ladylike skills, including dance and music as well as deportment, but also with fine dresses, luxurious underwear, jewellery and other adornments. She did not do so out of a spirit of lavish charity, however. She was investing in the monastery, as well as ensuring that the women, who were indebted to her for these donations, and for board and lodging too, were chained to the place unless wealthy admirers bought them out. Customers who attempted to persuade nuns to leave Santa Charlotta's without compensation for the proprietor were committing a grave breach of decorum, while those who offered presents to their favourites were in fact giving them to Charlotte.

Charlotte advertised her pampered charges by strolling with them in parks and pleasure gardens, and by gracing fashionable venues. At the opening in 1772 of the Pantheon,[79] the grand Oxford Street hall devoted to masquerades and concerts, she and several nuns were among the crowd of 1,500 in spite of an announcement by the Master of Ceremonies that actresses and courtesans would not be admitted. The edict failed, but the MC still tried to bar the dance floor to Betsy Coxe and her then lover, Captain Scott, who observed, 'If you turn away every woman who

[78] The painting hangs in the morning room at Waddesdon Manor in Buckinghamshire.
[79] Now the site of the Oxford Street branch of Marks & Spencer.

is not better than she should be, your company will soon be reduced to a handful!' Today, if a man took an 'escort' to a party, he would probably try to disguise her occupation; his eighteenth-century counterparts were not so squeamish.

The fashion-consciousness of Charlotte's profession is apparent in a picture entitled *A Nun of the First Class* (1773). The nun wears a tight hairdo, ascending to a point bearing a small bonnet, from which descends a row of orbs. She has a choker, a flower in her bodice, and a cheek patch[80] – these patches were originally coverings for smallpox scars, but became desirable adornments. In *A Saint James's Beauty* (1784) (which appears in this book's colour section), the nun wears a dress of some rich, heavy material; her hat sports feathers and a bow. She looks out of a window towards the palace – she is expecting a royal visitor. He may be the Prince of Wales (the future George IV), or his brother the Duke of York.[81]

In addition to royalty and lords, Charlotte's most favoured customers were Jewish merchants and financiers. The print *One of the Tribe of Levi, going to Breakfast with a Young Christian* shows an elderly gentleman at a breakfast table in a large reception room. Above him, a painting portrays a scene of seduction. A smiling, liveried black servant boy holds a seat for the nun, who stands richly dressed for the gentleman's inspection. E. J. Burford speculated that the woman observing them from the sofa – a rather crone-like figure – is Charlotte. Jewish men, he quoted her as saying, 'always fancy that their amorous abilities never fail'; they were civil, and spoke gently.

[80] E. J. Burford said that the cheek patch was there; it is invisible in the print I have seen.

[81] The previous Duke of York, brother of George III, had once, at the end of a visit, insulted the celebrated Kitty Fisher by leaving her only £50. Kitty, whose usual charge for a night was 100 guineas, illustrated her contempt by placing the banknote between two slices of buttered bread, which she ate for her breakfast.

George Stubbs's best-known painting of
Eclipse shows him at Newmarket, before
the toughest challenge of his career.

Scenes from the louche London over which Charlotte Hayes reigned: (**main picture**) Covent Garden, her spiritual home; (**left**) the Vauxhall pleasure gardens, where Londoners gathered to see and be seen; (**centre**) a gentleman is the centre of attention for some King's Place 'nuns'; (**right**) a St James's beauty looks out towards the palace, expecting her royal lover.

Above: Eclipse's long-undervalued sire Marske, painted by Stubbs.

Below: J. N. Sartorius's *Eclipse with Oakley Up*, showing the horse's low head carriage while galloping.

Country gentlemen, of the sort that Wildman and O'Kelly were not.

Stubbs's touching portrait of Wildman and his sons.

The Eclipse Macarony, a surely ironic title (a macarony was a dandy) for the gross, bearish Dennis O'Kelly.

Above: caricaturists did not hold back from depicting the Prince of Wales and his jockey, Chifney, as guilty of pulling their horse, Escape.

Below: Thomas Rowlandson's portrait of members of the Jockey Club, an assembly from which Dennis O'Kelly was excluded.

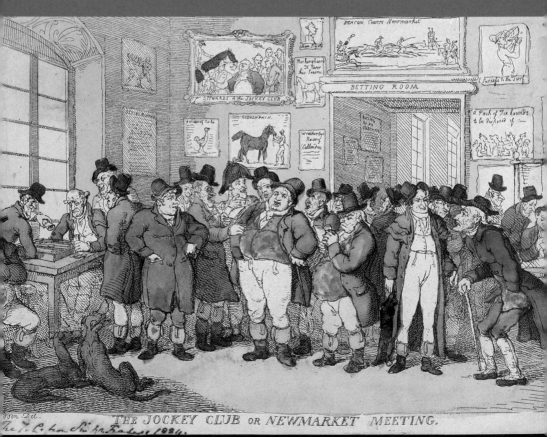

Dennis O'Kelly's nemesis, Sir Charles Bunbury (a.k.a. the first Dictator of the Turf) with (blue-coated) his trainer, Cox.

Eclipse by George Garrard, who painted the
horse at stud, with a stallion's high crest.

One of the Tribe of Levi, going to Breakfast with a Young
Christian *(1778). A scene from a King's Place nunnery. E. J. Burford*
thought that the crone-like figure in the background was 'probably'
Charlotte Hayes. She was to live for another thirty-five years.

Eighteenth-century men rarely allowed their enthusiasm for sleeping with prostitutes to wilt at thoughts of the risks involved. Gonorrhoea was widespread; worse, you might get syphilis (though the distinction between the diseases was not understood), guaranteeing a terrible decline and death. Charlotte's good name depended on healthy experiences for her customers. She employed a doctor, Chidwick, to give her nuns weekly check-ups, and she provided 'Mrs Phillips' famed new engines' – condoms, made of dried sheep's gut and tastefully presented in silk purses, tied with ribbon. Mrs Phillips owned a shop in Covent Garden that offered 'implements of safety for gentlemen of intrigue', in three sizes. A woman of advanced marketing skills, she promoted her wares with this advertising jingle:

To guard yourself from shame or fear
Votaries of Venus, hasten here;
None in wares e'er found a flaw
Self-preservation's nature's law.[82]

However, Charlotte's principles weighed lightly in the scales against commercial opportunities. In this business, you had to be flexible. *Nocturnal Revels* carried the anecdote of a nobleman who arrived at the nunnery with a plan to win a bet of 1,000 guineas against a rival, who was cuckolding him. The bet was that the rival would be afflicted with 'a certain fashionable disorder' within the next month, and the plan was this: Charlotte would provide an infected woman; the nobleman would sleep with the infected woman; the nobleman would infect his wife; the wife would infect the rival. Charlotte's first reaction to this scheme was a show of outrage. 'Heavens, you astonish me!' she cried. 'And I think you use me very ill, my Lord, considering the constant care I have

[82] Mrs Phillips retired to Jamaica, where she was elected to the appropriate post of mistress of the revels at carnivals.

always paid to your Lordship's health and welfare. I know of no such rotten cattle as you talk of; they never come under my roof, I assure your Lordship.' In response, his lordship produced a bank-note for £30. Charlotte said that she would see what she could do. The next time the nobleman met his rival in public, he demanded payment of his bet; the rival handed over the money.

James Boswell was, despite his careful use of 'armour complete', a frequent sufferer from the pox. So was the young William Hickey, who recalled treating himself with mercury (the standard medicine for the ailment) and enduring the unpleasant side-effect – exacerbated by his unwillingness to stop drinking – of 'salivation': black saliva flooded his mouth, and his tongue swelled up to prevent his ingesting anything other than fluids. Thus poisoned, he must have had a strong constitution to pull through and survive to the age of eighty.

In his entertaining account of his rackety life, Hickey noted that he was a frequent visitor to the 'house of celebrity' kept by 'that experienced old matron Charlotte Hayes'. However, he has caused confusion by referring also to 'Mrs Kelly and her bevy of beauties in Arlington Street'. A passage in the *Memoirs of William Hickey* recalled an episode from 1780. Hickey was in Margate, dining with his brother and two friends, when a sumptuous landau arrived, bearing Mrs Kelly, 'two nymphs' and a girl of twelve or thirteen. The girl, Mrs Kelly explained, was her daughter, off to a convent school in Ostend. At dinner, Hickey's brother got very drunk and made leering advances to the girl, offering such gracious observations as 'the young one's bosom had already too much swell for a nun' and 'no canting hypocritical friar should have the fingering of those plump globes'. He lunged at her, but fell to the floor, insensible. Mrs Kelly rushed the girl away, and roundly abused the whole company. Hickey, undeflected by the acrimony and farce into which the evening had descended, retired to bed with one of the nymphs.

Charlotte did start to style herself Mrs O'Kelly, and the 'O' was often treated as optional. But it is misguided to speculate that she and Dennis had a daughter and sent her abroad for a convent education.[83] Hickey's Mrs Kelly is clearly someone else, who is introduced only a few pages after a mention of Charlotte Hayes and her house of celebrity; and Burford wrote about Mrs Kelly of Arlington Street (not King's Place) – her first name, according to him, was also Charlotte – as a different person. In any event, the young girl in Hickey's anecdote may not really have been Mrs Kelly's daughter, but a ward of some sort – though one who got a more sheltered education than did Charlotte's Betsy Green and Emily Warren.[84]

Several of the nuns we have met in this chapter did well for themselves, escaping their cloisters to become the mistresses of wealthy men; some, such as Harriet Powell, made good marriages too. But of course they were exceptional. Most prostitutes, including those who spent their careers in the environs of St James's, endured miserable declines, which would begin before they were thirty years old. And although they were more likely to find grand lovers and husbands in Georgian London than at any other period of the capital's history, they did not enjoy complete social movement. Stigmas endured. Emily Warren became the mistress of a friend of William Hickey's, Captain Robert Pott, who on being posted to India commissioned Hickey to secure a passage for her to join him. Pott's father was dismayed. 'The unthinking boy,' he complained to Hickey, 'has taken that infamous and notoriously abandoned woman, Emily, who has already involved him deeply as to pecuniary matters, with him to India, a step that must not only shut him out of all proper society, but prevent his being employed in any situation of respect or emolument.' The story ended sadly.

---

[83] She is assigned a daughter and a role in the Margate episode in Hallie Rubenhold's *The Covent Garden Ladies*.

[84] The teenage Emma Lyon, later to become Lady Hamilton, may have danced at Mrs Kelly's.

The couple made a 'great impression' in Madras (Chennai), and set sail for Calcutta (Kolkata); but Emily died on board, mysteriously succumbing to fever shortly after drinking two tumblers of water mixed with milk.[85]

Charlotte, meanwhile, continued to prosper. In 1771, she opened a second King's Place brothel, at number 5, entrusting number 2 to a Miss Ellison. She also had an establishment in King Street, for the King's Place overspill. The German visitor Johann Wilhelm von Archenholz noted that King's Place was clogged with carriages in the evenings, and observed of the nuns, 'You may see them superbly clothed at public places; and even those of the most expensive kind. Each of these convents has a carriage and servants in livery; for the ladies never deign to walk anywhere, but in the park.'

Charlotte was in her pomp. Edward Thompson, who had followed her progress, wrote in the 1770 edition of his poem *The Meretriciad*:

> So great a saint is heavenly Charlotte grown
> She's the first lady abbess of the town;
> In a snug entry leading out Pell Mell
> (which by the urine a bad nose can smell)
> Between th'hotel[86] and Tom Almack's house
> The nunnery stands for each religious use;
> There, there, repair, you'll find some wretched wight
> Upon his knees both morning noon and night!

However, no businesswoman could afford to be complacent. Rivals were always threatening to challenge one's status as London's most fashionable hostess, and the entertainments at Mrs

---

[85] Hickey was to suffer a similar loss. In 1782, he travelled to India with his mistress, Charlotte Barry; she died the following year.
[86] The Golden Lion, at the corner of King's Place and King Street.

Cornelys's soirées or at the Pantheon might lure away customers. One had to innovate.

Accounts of James Cook's voyages in the Pacific had found an enthralled audience in England. When in 1774 Commander Tobias Furneaux returned from Cook's second voyage, he brought with him Omai, a young Tahitian, who made a great impression on society. An ode entitled *Omiah* was addressed to Charlotte Hayes, whom for some reason the poet enjoined to coax Lord Sandwich ('Jemmy Twitcher') to secure Omai's homeward passage.

> Sweet Emily, with auburn tresses,
> Will coax him by her soft caresses,
> And Charlotte win the day;
> Old Jemmy's goatish eyes will twinkle;
> Lust play bo-peep from every wrinkle;
> But first bribe madam Ray.[87]

What fired Charlotte's imagination were the sexual rites of the Pacific islanders. One ceremony involved the deflowering of a young girl in front of an audience of village notables, with a venerable woman called Oberea presiding. Charlotte decided to recreate the spectacle in King's Place, but to introduce more variety to it: there would be not one virgin, but a dozen (as her definition of virginity was loose, the casting did not present a challenge). She hired a dozen lusty young men, with whom the 'unsullied and untainted' nymphs would perform under the tutelage of Queen Oberea, 'in which character Mrs Hayes will appear on this occasion'. Charlotte's invitation advised that the rites would begin 'precisely at seven'. Twenty-three men accepted, mostly including 'the first nobility', along with a few baronets, and five commoners.

---

[87] Martha Ray was Sandwich's mistress. In 1779, she was assassinated by a jealous former lover, James Hackman.

The spectacle entertained these dignitaries for two hours, and 'met with the highest applause from all present'. When a collection came round for 'the votaries of Venus', there was a generous response. Their blood up, the distinguished gentlemen now got their own opportunity to perform with the young women. The evening ended on a festive note, with champagne and musical entertainment in the form of catches and glees. In the account in *Nocturnal Revels*, an exhausted but exultant Charlotte, her last guest having departed at four in the morning, 'threw herself into the arms of the Count, to practise, in part at least, what she was so great a mistress of in theory'.

It was the greatest triumph of Charlotte's career, her equivalent of the moment in April 1770 when Eclipse galloped clear of Bucephalus. She was established, and rich, recognized as the nonpareil of her profession. She was the companion of the owner of the greatest racehorse of the day. Charlotte and Dennis were at the summits of two of the most important leisure industries in Britain.

11

The Stallion

FIFTY GUINEAS, THE SUM Lady Loveit paid for her romp with Captain O'Thunder, was also the cost of sending a mare to Eclipse. In 1771, it was the highest stud fee in England. Like the modern champions Nijinsky and Secretariat, Eclipse had achieved fame that transcended his sport, and his transfer to a role as a begetter of future champions generated huge interest.[88] His sexual attention, Dennis O'Kelly could assume, was a privilege for which owners of mares would fork out an expensive premium.

Eclipse, who had spent most of his racing career in dark stables, now began to enjoy more of the open air. He passed a happy, idle winter in 1770–71, grazing in his paddock at Clay Hill. He put on condition – the equestrian equivalent of a paunch; his neck began to thicken too, slowly transforming him into the imposing, high-crested figure that features in the later portrait by George Garrard (see this book's colour section).

His new career probably began in February 1771. There were sixty or more mares to impregnate in time to enable them to give birth, after an eleven-month pregnancy, in the early months

---

[88] In the TV sitcom *Cheers*, a husband whose broody wife was demanding constant sex complained, 'Even Secretariat gets a break now and again!'

of the following year. The foals' official birthdays would be on 1 May. Today, when horses have their birthdays on 1 January, a foal born after 1 May is considered late. Stallions have to pack a lot of virile activity into a short space of time.

Breeders in the eighteenth century did not know a great deal about when their mares would ovulate.[89] Then, as now, they brought the horses to the stud and left them there, perhaps for a month. Stallion owners advertised in the *Racing Calendar* that the mares would get 'good grass', at a weekly fee of about five shillings. The mare enjoyed this grass for a day or so before her rendezvous.

One of the first mares to meet Eclipse was not a visitor. Clio, a great-granddaughter of the Godolphin Arabian, was one of several mares bought by Dennis to breed to his stallion; by the time of his death, he had amassed a broodmare band of thirty-three. Clio faced an experience that was little different from what would happen at a contemporary stud farm – the central act is the same, after all. A stable boy led her to the breeding shed, or per-haps to a fenced-off area of a paddock. She would not simply allow the stallion to turn up and ravish her: she required foreplay, a task from which, on a stud farm, the stallion is exempted. In his place, the horse with the unfulfilling job of 'teaser' arrived and nuzzled Clio's hindquarters for a while, until she lifted up her tail and released a small stream of urine. It was a signal that she was in season, although the procedure might go ahead even if she did not give such encouragement. It was also the teaser's only reward: once Clio had given it, he was led away. Now Dennis's staff took steps to protect their stallion, binding Clio's hind legs or tying them to posts, because mares in this circumstance were apt to kick out, and had been known to deal fatal blows to their valuable would-be paramours.

[89] The breeder is not the provider of the stallion. To breed is to own brood-mares, and to produce a foal by sending a mare to a particular stallion.

Eclipse and his stud groom approached. Inexperienced as he was, the stallion knew what was on the menu, and as he got close to Clio he let out an unearthly bellow, a neigh transformed into something deep and resonant and scary. He reared, and the staff moved into panicky action. One tried to soothe the mare; another lifted her tail; another two, one of them pushing from the rear, guided the half-ton Eclipse towards docking. Once there, he did not hold back, and was done in a few seconds. He rested on Clio for a couple of moments longer, before withdrawing. As Dennis's was a well-managed stud with a regard for hygiene, Eclipse had his penis and testicles washed before he returned to his paddock – the importance of this procedure would be demonstrated a few years later when the great stallion Herod, bred like Eclipse by the Duke of Cumberland, died following an inflammation of his penis sheath. Eclipse was probably due to be on duty again later in the day.

The mare, calm now, returned to her paddock. Everyone hoped that Eclipse's sperm was fusing with Clio's ovum to produce an embryo, but, as this was 1771, they could not scan to check. The best that the stud managers could do was try to maximize Clio's chances of getting pregnant. They may have arranged for Eclipse to cover her again, the same day or within a day or two. Over the course of the next month, they presented her to the teaser a couple of times more; when she showed no interest, they assumed that she had conceived. While Clio remained in her own paddock, visiting mares would return home at this stage. Their grooms and other staff from their studs would arrive, pay the fees (fifty guineas, a guinea for the groom, and grazing fees) and take them away. If any mares turned out not to be 'in foal', Dennis would offer a special deal next season.[90]

The greater frequency of double coverings is the main dif-

[90] Today, when the science of breeding is more accurate, stud owners usually give a live foal guarantee, offering a free subsequent mating if the first one is unproductive.

ference between the eighteenth-century stud and a modern farm. Now that scanning has reduced the reliance on double coverings, stallions are able to cover more mares. Eclipse, in his first season, covered sixty mares, as well as those owned by Dennis; a leading contemporary sire such as Montjeu, standing at the Coolmore stud in Ireland, covers a hundred mares or more each spring. In 2007, the National Hunt sire Oscar managed, with unflagging virility, 367 different coverings. Some stallions do not even get a holiday. At the end of the season, 'shuttle stallions' travel to the southern hemisphere and put in another stint there. It is a busy job; but they have to do it, because the Thoroughbred industry, wishing to preserve the integrity of the breed, has never contemplated the introduction of artificial insemination.

In spring 1772, Clio gave birth to a male foal, named Horizon. By the time Horizon was a yearling, Dennis faced the quandary of all owner-breeders: whether to sell the horse, or train him for racing. If he sold, he earned instant money. If he raced the horse, and other home-bred colts and fillies, he might find that they would show the ability to become valuable stallions and broodmares of the future; on the other hand, he could not afford to give the impression that he was holding on to the best ones and selling only the dross. He held on to Horizon. Two years later, Horizon became the first offspring of Eclipse to race, and won a match over a mile at Abingdon, earning 300 guineas. But his subsequent career was moderate, and he did not graduate to become a stallion.

Such is the story of the vast majority of horses in training, including impeccably bred ones. Great racehorses are rare, only a small percentage of that rare group become successful stallions, and only a small percentage of those successful stallions become part of an enduring line in a Thoroughbred dynasty. In 1771, there were three stallions – Herod, Matchem and Eclipse – who were to join this elite group; and the Eclipse line was to dominate those of the other two by a ratio of more than nine to one.

*

Actually, there were four stallions in this elite group, because Eclipse's sire, Marske, was still in business – indeed, after fifteen years at stud, he was only now, thanks to Eclipse's exploits, coming into fashion. As mentioned earlier, William Wildman had bought him from a Hampshire farmer for twenty guineas, and in 1769 stood the horse at the Gibbons Grove stud in Mickleham at a fee of five guineas. That was the year when Eclipse hit the race-course, winning five King's Plates and suddenly suggesting that his neglected father might be worth something after all. Wildman raised Marske's fee accordingly, to ten guineas; by 1772, he was asking for thirty guineas, and was also taking steps to quash a threatening rumour that was circulating, to the effect that a stal-lion called Shakespeare, and not Marske, was Eclipse's real father. Wildman's advertisement for Marske in the *Racing Calendar* included the statement: 'Mask [*sic*] was the sire of Eclipse. Witness my hand, B. Smith, stud groom to the late Duke of Cumberland.' Most people believed him, but not everyone.

The believers included the Earl of Abingdon. Once again – following his sales of Gimcrack and Eclipse – Wildman decided to offload an asset once its value started to rise, and he sold Marske to Abingdon, who paid 1,000 guineas for the horse. The Earl, who sported the Wodehouseian name of Willoughby Bertie, bumped up Marske's stud fee and earned back the purchase price within a season. Standing him at Rycot in Oxfordshire, Abingdon set the fee at fifty guineas, and a year later he doubled it. One hundred guineas was the highest sum commanded by any stallion of the era. *The Sporting Magazine* claimed that Abingdon demanded 200 guineas for Marske's services one year, and the equestrian writer John Lawrence trumped that claim with 300 guineas, although there is no corroboration of these figures in the racing calendars of the period. Marske became champion sire[91] in 1775, and again in 1776.

[91] The sire whose offspring earn most money through racing.

His involvement with Eclipse and Marske apart, Wildman remains of interest to us on account of his association with George Stubbs. One of his commissions from the artist was rediscovered recently, and fetched a small fortune. It is a painting of Wildman's horse Euston, a grey son of Antinous bred by the Duke of Grafton and the winner of twelve consecutive races, including two King's Plates, in 1773 and 1774. Euston, alert head turned inquisitively, is tall and fine-framed, and carries a jockey wearing crimson silks, which Wildman presumably adopted on passing his original colours to Dennis O'Kelly. The horse is set against a country land-scape, possibly Grafton's estate, with the land behind him falling to a lake with a walled tower on the furthest bank, and beyond that hills rolling into a misty distance. As in many of Stubbs's paintings with country settings, the horse is posed next to trees – in this case, an oak and a willow, of a slenderness to match Euston's physique. What is he doing here, ready to race and with a jockey on his back but far from a racecourse? The answer is prosaic, though the effect of the painting is not. Stubbs was not greatly interested in racing scenes, and quite often plopped down his racehorses against backgrounds chosen simply because his clients would find them pleasing. It gives his work an other-worldly, haunting quality.

Stubbs exhibited the painting at his first, 1775 exhibition at the Royal Academy. After the Wildman dispersal sale, *Portrait of a Horse Named Euston, Belonging to Mr Wildman* passed through several hands, until no one knew, or could discern, the identity of the horse. Only when the painting went for cleaning in the late 1990s was the title revealed. Restored, the portrait went on sale at Sotheby's in November 2000, and fetched £2.7 million – the third highest price ever paid for a work by Stubbs.

The most touching legacy of the relationship between Wildman and Stubbs is the study – some call it a 'conversation piece' – *Eclipse with William Wildman and His Sons John and James*. It is one of the rare Stubbs paintings of a racehorse and owner, leading you to suppose that he was friendlier with Wildman, a fellow self-made man, than with his aristocratic patrons. It shows family members at ease with one another and proud of their horse, and is especially poignant in the light of Robert Fountain's evidence, in his essay *William Wildman and George Stubbs*, that one of these boys and maybe both did not survive their father.[92]

William Wildman — meat salesman, first owner of Eclipse, and art patron — died on Christmas Day, 1784, aged sixty-six. At his dispersal sale at Christie's in 1787, the lots formed, however you count them (there were nineteen paintings according to Fountain's sums, and seventeen according to Judy Egerton's), the most important contemporary collection of Stubbs's work along-side the Prince of Wales's. They depicted racehorses, dogs, a lioness and a panther; a series of four paintings may show Wildman and a friend, two hearty men of middle age, as the visitors from the 'smoaky town' on a shooting expedition at the estate of the Duke of Portland. The sale included some 150 other paintings, including a Rubens and a da Vinci, and fetched, according to Fountain, the very modest-seeming sum of £665 — a figure that, translated to the present-day equivalent of £67,000, is insignificant in the context of subsequent valuations.

Marske, also painted by Stubbs (see colour section) following a Wildman commission, died in July 1779. He had sired 154 winning horses, whose 352 victories earned £72,000. A poet called Samuel Harding, perhaps at the behest of Abingdon, made the following attempt to immortalize him:

> Dissolved in tears, ye sportsmen, mourn the loss,
> Renowned Rycote bears the heavy cross,
> Old MARSK is dead! the King of horses gone,
> Sire to Eclipse, who ne'er was beat by none,

[92] There is a fuller discussion of this painting in chapter 18.

Eclipse doth mourn, Transit, Shark, Pretender;
He was their sire. – grim Death made him surrender.

If that effort had been his only memorial, Marske would not have been remembered for long. Fortunately, his descendants did a more eloquent job.

Eclipse stood at stud from 1771 to 1788, and sired, at a rough estimate, 930 colts and fillies. The best of them, and the one who was to continue the male line that is most influential today, came early. In 1772, the Earl of Abingdon, who had not yet bought Marske, sent his mare Sportsmistress from Oxfordshire to Clay Hill. The following spring, Sportsmistress gave birth to a colt, chestnut like both his parents, and with a white blaze like his father's. Abingdon's stable staff referred to the foal as 'Potato', a name, according to legend, that one lad rendered in writing on a corn bin as 'Potoooooooo'. The horse became Pot8os. His later owner, Earl Grosvenor, tickled his audience at White's club by observing, 'Must say the boy could count, even if he couldn't spell.'

In a five-year career from 1777 to 1782, Pot8os won numerous races at Newmarket, including two Jockey Club Plates and two prizes worth 700 guineas each, and he also enjoyed three victories in a race called the Clermont Cup, all by walkovers. At ten, he retired to Grosvenor's Oxcroft Stud in Cambridgeshire. By that age, most twenty-first-century stallions have been at stud for six seasons. Nevertheless, Pot8os had time to sire 172 winning sons and daughters, among them Waxy, who continued the Eclipse male line from which a huge majority of contemporary Thoroughbreds descend.

Pot8os's defeated opponents included another son of Eclipse, King Fergus. Out of a mare called Creeping Polly, King Fergus was sold by his breeder, Mr Carver, back to Dennis, and forged a racing career of moderate distinction, with highlights including several valuable matches at Newmarket. He seemed unlikely to become a prized stallion, and passed an unsuccessful spell at stud in Ireland before returning to England, where he caught the eye of an owner and breeder called John Hutchinson. Like the jockey and trainer John Singleton,[93] Hutchinson was a horseman of modest birth who had managed to climb the social rankings. Starting out as a stable boy to Sir Robert Eden, who bred Eclipse's dam Spilletta, he went on to train for Peregrine Wentworth, owner of Eclipse's defeated opponent Bucephalus, and rose to become an owner and breeder. He took a liking to King Fergus's 'wonderfully clean legs' and 'mak' an' shap' (he meant, one supposes, the horse's conformation), judgements that were to prove sound. The stallion sired numerous good horses, including Hambletonian – the hero of *Hambletonian, Rubbing Down*, widely considered to be George Stubbs's greatest painting. Through Hambletonian, the line continued to the great and un-defeated St Simon (born in 1881); the Prince of Wales's Derby winner Persimmon (b. 1893); the Italian champion Ribot, twice a winner (in 1955 and 1956) of the Prix de l'Arc de Triomphe; and Alleged, another dual Arc winner (1977 and 1978).

You can see how rare it is to make an enduring mark in bloodstock breeding. Eclipse is the most influential sire of all time thanks to only two of his hundreds of sons. While some others did well at stud, their male descendants, sooner or later, flopped, and their male lines died out.

Breeders of the era could not foresee these developments. All they had to go on were the performances of Eclipse's sons and daughters on the racecourse. What particularly strikes the con-temporary observer is that Eclipse sired three of the first five winners of the Derby: Young Eclipse (1781), Saltram (1783), and Sergeant (1784). But the Derby was not yet the most prestigious horse race in the world. It was a new contest, and over what was, by the standards prevalent when Eclipse was racing, a short dis-

---

[93] See chapter 8.

tance. For breeders, the victories confirmed the impression that although the progeny of Eclipse were speedy, they did not necessarily have 'bottom'.

In the 1770s, Eclipse faced competition as a stallion from highly regarded rivals such as Matchem and Snap, about whom the breeding adage went, 'Snap for speed, and Matchem for truth and daylight' — truth and daylight in this context meaning soundness and stamina. Then there was Marske, Eclipse's own father. Marske was succeeded, following his two years as champion sire, by Herod, who held the title from 1777 to 1784 and who handed over the crown to his son, Highflyer, champion from 1785 to 1796, and again in 1798. (King Fergus managed to intervene in 1797; one historian thinks that Pot8os, another Eclipse son, was the true champion in 1794.) The writer John Lawrence introduced the now-insignificant Goldfinder as another competitor: 'The produce of Eclipse ran too generally and exclusively to speed; and that, in toughness and continuance, they were greatly surpassed by their competitors on the course, the stock of King Herod and Goldfinder.' Eclipse was in fact never champion sire, finishing runner-up to Herod and then to Highflyer every year from 1778 to 1788.

How could this be? Eclipse's celebrity, and the subsequent records of his descendants, make his failure to win a single sire's championship appear extraordinary. Every contemporary reference to Eclipse indicates that he was a household name: the Seabiscuit, the Red Rum, the Desert Orchid of his day, only with a far more awesome reputation as a racer. The flamboyant, dodgy personality of his owner, Dennis O'Kelly, heightened the mystique, as did Dennis's talent for hype. Yet the words of John Lawrence — one of Eclipse's greatest admirers — hint that a few observers may have been able to separate their awe for Eclipse from their assessment of his progeny. There were also class considerations: some men of the Turf preferred not to do business with a scandalous Irish upstart.

Richard Tattersall, who had supported the rumour that Shakespeare was Eclipse's sire, was gleeful when a colt called Noble won the 1786 Derby. Noble, who had started at the huge price of 30-1, was a son of Tattersall's stallion Highflyer, and defeated the favourite, Eclipse's son Meteor. Eclipse had had his day, Tattersall exulted. Described in a nineteenth-century history of the Jockey Club as 'an auctioneer, though of excellent repute' (the same work characterized Dennis O'Kelly as 'a disreputable adventurer'), Tattersall was hugely proud of Highflyer. He built a mansion called Highflyer Hall, and was pictured there, bluff of countenance and sporting a wide-brimmed hat, standing in front of a painting of the horse and with his hand resting on a document bearing the instruction 'Highflyer not to be sold' (see colour section). When Highflyer died, in 1793, Tattersall's tribute to him – more touching than Harding's ode to Marske – was this grave-stone inscription: 'Here lieth the perfect and beautiful symmetry of the much lamented Highflyer, by whom and his wonderful off-spring the celebrated Tattersall acquired a noble fortune, and was not ashamed to acknowledge it.'

Tattersall and his contemporaries would have expected the Herod and Highflyer male line, and that of Matchem, to have sur-passed Eclipse's in later generations. But Eclipse has come out on top – by a distance. It is estimated that 95 per cent of contempo-rary Thoroughbreds are Eclipse's male line descendants. A check of the lists of top contemporary stallions suggests that the per-centage may be even higher than that: the representatives of the Herod and Matchem lines are sparse. How did Eclipse become, in the words of racing historian Arthur FitzGerald, 'the most influ-ential stallion in the history of the Thoroughbred'?

Herod and Highflyer have a good deal to do with it. Georgian breeders noted that uniting the Herod and Eclipse lines was a remarkably effective 'nick' – a cross that produced out-standing racers. At his death, Dennis O'Kelly owned nine daughters of Herod, whom he had bought to breed with Eclipse and with Eclipse's sons. The nick also worked the other way round, when Herod covered Eclipse's daughters, and it worked when Herod's son Highflyer covered Eclipse's daughters.[94] 'Send me your Eclipse mares,' Richard Tattersall said, 'and you shall have the best racehorses in England as a result.' It was no vain boast; and it offered a formula for the breeding of champions for years to come.

[94] I apologize for neglecting the female role in my discussion of Eclipse's male descendants. His daughters are also significant presences in pedigrees. Horses, of course, inherit half their genes from their fathers and half from their mothers, so there is no reason to treat the sire as more important. However, a successful sire produces hundreds (these days, thousands) of offspring, whereas a successful dam produces, if she is particularly fertile and robust, about ten. Moreover, the Thoroughbred is an inbred animal, so the male line saturates pedigrees to an ever greater extent as the generations continue. That is why the Eclipse male line is so important.

12

The Most Glorious Spectacle

IN THE LAST QUARTER of the eighteenth century, one world began to make way for another. Concepts of citizenship, alien to Britain's royalist traditions, fuelled revolutions in America and France. Wars transformed the map of Europe. Industrialization gathered pace, bringing with it a more turbulent social structure. The press became a mass medium. There was a new imaginative atmosphere: in place of the earthy humour of Henry Fielding, there was the fine moral discrimination of Jane Austen, and the robust intellectual conservatism of Samuel Johnson was followed by the Romantic idealism of William Wordsworth, Samuel Taylor Coleridge and Percy Bysshe Shelley. Gentlemen and ladies were expected to behave with far greater decorum than had their scandalous predecessors. There was a new notion of personality. Observing the likes of Charles James Fox, William Hickey and even Dennis O'Kelly, you get the impression of a certain self-consciousness, as if these men were playing a game or had adopted roles: the flamboyant statesman, the rake, the sporting dandy. While the ideal of the British sporting gentleman persisted, a new ideal, of sincerity to the true self, came to inspire people's behaviour.

One risks bathos by appending horseracing, aptly described

as the 'great triviality',[95] to this list. But remember the scene on Derby day. No other sport has so many ties to so many levels of society. It was bound to change too.

In essence, the eighteenth-century gentlemanly pursuit became a mass entertainment, and more professional – more industrialized, if you like. Three men were at the heart of the transformation of racing, driving innovations that continue to shape the sport today; and they were all Eclipse's contemporaries.

In about 1750, a group of sporting gentlemen took to meeting regularly in the Star and Garter pub in St James's. Calling themselves the Jockey Club, they established a race to be staged during the spring meeting at Newmarket, where they acquired premises: 'A contribution free plate [the entrants did not have to pay a fee], by horses the property of the noblemen and gentlemen belonging to the Jockey Club at the Star and Garter in Pall Mall, one heat on the Round Course, weight eight stone, seven pound.'

The Jockey Club, which evolved into an administrative body and later moved into estate management, is not what we normally understand by the word club, and it has no jockeys in it. In the eighteenth century, groups of men meeting frequently, such as those taking regular rooms in coffee houses or taverns, tended to call themselves clubs. Jockeys were owners and others connected to the Turf. At first, the noblemen and gentlemen probably thought of the JC as a forum for socializing, drinking, and challenging each other to races, but soon they began giving instructions on how races were to be run, and they gradually assumed the status of the governing body at Newmarket. Later, they were to govern the whole of British racing, with responsibilities such as compiling the fixture list, controlling the rules of the sport, disciplining miscreants, licensing trainers and jockeys and other staff, and ensuring proper veterinary care; they also

[95] By Phil Bull, the founder of the ratings organization Timeform.

acquired a good deal of land, as well as various racecourses.[96]

In 1762, the Jockey Club announced the official colours that members would use consistently thenceforth. The men who registered their colours included a royal duke (Cumberland – riders of his horses wore purple), five other dukes, a marquess, five earls, a viscount, and a baron. A historian of the JC wrote that the members were 'almost to a man, of royal or noble or hereditarily gentle birth; and they were, almost to a man, either hereditary or elective legislators, for nearly all the commoners, or at any rate a large proportion of them, were Members of Parliament'. (That was exactly the profile of the clientele at Charlotte Hayes's King's Place nunnery.) An industrialist commented, perhaps with bitterness, that 'To become a member of the Jockey Club you have to be a relative of God – and a close one at that.'

Such breeding did not mean that JC members were not rackety. They gambled, they drank and they womanized. Their first home, the Star and Garter, was where Lord Byron (great-uncle of the poet) killed a man called Chaworth following an argument about dealing with poachers, and where Lord Barrymore bet successfully that he could find a man who would eat a live cat. (It was also where, in 1774, the rules of cricket were refined.) In 1792, a member called Charles Pigott broke ranks to write *The Jockey Club: Or a Sketch of the Manners of the Age*, a scandalous collection of portraits of contemporaries from the Prince of Wales down. Pigott was expelled.

One member who remained above reproach, however, was

---

[96] Having argued that horseracing reflects society, I must concede that sometimes the adaptation to wider influences is sluggish. The Jockey Club, a self-selecting body, ran British racing, the tenth largest industry in the country, until 1993, when it transferred its administrative responsibilities to the British Horseracing Board. In 2006, the JC handed over the policing of the sport to the Horseracing Regulatory Authority. A year later, the BHB and HRA merged, to form the British Horseracing Authority. Now, the JC concentrates on the administration of its racecourses and other estates.

the baronet Sir Charles Bunbury, the man who cemented the JC's position as the authority of racing. Uninspiring both as an MP and as a husband, Bunbury did not allow the elopement of his wife Lady Sarah to deflect him from his real passion, Turf affairs. (He had, briefly, entertained the notion of challenging Sarah's lover Lord William Gordon to a duel, until it was pointed out to him that if adultery were to be the grounds, he might have to issue challenges to quite a few other men as well.) He immersed himself in racing and in his role as steward of the Jockey Club, of which he was later recognized as perpetual president, or 'Dictator of the Turf'.

Bunbury's sturdiness was the making of the Jockey Club. When the Prince of Wales became involved in a racing scandal, Bunbury did not hesitate to instruct the heir to the throne on how he was expected to behave.[97] His inflexible nature could cause him to be mean, however. When his colt Smolensko, ridden by Tom Goodisson, won the 1813 Derby, Bunbury and others won a considerable amount of money from a bookmaker called Brograve. Unable to honour the bets, Brograve shot himself. Paying Goodisson, who had ridden Smolensko to three victories, Bunbury handed over just a modest sum; Brograve's drastic default, he explained, meant that it was all he could afford.

Today, Eclipse's peerless status has biblical authority in the racing world. He is one of the rare historical figures to achieve a reputation beyond dispute. Sport, in which achievement is usually measurable, arouses just as much disagreement among aficionados as do more subjective matters such as the arts – tennis fans, for example, differ about the relative merits of Bjorn Borg and John McEnroe, in spite of the existence of records, and even head-to-head results, that might settle the issue. But at least there is a record of Eclipse's achievements: we know the races he won, who

[97] This was the Escape Affair. See chapter 17.

his opponents were, in some cases how easily he won, and how favoured he was in the betting. We can also trace his extraordinary influence as a stallion.

The man largely responsible for introducing authority to racing records, as Bunbury brought it to the sport's governance, was James Weatherby. A Durham solicitor, Weatherby came to Newmarket in 1770 as keeper of the match book – the record of match races arranged and run – and secretary of the Jockey Club. We do not know a great deal about him, except that he was quite an operator.

The first 'racing calendar', John Cheny's *An Historical List of All Horse Matches Run, and of All Plates and Prizes Run for in England*, had appeared in 1727. Before that, when record keeping was in the hands of keepers of private stud books, accounts of races were rare – a fortunate exception being this glimpse, from the Duke of Devonshire's stud book, of the brilliance of Flying Childers: 'Chillders [*sic*] & Fox run over ye long course, Chillders carried 9 stone, Fox 8 stone. Chillders beat Fox a distance and a half.' Cheny's and subsequent calendars included race results, notices of rules, selected records of cock fights, advertisements promoting stallions, and advertisements for medicines such as 'Watson's Cambridge horse balls'. However, when Weatherby arrived on the scene, during Eclipse's second season, there were rival calendars, one edited by Mr B. Walker, the other by William Tuting and Thomas Fawconer.

After Walker withdrew from the market, Weatherby, who had supplanted Tuting as keeper of the match book and Fawconer as Jockey Club secretary, set about supplanting their racing calendar as well. He persuaded Tuting to abandon Fawconer; then he seized and concealed 1,600 copies of Fawconer's calendar before it came out. Why were Fawconer's subscribers not furious with him? Whatever Weatherby's tactics were for deflecting the blame for the disappearance of the books, they worked, and in 1774 he found a healthy collection of subscribers for his own publication (a record of the 1773 season). Fawconer carried on nonetheless, but died in 1777. At this point, Weatherby announced brazenly that Fawconer's 1772 edition, 'having hitherto been distributed to but a few of the subscribers, the rest of the subscribers, and others, are hereby informed that the same may be had of Mr Weatherby'.

Racing results were only half of the records that racing, if it were to be an efficient industry, required. They needed to be supplemented by, and linked to, pedigrees. In the words of a modern historian, a fair market in horses requires accurate pedigrees as surely as the motor market requires vehicle registration documents. Anyone making a commercial decision about bloodstock will ask: what is a horse's breeding, what were the performances of its ancestors, and what does that evidence suggest about the horse's potential? The answers, until Weatherby came along, were usually vague.

Weatherby's nephew, also called James, set about producing a comprehensive account of racing bloodlines, commissioning an author called William Sydney Towers to research in old racing calendars and in whatever private stud books he could lay his hands on. In 1791, *An Introduction to a General Stud Book* (compiled by Towers) began the job of rescuing the Turf 'from the increasing evil of false and inaccurate pedigrees'; it was succeeded by further introductions, until the volume regarded as the definitive first edition of the *General Stud Book* appeared, in 1808.

The *GSB* listed mares with their offspring. Looking for Eclipse in the index, we are directed to Spilletta, 'Bred by Sir Robert Eden, foaled in 1749, got by Regulus, her dam (Mother Western) by Smith's Son of Snake – Lord D'Arcy's Old Montagu – Hautboy – Brimmer.' (These last three names are the damsires in the tail female line – the bottom line of the pedigree, from mother to her mother, and then to her mother's mother, and so on.) Spilletta's foals are a bay filly (foaled in 1759) by the Duke of Cumberland's Crab; Eclipse (1764) by Marske; Proserpine (1766) by Marske; Garrick (1772) by Marske; and Briseis (1774) by Chrysolite.[98] We can trace further male lines in the pedigree by looking for Eclipse's sire Marske (out of the Ruby Mare) in the index, and then for Marske's sire Squirt (out of Sister to Old Country Wench), and so on. A later volume of the *GSB* authorized Eclipse's date of birth as 1 April 1764: 'Eclipse was so called, not because he eclipsed all competitors, but from having been foaled during the great eclipse of 1764.'

Assembling this information, from inconsistent calendars and private records of fitful reliability, must have been a painstaking and frustrating job. But Weatherby and Towers performed it with remarkable accuracy. There were further, even thornier problems for compilers of later editions, as more and more horses came up for inclusion. Who should be in, and who out? The editors explained that 'half-bred' animals were not eligible; and in 1821, they first mentioned the implied contrasting term, 'Thoroughbred'. By it, they meant a horse descended from a particular group of mares, accepted as the foundation mothers of the breed.

One of the earliest quandaries concerned a horse who was, like his grandfather Eclipse, a national celebrity. Copenhagen was Wellington's charger at the Battle of Waterloo. He had inherited the Eclipse temperament: when Wellington dismounted following the battle and gave him a pat, Copenhagen lashed out, nearly achieving the fatal blow that Napoleon's forces had failed to land. Not bearing a grudge, Wellington said of him, 'There may have been many faster horses, no doubt many handsomer, but for bottom and endurance I never saw his fellow.' The problem was Copenhagen's inheritance from Lady Catherine, his mother. Lady Catherine's owner, General Grosvenor, had lobbied to get her included in the *GSB*, and Copenhagen appeared in one edition as well. But the editors later removed them, on the grounds that

[98] Eclipse's pedigree is examined in Appendix 2.

among Lady Catherine's ancestors was 'a hunting mare not thorough-bred'.

There were more incendiary issues than this to come, with implications for international diplomacy. The term 'Thoroughbred' evolved to mean, in effect, 'horses granted admission to the *General Stud Book*'. But that caused a problem when racing developed as an international sport and industry, because Weatherbys could not trace back a good many American horses, for example, to the English foundation mares. Much ill feeling ensued: while English bloodstock experts argued that 'the pages of the *Stud Book* should be zealously safeguarded', American breeders thought that the dastardly British were closing off the market by stigmatizing American horses as half-bred. The dispute did not begin to be resolved until the middle of the twentieth century, and a more practical definition of 'Thoroughbred' at last appeared in 1969.[99] More recently, Weatherbys has granted admission to horses traced to sources in the stud books of other countries. The ancestry of the Thoroughbred is no longer exclusively English.[100]

Dealing with such matters is more than a simple publishing job. Weatherbys, which is still in business and still a family firm (and which, after James Weatherby's initial shenanigans, has maintained a fine reputation for integrity), continues to compile the

---

[99] 'Any horse claiming admission to the *General Stud Book* should be able: 1. To be traced in all points of its pedigree to strains already appearing in pedigrees in earlier volumes of the *General Stud Book*, those strains to be designated "thoroughbred". Or: 2. To prove satisfactorily eight "thoroughbred" crosses consecutively including the cross of which it is the progeny and to show such performances on the Turf in all sections of its pedigree as to warrant its assimilation with "thoroughbreds".'

[100] Or rather, traceable to imported sires and to English-domiciled mares whose precise breeding is unknown, but that may have included a good deal of Eastern blood. British racing, both Flat and National Hunt, has always been open to non-Thoroughbreds: in 1948, two English Classics, the 2,000 Guineas and St Leger, were won by horses (My Babu and Black Tarquin respectively) whom the *GSB* considered unacceptable.

Racing Calendar and *General Stud Book*, and also manages race entries, issues lists of runners and riders, allocates weights, registers horses and owners, and collects and distributes prize money. It is a kind of civil service of British racing.

Our third influential man of the Turf left us the race that was to represent the summit of Thoroughbred achievement, as well as one of the most widely used of all eponyms: Derby.

 From the 1770s, racing's organizers began to introduce new kinds of contests, both to encourage the speediness that stallions such as Eclipse were engendering, and to offer better spectacles to the public. Four-mile heats went out of fashion, and in came shorter races, which you might be able to see from start to finish if you had a decent vantage point, and which took a few minutes, rather than a whole afternoon, to decide[101] (they were to heat races roughly what limited-overs cricket matches are to five-day Tests). Racecourses also staged races that encouraged ordinary people to bet. At matches and plates, huge sums were bet by racing insiders and their friends, who felt that they knew what was going to happen. Now handicaps, which assigned weights to horses according to their abilities, created – at least in theory – a more open betting market. In 1791, forty thousand people gathered at Ascot to watch the Oatlands Stakes, in which the bottom weight and officially least able horse carried 5st 3lb (it is hard to form a mental image of his jockey), and the top weight and officially best horse carried 9st 10lb. The winner, at 20-1, was

---

[101] Match racing took longer to decline. One of the most celebrated races of the nineteenth century, drawing a hundred thousand spectators to York in spring 1851, was the match in which The Flying Dutchman (the 1849 Derby winner) defeated Voltigeur (the 1850 winner), avenging a shock defeat the previous autumn. A few matches continued to take place in the twentieth century, most famously – the fame of the contest revived by a hit book and film – between Seabiscuit and War Admiral on 1 November 1938, when Seabiscuit triumphed by four lengths.

Baronet,[102] owned by the Prince of Wales. As a betting magnet, the race was a huge success, with £100,000 staked on the result; as an enricher of punters, however, it was a disaster. So few people had backed Baronet that, a contemporary wrote, 'Horses are daily thrown out of training, jockeys are going into mourning, grooms are becoming EO [roulette] merchants and strappers are going on the highway.'.

Some of the most venerable races in the calendar followed the Oatlands Stakes model: the Ebor, the Cambridgeshire and the Grand National are among the examples. The Melbourne Cup, the race that stops Australia, is also a handicap. The Santa Anita Handicap is the event that Seabiscuit's owner, Charles Howard, most wanted to win. However, it is the Classics and prestigious weight-for-age races (older horses carry more weight, but otherwise the weights are level) that reveal the greatest champions: the St Simons, Nijinskys and Secretariats. These races have also revealed the supremacy of the Eclipse line.

The first of these races, which came to be known as the Classics, was the St Leger. In 1776, a group of sportsmen subscribed to a new sweepstakes – a relatively recent innovation, in which several owners advanced entry fees that formed the prize money – at Doncaster. The race was over two miles (later reduced to its current distance of an extended one mile, six furlongs), and it was won by Lord Rockingham's Allabaculia.[103] In 1778, the sportsmen voted to name their race after one of their number, General Anthony St Leger, an Irish-born, Eton and Cambridge-educated former MP who bred and raced horses from the nearby Park Hill estate.

The catalyst for the next two Classics was another Eton and

---

[102] Baronet was a son of Vertumnus, who was standing at the O'Kelly stud. Vertumnus's sire was Eclipse.
[103] By a sire called Sampson, Allabaculia – unnamed, as was the race, in the first records – was a great-granddaughter of Flying Childers. Her dam is unknown.

Cambridge man. Edward Smith-Stanley, the 12th Earl of Derby, began his association with Epsom in 1773, when at the age of twenty-one he took over the lease of a nearby house called The Oaks. A year later, he married Lady Elizabeth Hamilton. The wedding was grand. General John Burgoyne, who had owned the property previously and who three years later was to surrender to American forces at Saratoga, played host and wrote a masque, *The Maid of the Oaks*, for the occasion; David Garrick, the actor and impresario, stage-managed the drama; Robert Adam, the great architect, designed the dance pavilion. But despite this splendid inauguration, and the arrivals of two daughters and a son, the marriage foundered. While playing cricket at The Oaks, Lady Derby met the Duke of Dorset, fell in love, and ran off with him. Lord Derby declined to divorce her, so preventing her from marrying the Duke, but also preventing himself from marrying the woman he loved, the actress Elizabeth 'Nellie' Farren. Lady Derby's death in 1797 cleared the way. This second union was much happier, even though Lord Derby's new bride did draw the line, the historian Roger Mortimer wrote, 'at cock-fights staged in her drawing room'.

In other respects, Derby was a jovial, convivial figure. He hosted regular house parties, and at one of them the company agreed to establish on nearby Epsom Downs a new race, over a distance of a mile and a half, for three-year-old fillies. In tribute to the hospitality that brought it about, they named the race the Oaks. It was a sweepstakes, and the first running, in 1779, attracted seventeen subscribers contributing fifty guineas each to the prize fund, with twelve fillies eventually going to post. One of them, a daughter of Herod called Bridget, was Derby's; she was the 5-2 favourite, and she won. Down the field was an Eclipse filly with the bare name Sister of Pot8os. She was owned by Dennis O'Kelly.

Reconvening at The Oaks, Derby and his guests agreed that their fillies' race had been a great success, and that they should

Lord Derby's house The Oaks, after which the classic race for fillies was named, and where, reputedly, Derby and Charles Bunbury agreed the naming of the Derby Stakes on the toss of a coin.

supplement it with another new sweepstakes, this time for both colts and fillies and over a mile, the following year. But what to call the race? Sir Charles Bunbury was among the party, and he, intent on encouraging speedier Thoroughbreds, had been a great promoter of these shorter races, for younger horses, carrying lighter weights. Perhaps the race should be named after him? And so we come to another racing legend: Bunbury and Derby competed for the honour by tossing a coin, and Derby won.[104] Had Bunbury called the toss correctly, we assume, the great race would have been named the Bunbury; the 'Run for the Roses' at Churchill Downs would be the Kentucky Bunbury; a football match between Arsenal and Tottenham would be a North London bunbury; and motor cars would crash into one another in demolition bunburys. As it is, we remember Sir Charles with the Bunbury Cup, a seven-furlong handicap at the Newmarket July meeting.[105]

A year later, on 4 May 1780, Bunbury gained compensation when his colt Diomed (6-4 favourite) became the first winner of the Derby Stakes. Second was Dennis O'Kelly's Boudrow (4-1), by Eclipse. The nine competitors raced over the last mile of the course that Eclipse had graced eleven years earlier. This race was even more popular than the Oaks, attracting thirty-six subscribers who each contributed fifty guineas to the prize fund, Bunbury's winning share of which was 1,150 guineas.

Diomed, by a son of Herod called Florizel, was not at first a shining advertisement for the Derby Stakes. His subsequent racing record was mixed, and his stud career was so undistinguished that

---

[104] This famous story first appeared in print some 120 years later, in the second edition (1911) of *The History and Romance of the Derby* by Edward Moorhouse, who cited 'tradition treasured by the descendants of Sir Charles Bunbury'.

[105] 'Bunburying', which probably has nothing to do with Sir Charles, is what Algernon does in Oscar Wilde's play *The Importance of Being Earnest*: it is the invention of a friend who must be visited, and who offers an excuse for pursuing one's interests.

by 1798, when he was twenty-one years old, he was commanding a fee of only two guineas for each mare he covered. Bunbury gave up on him, and sold him to America. As the horse crossed the Atlantic, so did a message from James Weatherby's secretary: 'Mr Weatherby recommends you strongly to avoid putting any mares to [Diomed]; for he has had fine mares to him here, and never produced anything good.' Diomed also had a reputation for firing blanks, semen-wise.

However, just as there was a wonderful alchemy when Arab stallions met English mares on English soil, so was there when Diomed met American mares in Virginia. The stallion would emerge from his stable at a gallop, and set about his procreative task with the enthusiasm and vigour of a horse half his age.[106] Diomed sired numerous champions, right up until his thirtieth year, by which time his covering fee was $50. He died at thirty-one. 'Without Diomed,' a US historian observed, 'the most brilliant pages of our Turf story could never have been written.' Four generations down his male line came Lexington, a stallion who by the end of the nineteenth century was to saturate the pedigrees of the best American racehorses – and who created a headache for the compilers of the *General Stud Book*, because, like Copenhagen, he had dubious ancestry on his dam's side.

Several of Lord Derby's guests, and particularly Sir Charles Bunbury, would have been dismayed if the rogue Dennis O'Kelly had won the first running of the Derby Stakes. But Dennis had come close, and in 1781 he won the second running, with Young Eclipse. 'Jontlemen,' he told the Munday's coffee house crowd in the weeks before the race, 'this horse is a racer if ever there was one.' Alas, the Derby turned out to be Young Eclipse's finest hour, as it had been Diomed's; and Young Eclipse was not a successful stallion. Describing the horse as 'not a bit too honest', a writer – probably John Lawrence – noted in *The Sporting Magazine*,

---

[106] According to the Thoroughbred expert Peter Willett in *The Classic Racehorse*.

'O'Kelly on first training this horse for the Derby, which he won, was certainly deceived, having flattered himself that fortune had favoured him with another Eclipse! Vain expectation, that two such phenomena should appear together in the world! Between Flying Childers and Eclipse, there was an interval of between 40 and 50 years, and we shall be in high luck, indeed, if we can produce a third to those – what a trio! – within 50 years of the latter.'

The writer went on to note that it was not always possible to take the inconsistent form of Dennis's horses at face value: 'race-horses, more particularly in hands such as those of Dennis O'Kelly, are extremely apt to run according to the immediate pecuniary interests of their proprietors'. If the owner wanted to lay against a horse, the horse was apt to run slowly; next time, with the owner's money down at a bigger price, the horse would show miraculous improvement. Such practices, or at least suspicions of them, have not gone away.

Dennis's horses were probably all trying in the Derby, though. It was too valuable a race to mess about in. He had the Derby second again in 1783, when Dungannon, later to stand at his stud, lost out to Saltram, also by Eclipse; and he won for the second time the following year, with another son of Eclipse called Sergeant.[107]

Lord Derby triumphed in his own race in 1787. He and Lady Elizabeth were still married, but living apart, and he and Nellie Farren were conducting a relationship of apparently irreproachable propriety. 'The attachment,' James Boswell wrote, 'is as fine as anything I have ever seen: truly virtuous admiration on his part, respect on hers.' One of Nellie's most celebrated roles was Lady Teazle in Sheridan's play *The School for Scandal*. Lord

---

[107] The Derby distance had been extended to a mile and a half, and the runners set off on the opposite side of the Downs to the winning post, taking a course behind Downs House, where Dennis now had his training stables (see map on p. 88). A course on the near side of Downs House came into use in the late 1840s.

Derby ran a filly called Lady Teazle in the 1784 Oaks, finishing second; three years later, Sir Peter Teazle, his only Derby winner, gave Derby's virtuous admiration an enduring symbol in the sporting record books. He later turned down a bid for the colt of 500 guineas from, according to The Times, the Duke of Bedford and Dennis O'Kelly.[108]

Sir Charles Bunbury was to win the Derby twice more. There was Smolensko, whose jockey was so meanly rewarded, and before that, in 1801, a filly called Eleanor. Some time before the 1801 race, Bunbury's trainer Cox fell mortally ill. Close to death, with a parson standing by, Cox indicated that he had something to say. The parson bent low; Cox breathed in his ear, 'Depend upon it – that Eleanor is the hell of a mare.' He was right: Eleanor beat the colts in the Derby, and a few days later won the Oaks as well. She is one of only four fillies – 'filly' is a more usual term than 'mare' to describe a horse of three – to achieve the double.[109]

The Derby was not yet the most important race in the calendar, but it was getting there. The founding in 1809 of the 2,000 Guineas (one mile, for three-year-old colts and fillies) and in 1814 of the 1,000 Guineas (one mile, for three-year-old fillies) facilitated the rise in prestige, because these races became preludes to the Derby and the Oaks, which in turn led to the St Leger. The five races became the English Classics, the prizes that all owners dreamed of winning, and that were the highest goals of the breeding industry. By 1850, the Derby was stopping the nation: Parliament adjourned during the week of the race. 'We declare Epsom Downs on Derby Day to be the most astonishing, the most

---

[108] Lord Derby's family was not to record another victory in the race until Sansovino triumphed for the 17th Earl in 1924. The current earl, the 19th, won the 2004 Oaks with Ouija Board, his only horse in training.
[109] The others are Blink Bonny (1857), Signorinetta (1908) and Fifinella (1916). The other fillies to have won the Derby are Shotover (1882) and Tagalie (1912). At the time of writing, the last filly to contest the Derby was Cape Verdi (1998); she went off favourite, but was unplaced.

THE DERBY.—AT LUNCH.

The Derby — At Lunch *by Gustave Doré (1872). 'The Derby is emphatically,
all England's day,' wrote Blanchard Jerrold in his accompanying text.*

varied, the most picturesque and the most glorious spectacle that ever was, or ever can be, under any circumstances, visible to mortal eyes,' the *Illustrated London News* asserted.

In the middle of the twentieth century, the owner and breeder Federico Tesio – who bred the champion Nearco – could say, 'The Thoroughbred racehorse exists because its selection has depended not on experts, technicians or zoologists, but one piece of wood: the winning post of the Epsom Derby.' And it was this piece of wood that reinforced Eclipse's dominant role in racing history. Five of the ten Derby winners in the 1850s, when the *Illustrated London News* hailed the glorious spectacle, were from the Eclipse male line. By the first decade of the twentieth century, the figure had risen to nine out of ten. In the past fifty years, all but three Epsom Derby winners have been Eclipse's male-line descendants. The history of racing's greatest race is a tribute to the sport's greatest horse.

Cross and Jostle

DENNIS O'KELLY WAS A larger-than-life figure in the world of Sir Charles Bunbury, James Weatherby and the Earl of Derby. He competed against them, often with success. As the owner of Eclipse, he had bragging rights that they could not match. But he was never one of them.

In part, Dennis acknowledged this disparity. Although he referred to himself and his companions as 'jontlemen', he did not make much effort to assume the disguise of a gentleman of the Turf. No top hat, embroidered waistcoat and lace-adorned cravat for him; he went about with battered headgear and an elderly, striped coat. An unmistakeable, bearish figure, he was at the centre of a kind of court at race meetings, gambling on the horses during the day and on dice in the evenings. When he was the caster – the player throwing the dice – at hazard, he demanded generous sums as stakes, and liked to brandish large wads of banknotes. One fellow, seeing Dennis apparently unable to find the note he wanted, asked to help. 'I am looking for a little one,' Dennis told him, flicking through his collection of hundreds. 'I want a fifty, or something of that sort, just to set the caster.' Fifty pounds was more than a year's wages for many people.

Dennis's bravado implied that no pickpocket would dare to

tackle him. One did, in an upstairs room at an inn during Windsor races, and was spotted before fully extracting the notes. The assembly clamoured that they would drag the miscreant before a magistrate, but Dennis grabbed hold of him, hauled him to the door, and booted him down the stairs. ''Tis a sufficient punishment to be deprived of the pleasure of keeping company with jontlemen!' he observed.

The wad of notes also served to put people in their place. At the racecourse, a gentleman placing a bet with him asked, snootily, 'Where lay your estates to answer for the amount if you lose?' 'My estates!' Dennis exclaimed. 'Oh, if that's what you *mane*, I've a map of them here.' He got out his wallet, revealing notes worth many times the value of the gentleman's money – which also went into the wallet, and stayed there.

Dennis liked to bet on boxing matches too. Bare-knuckle fights were sometimes staged among the attractions at race meetings, usually on demarcated patches of ground; spontaneous bouts at venues such as Vauxhall Gardens and Marylebone Fields were also common. Jack Broughton, a boxer and author of the first set of rules for the sport, constructed a boxing amphitheatre on Oxford Street in London, with a rectangular platform for the combatants. Here, in 1750, the Duke of Cumberland was said to have lost a bet of £10,000 when Broughton, amid allegations of match-fixing, suffered defeat at the hands of John Slack. A print of the fight has the title *The Bruiser Bruis'd: or The Knowing Ones Taken-in*. Cumberland, who had sponsored the amphitheatre, was furious, and closed it. Just over twenty years later, Dennis was also involved in a bent fight. The difference between Eclipse's breeder and Eclipse's subsequent owner was that Cumberland lost his money, whereas Dennis made sure not to.

The notorious fight between Peter Corcoran and Bill Darts took place at the Epsom race meeting in the spring of 1771. Corcoran, like Dennis, was born in County Carlow, and like him had been a chairman on coming to London. He had also heaved coal, and was a natural boxer. 'His aim was generally correct, and he scarcely ever missed the object in view,' Pierce Egan later recorded in *Boxiana* (1812), a collection of boxing anecdotes. But Darts was the better known, with a reputation as 'one of the most desperate hitters of the time', and was the favourite for the contest.

When, on entering the ring, Darts fought cagily, and before long threw in the towel, there were jeers and boos from the crowd, and soon reports circulated that Dennis, having backed his countryman Corcoran, had bribed Darts with £100 to lose. In his report of the affair, Egan protested, with a vehemence that may have been ironic, 'Surely, no thorough-bred sportsman could commit such a bare-faced robbery!', adding that there had been no need for fixing, because Corcoran, according to the 'best information', was twice the fighter that Darts was anyway.

Corcoran was not above taking a fall himself. At a fight against an opponent called Sellers, he began by knocking Sellers down; then, strangely, he backed off, put up little defence against a series of blows, and surrendered. 'The poor Paddies were literally ruined,' Egan – writing in the days before political correctness – noted, 'as many of them had backed their darling boy with every farthing they possessed. St Giles was in a complete uproar, with mutterings and disapprobation at [Corcoran's] conduct!' Previously in dire financial trouble, Corcoran was suddenly flush again. But he soon sank back into poverty, 'and was as much despised as he had been before respected; and was so miserably poor at his decease, that his remains were interred by subscription'.

Dennis was never poor again, although he did sometimes run short of funds. Eclipse was earning well; however, Dennis owned only one other stallion, Sultan, whose fee was just five guineas, and he was also paying for the upkeep of some fifteen racehorses, as well as various broodmares. He was acquiring land and properties too. In 1771, he bought nine acres on Epsom Downs next to the racecourse, stabled his racers there, and built a house. Continuing to expand his portfolio of properties in the town, he eventually, in the 1780s, built his own house and stables on Clay Hill. A traveller, describing the 'beautiful and elegant villa', reported that the drawing room at the O'Kelly residence was forty feet by twenty feet, and that there were twenty-five paddocks, as well as a fine garden. 'Here,' the traveller added, 'I was entertained with a sight of Eclipse.' This bare mention dismayed one local historian, who lamented, 'Oh! Casual and unresponsive scribe, who was entertained with a sight of the famous Eclipse and was satisfied to dismiss the subject in nine words.'

Like Lord Derby, Dennis and Charlotte entertained generously during race meetings. Their guest list was prestigious, with, in the 1780s, the Prince of Wales at the head; another royal, the Duke of Cumberland,[110] joined the party, as did nobles such as Lord Egremont and Lord Grosvenor, mingling with a selection of Dennis's less reputable associates, Dick England and Jack Tetherington among them. No doubt Charlotte brought her most lovely King's Place nuns to adorn the gatherings. While the entertainment may have been wild, Dennis insisted upon one rule: that no gambling should take place under his roof – 'Nor would he ever propose or accept the most trifling wager in private company.'[111] Did he think that gambling lowered the tone? It seems, from him, a somewhat hypocritical scruple.

The author of *The Genuine Memoirs of Dennis O'Kelly* pretended, with a rhetorical flourish, that this was when Dennis acquired his 'O':

Who keeps the best house in England? was the frequent question – O! Kelly, by much. Who the best wines? O! Kelly, by many degrees. Whose the best horses? O! Kelly's beat the world. Who the pleasantest fellow? Who? O! Kelly. In short, such was the

---

[110] Nephew of the Cumberland who bred Eclipse.
[111] From *The Genuine Memoirs of Dennis O'Kelly*.

frequent use of that ejaculatory vowel upon referring to the
Count, that at length it became incorporated with his original
name, and the harsh guttural of the consonant K was softened by
the modest melody of the liquid O. No more humble Dennis
Kelly. No more Mr Kelly. No more Count Kelly!

Dennis did not play the grand host with total authenticity,
however, and his servants amused themselves with anecdotes
about his gaffes. 'John, bring us the apples,' he would say, when
referring to pineapples. One servant, ordered to buy fish in Epsom
but reporting that he could not procure any, was told, 'Go back,
sirrah! Go back; and by Jasus, if you can't get fish, bring herrings.'

Like many wealthy people, Dennis could be generous in
some respects, and mean in others. He would spare no expense in
entertaining; he would throw money around with apparent care-
lessness at the racecourse; and despite the report that he had
vowed never to be charitable again after the donation enforced by
his misbehaviour with Miss Swinburne at York, he gave to good
causes, such as the Benevolent Society of St Patrick. At a Society
evening in 1786, Dennis succeeded the Marquis of Buckingham in
the chair, and proposed toasts to the Marquis and to 'the inland
navigation of Great Britain and Ireland' – this being the period of
intensive canal construction, offering work for Irish labourers. At
the same time, some of his employees, particularly jockeys, complained about his evasiveness over payments. One, Tom Cammell,
was very indignant: 'Damn his fat, pampered guts; I have kept
mine thin, and rode many a hard race to stuff his, and now can't
get my money, without a still harder run over the course at
Westminster Hall.' The reporter of this outburst suggested that
Cammell was a victim of a temporary, gambling-induced cash flow
crisis. Dennis, this reporter (John Lawrence) added, occupied a
rare position in between sporting aristocrats and gamblers; though
'not overladen and depressed in his career by scruples', he was no
worse a man than his supposed superiors.

Class, however, is not a matter of achievement, nor of morality. While the Duke of Grafton could scandalize society without jeopardizing his Jockey Club membership, Dennis, the partner of a madam, had no prospect of gaining election. Similar, unspoken rules apply today. Current JC members, all upstanding people no doubt, could commit quite a few indiscretions without loss of status. Yet the porn baron David Sullivan, despite ownership of a string of racehorses and a victory at the Eclipse Stakes,[112] is unlikely to be joining any time soon.

Once a blackleg, always a blackleg, was the JC's unbending view of Dennis. Not being what Daniel Defoe called (satirically) a True-born Englishman was another of his demerits, as it has been for many others. His older contemporary, the Jewish financier Sampson Gideon, attained fabulous wealth and converted to Anglicanism, but failed to be awarded a title, only to see his son gain a baronetcy. This pattern, of recognition held over to the next generation, was also to be the O'Kelly story.

Dennis aspired to be a member of the Turf elite; he thought he should be a member. He was one of those people who believe that anything they set their minds to achieving is within their reach. Possessing a mixture of naivety and chutzpah, they often do get what they want, and they rise to a new floor in the social hierarchy; but they have failed to see, and are dismayed and bewildered to discover, that certain rooms on that floor are barred. Using a slightly different metaphor, the historian Roy Porter wrote in his history of the eighteenth century, 'It was easy to rise *towards* the portal of the next status group. Crossing the threshold was more difficult, and required special visas.'

It has been an unvarying feature of society that no matter how successful or eminent you are, you always have to know your place. The late Auberon Waugh, son of one of the great novelists of the twentieth century (Evelyn Waugh) and a self-confessed

[112] His horse David Junior won the 2006 running.

member of the 'bourgeois cultural elite', discovered on arrival at Oxford University that he was excluded from the smart set that congregated round the dons Maurice Bowra and Isaiah Berlin. What he lacked, he concluded sourly, was 'an ancient name, a stately home and a couple of thousand acres'. Friends of the late Princess Margaret took care always to address her, in line with royal protocol, as 'Ma'am', while very dear friends called her 'Ma'am darling'. We might conclude, on hearing that Dennis and Charlotte entertained royalty and lords at Clay Hill, that eighteenth-century society was more fluid; but away from Epsom – or from the King's Place brothel – the barriers were up.

Dennis was bitterly uncomprehending that men with no obvious claim to pre-eminence, and who socialized with him and played sport with him, in effect continued to say, 'You are beneath us.' The key man who held that attitude kept the social contact to a minimum as well. During the Epsom races, Sir Charles Bunbury partied at The Oaks, not at Clay Hill. It seems that he would not send his mares there either, and he owned, throughout his racing career, only one horse sired by Eclipse. Bunbury ran the Jockey Club, he determined its rules, and he did not like the cut of Dennis's jib.

Dennis's feelings came out when he offered a jockey[113] a huge salary of £400 to be his retained rider, and promised to double the sum if the jockey agreed never to ride for 'any of the black-legged fraternity'. The jockey asked whom he meant. 'O, by Jasus, my dear,' Dennis shouted, 'and I'll soon make you understand who I mean by the black-legged fraternity! There's the D of G, the Duke of D, Lord A, Lord D, Lord G, Lord C, Lord F, the Right Hon. A, B, C, D, and C, I, F, and all the set of *thaves* that

---

[113] 'Thormanby' (William Willmott Dixon), writing more than a hundred years later, said that the jockey was Frank Buckle. Born in 1766, Buckle began riding at seventeen, so the story is feasible. He succeeded Sam Chifney as the leading jockey of his era, and was noted, unlike some of his contemporaries, for his unassuming manner and honesty.

belong to their humbug societies and clubs, where they can meet and rob one another without detection!'

One of these 'thaves', Lord A (Abingdon), offered Dennis a classically patrician put-down one evening at Burford races. The company at dinner were proposing matches for the following year, and Abingdon – owner of Eclipse's sire, Marske – offered to race a horse against one belonging to a Mr Baily, who appealed to Dennis for help over the terms. Giving a succinct precis of the English sportsman's attitude that professionalism is infra dig, Abingdon observed loftily, 'I, and the gentlemen on this side of the table, run for honour; the Captain [Dennis] and his friends for profit.'

The match was made, and Baily asked Dennis to stand half of the 300-guinea stake. Dennis, who did not approve of the terms, declined, adding fiercely: 'If the match had been made cross and jostle,[114] as I proposed, I would have stood all the money; and by the powers I'd have brought a spalpeen [young ruffian] from Newmarket, no higher than a two-penny loaf, that should (by Jasus!) have driven his lordship's horse and jockey into the furzes, and have kept them there for three weeks!'

Dennis also made a bid for social cachet through the military. While he happily brandished his bogus rank of 'Count', bestowed by a fellow inmate in the Fleet, he recognized that a more prestigious title might carry more weight. His opportunity came when a noble, to whom he had given some 'secret services' in the course of a legal action, secured him a captaincy in the Westminster Regiment of the Middlesex Militia.

The militias, which were the responsibility of lord lieutenants of counties, were raised with the aim of securing England against enemy invaders. They recruited through a form of national service: your name went into a ballot, and if it was drawn, you had to join up; you also had to make yourself available each year for

---

[114] A race in which contestants have licence to try to impede the other horses.

training. A typical order stated: 'Every militia man (not labouring under any infirmity incapacitating him) who shall not appear at the time appointed for the annual exercise shall be deemed a deserter and forfeit £20 or six months in gaol, or until he has paid.'

The Genuine Memoirs of Dennis O'Kelly may have been unreliable, but they offered a plausible portrait of a regiment comprising a motley assortment of officers and soldiers – a Georgian Dad's Army. 'Lamb, the Major, was a common mechanic, we believe, a watch-maker; and the Captains and Subalterns were, in general, really so low and obscure, as to be beneath the level of contempt or observation.' By the 1770s, the regiment had found roles for further obscure personages, whom the author of the *Memoirs* gleefully caricatured. There was Burbridge, a farmer, who despite his rank of lieutenant colonel responded to every enquiry about regimental business with the words: 'What do you ask me for? I do not know.' There was Barlow, the major, 'a superannuated mercer', incapable of marching because of gout, but useless on horseback as well. Dennis's fellow captains included a Dutchman called William Hundeshagen, whose frame held 'not six ounces of flesh' and whose misshapen hands and feet were evidence, like those of a castrato, of 'nature diverted from its regular courses'. Our hero, though, 'bore the most soldierly appearance of any officer in the regiment'.

This was the time of the American War of Independence (1775 to 1783), when Britain's enemies also included the French, Spanish and Dutch. Dennis's regiment travelled round the country on manoeuvres. In 1781 to 1782, for example, there were musters in Kent, Liverpool and Lancaster. Dennis journeyed in style, with accompanying carriages and servants, and Charlotte followed, with her own lavish retinue. He also found time – as no doubt did she – for his 'more profitable avocations'. But he was present at every important military exercise, and he stood firm whenever there appeared to be a threat, while his fellow soldiers panicked – or so the *Genuine Memoirs* had it. Resorting to crudity, the author reported that when enemy ships could be seen off the coast, 'the temple of Cloefina [the lavatory] became the alternate and eternal citadel of [Dennis's fellow officers'] prowess'. Dennis petitioned the Lord Lieutenant to dismiss these officers, without result. There would soon be peace, the Lord Lieutenant observed; and the men were old.

By the beginning of 1781, Dennis had risen to the rank of major, in charge of one of the regiment's nine companies, and had led the regiment before the King in St James's Park. He became Lieutenant Colonel Dennis O'Kelly in 1782. He failed to show gratitude to his supporters for his elevation, though. The *Genuine Memoirs*, switching as they often did from eulogy to censure, reported that Dennis did not invite any of his fellow soldiers to a grand entertainment in Lancashire attended by Lord Derby and various other nobles: 'A conduct so ungrateful, and so strongly tinged with upstart insolence, could not fail of producing great enmity and ridicule, and it is a fact, to the honour of those who were of that party, that even they joined in the general censure and disgust.'

Although Dennis's overtures to the Jockey Club made no headway, in other respects his Turf affairs were beginning to thrive. In *Eclipse and O'Kelly*, Theodore Cook recorded some of his impressive transactions. One of Dennis's broodmares, the Tartar mare, proved especially valuable, throwing ten chestnut offspring to Eclipse between 1772 and 1785; and Dennis made good money by selling them. The colts Antiochus and Adonis went to Sir John Lade (1,500 and 1,000 guineas; at the Cumberland dispersal sale, the renowned Herod had fetched only 500 guineas, and Eclipse only 45), Jupiter to Mr Douglas (1,000 guineas), and Mercury to Lord Egremont (2,500 guineas). Mr Graham offered 5,000 guineas for Volunteer, but was turned down. The fillies were in demand too: Venus went to Lord Egremont (1,200 guineas), the dam of a racer called Crazy and a Herod mare went to Mr Broadhurst (300 guineas), Lily of the Valley went to the Duke of

Bedford (700 guineas), Boniface and a Herod mare to Mr Bullock (250 guineas), and Queen Mab to the Hon. George Bowes for 650 guineas. The *Annual Register*, the chronicle of events of the year, reported of the Jupiter transaction that it involved a bonus of £500, payable to Dennis if the colt won on his debut.

Amid these transactions, Dennis was never tempted to part with his most valuable asset. Lord Grosvenor, owner of Eclipse's outstanding son Pot8os, offered 11,000 guineas for Eclipse; Dennis responded to the offer with the impossible demand of 20,000 guineas, a £500 annuity, and three broodmares. When another interested party (the Duke of Bedford, perhaps) asked about the stallion's selling price, Dennis replied, 'By the Mass, my lord, and it is not all Bedford level that would purchase him.'

The fame of stallion and owner are apparent in contemporary references. In a heavy-handed satire entitled *Newmarket: Or an Essay on the Turf* (1775), the author wrote, with galumphing jocularity:

> I think I never met with a stronger proof of this, nor with any thing that ever pleased me better, than the following important article of intelligence. 'On Sunday last arrived in town, Count O'Nelly, master of the famous horse Moonshade.' See how honour, coy mistress as she is, yet mounted this gentleman's horse, and announced his arrival in town.
>
> I only urge, that the following titles, given to an excellent horse, would sound very nobly, and be bestowed with admirable justice. Kelly's Eclipse. Creations: Duke of Newmarket; Earl of Epsom and York; General of the Race-grounds; Baron Eclipse of Mellay; Viscount Canterbury; Lord of Lewes, Salisbury, Ipswich, and Northampton; Marquis of Barnet, and Premier Racer of all England.

An Example to the Turf

IN HER PROFESSIONAL LIFE, Charlotte remained Charlotte Hayes or Mrs Hayes. But away from the King's Place nunnery, she was Charlotte O'Kelly. Whether there was ever a Mr Hayes, we do not know, and we have no evidence that Charlotte and Dennis ever became wife and husband. It has been suggested that theirs was an unofficial union, like the 'Savoy Chapel wedding' performed by the impious clergyman John Wilkinson with which the younger Dennis was reported to have duped a young lady of fortune. The *Genuine Memoirs of Dennis O'Kelly* had this to say on the subject: 'Whether the God of love had . . . presented [Charlotte] at the altar of Hymen, we do not presume to ascertain. Certain it is, that if reputation, and cohabitation, were sufficient evidences of matrimony, the performance of that ceremony must have been confirmed in the eyes of the world.' Which is a nice way of saying that no marriage ever took place.

Charlotte was wealthy, successful, extravagant, and careless. An astute and often unscrupulous businesswoman, she was also wayward and nervy, and often landed in trouble. In 1776, the creditors of a bankrupt haberdasher, James Spilsbury, got her imprisoned in the Marshalsea for unpaid debts concerning 'the use and hire of certain clothes and garments . . . let to hire to the said Charlotte at her special interest and request . . . and also for work and labour before that time done performed and bestowed . . . in making fitting adorning and trimming diverse clothes, garments and masquerade dresses'; 'the said Charlotte not regarding her said several promises and undertakings so made as aforesaid but contriving and fraudulently intending craftily and subtly to deceive and defraud . . . hath not yet paid the said several sums of money or any part thereof . . .' The creditors sued for £50. Charlotte spent several months in jail before Dennis secured her release. Whether his delay was a symptom of lack of gallantry or lack of funds is not altogether clear.

The author of the *Genuine Memoirs* certainly showed gallantry. 'No woman could have maintained a better conduct,' he insisted. '[Charlotte's] conversation was delicate and agreeable, and her manners conciliating, from gentleness and modesty.' This paragon would never have defrauded anyone: her debt was 'rather neglected than withheld'. Such was the respect due to Charlotte, the *Genuine Memoirs* added, that the arresting officers were inclined to dismiss the claim against her, and they allowed her bail instead so that the true extent of the debt could be revealed and discharged. Dennis was in York at the time, and about to land himself in the 'unfortunate adventure' with Miss Swinburne. The evidence belies this account, however. Charlotte did indeed go to prison, and Dennis was not in York. His adventure there had taken place six years earlier.

When at liberty, Charlotte spent much more of her time in London than in Epsom. She lived in a newly acquired property in Half Moon Street, Piccadilly, where, as she began to take life more easily, she delighted especially in the company of her pet parrot. Polley had been procured by Dennis from Bristol, and had cost fifty guineas – the sum that was Eclipse's highest covering fee. (One report says that Dennis paid 100 guineas for Polley.) Owing to her rarity, and to her reputed status as the first parrot to be bred in England,[115] Polley was credited with miraculous abilities. She sang a variety of tunes, on request, beating the time with her wings, and if ever she made a mistake, she would return to the appropriate bar, and resume. According to the *Gentleman's Magazine*, her repertoire included 'the 114th Psalm, "The Banks of the Dee", "God Save the King" and other favourite songs'. What Eclipse was among horses, another report enthused, Polley was among parrots.

In the 1780s, Dennis – born in about 1725 – entered what was considered to be old age. Life expectancy during this period was a little more than thirty-five years. While that figure reflects high levels of infant and child mortality, it also shows why people who lived into their late fifties and beyond were thought to be doing especially well. Not until the twentieth century, and then only in affluent societies, did the biblical lifespan of three score years and ten become a feasible standard. Charlotte Hayes – roughly Dennis's contemporary, and destined to live for another thirty years – was in 1780 'that experienced old matron', in the words of William Hickey.

So, in his late fifties, Dennis began to assume elderly habits. Whatever the Jockey Club thought, he was leaving behind the anarchic life of the blackleg, and he was no longer in tune with some of his old associates, Dick England among them. One evening in the 1780s at Munday's coffee house, Dennis and a certain Lieutenant Richard were comparing notes about what a vile scoundrel England was. An eavesdropper reported the conversation to England, who was elsewhere in the house. England came charging into the room, took on both Dennis and the Lieutenant, and beat them up. Dennis was so bruised that he was unable to leave the premises, and had to accept the hospitality of the proprietor, Jack Medley, who gave him a bed for the night. Unwisely,

[115] Another version has it that she arrived on a ship from the West Indies.

Dennis and the Lieutenant sued. The case came before the King's Bench, where England pleaded guilty; the judge, ruling that the defendant had been severely provoked, awarded only one shilling in damages.[116]

It was inevitable that a man enjoying Dennis's successes would find an extended family popping up and making claims on his charity. For the most part, he did the right thing. In the early 1770s, he had brought his brother Philip over to England, and put him in charge of the stables and stud at Epsom. Philip arrived with his wife, Elizabeth, and son, Andrew Dennis, who received a fine education at Dennis's expense. Although Andrew would inherit the O'Kelly talent for controversy, he gained more ease in society than Dennis ever enjoyed.

The *Genuine Memoirs* said that Dennis also helped two nieces. Who they were is not clear, because they receive no mention in the notes about the family in the O'Kelly papers, lodged at the University of Hull. One of the documents, an importuning letter to Dennis, refers to 'your sister Mrs Mitchell' and her daughter 'Miss Mary Harvey', who had travelled to England with Philip. Again, this is puzzling. Dennis's sister Mary married a man called Whitfield Harvey, so perhaps Miss Mary was the daughter of that marriage (before a second marriage, to Mitchell).[117] The letter writer is Thomas Gladwell, who was married to Dennis's cousin. With what must have been lack of tact, he said that 'friends were not pleased with my marriage', and reported that 'I could have

---

[116] In 1784, Dick England fled the country after shooting a man called Le Rowles (or, possibly, 'Rowlls') in a duel. He returned twelve years later to face trial. After support from the witness box from the Marquis of Hertford and Lord Derby, who surprisingly described him as 'a very civil, well-bred, polite gentleman', England got away with a verdict of manslaughter and a sentence of a year in Newgate. On his release, he enjoyed a comfortable old age, and died 'peacefully in his bed' at eighty.

[117] A second sister, unnamed in the papers, married someone called Sterne Tighe. See Appendix 3.

made a more advantageous match'. Gladwell was struggling to get by on a clerk's wages of £30 a year. 'Hearing of your goodness of heart to all your relations and others who have applied to your assistance emboldened [my wife] to lay this state of our circumstances before you. Be pleased to grant us some relief.' Dennis kept the letter, but whether he responded to it is doubtful: Gladwell mentioned three previous requests that had received no acknowledgement. Another letter in the collection is from a family member recommending one Patrick O'Fallon, and presuming on 'the general good nature of your character' to request that O'Fallon be found some 'small place', perhaps in the Custom House.

By this time, Dennis was considerably, though precariously, affluent. He owned various properties and a good deal of land in Epsom, as well as a substantial racing operation; and he owned, or at least rented, properties in London too. Sometimes, he raised cash through leasing arrangements, and he also went in for subletting. The O'Kelly papers include an aggrieved letter from James Poole, writing to say that he is 'by no means satisfied' with the condition of a house he let to Dennis several years earlier: it 'has been turned into separate habitations for poor persons', who have left it in a state of disrepair. Poole demanded that the house be returned to its original state, and that the overdue rent be paid.

Of the Epsom properties, only a barn from the Downs House stables survives. But Dennis's last and most impressive acquisition still stands. Cannons[118] in Edgware had been, in the early part of the eighteenth century, the site of an ostentatiously grand palace built by James Brydges, Duke of Chandos. A drawing in the British Library shows a colonnaded structure of overweening vulgarity. There were ninety-three servants in the house; in the grounds were storks, flamingos, ostriches, blue macaws, eagles and, at one time, a tiger. By reputation, this was the model for

---

[118] The current spelling is Canons.

Cannons (now spelled Canons) in Edgware, the villa built by Hallett, the last home of Eclipse and of Dennis O'Kelly. The house is now part of the North London Collegiate School for Girls.

'Timon's Villa' in Alexander Pope's *Epistle to Burlington* ('At Timon's villa let us pass a day / Where all cry out, "What sums are thrown away!"') – although scholars are inclined to accept, at least partially, Pope's denial of the connection. Some of Chandos's expenditure nevertheless resulted in achievements of enduring value. He appointed George Frideric Handel as composer in residence: Handel wrote the eleven Chandos Anthems to be performed in the adjoining church, Whitchurch, where he played the organ; and *Acis and Galatea*, his wonderful masque (or chamber opera), received its first performance in the Cannons grounds.

If you were going to spend a fortune at this time, you did not want that fortune to be secured by South Sea stock. Unfortunately, Chandos was an investor in the apparently booming South Sea Company, and he took a heavy hit when the share price collapsed.[119] He carried on, undaunted, but bequeathed family finances that were seriously in the red. In 1747, the second Duke sold Cannons, with the result that the palace, completed just twenty-five years earlier, was broken up and dispersed. The marble staircase went to Lord Chesterfield's Mayfair house – which was later demolished too. According to a history of Cannons, the eight Ionic columns in front of the National Gallery in London are from the Cannons colonnade. The ornamental gates stand at an Epsom mansion called The Durdans. A cabinet-maker called William Hallett bought the estate, and built a more modest villa there, of Portland stone.

In 1785, Dennis bought Hallett's villa, with some of the grounds, and the following year he struck a deal for the remainder of the estate. A document in the London Metropolitan Archives tells us that the second purchase cost him £10,500. He took

---

[119] This was 'The South Sea Bubble'. Investors bought into the South Sea Company, and into other companies, with the blind enthusiasm that was to greet internet stock nearly three hundred years later. Then the realization dawned that these companies – like a good many internet ventures – were unprofitable. Panic selling ensued, and fortunes were lost.

possession of a park some two miles round, containing between three and four hundred deer, with lakes and avenues, as well as smallholdings with cows, sheep and horses.

Horace Walpole, that barbed critic, disapproved of Hallett's taste, referring to his decorations as 'mongrel chinoise'. The third Duke of Chandos also had criticisms of the new Cannons house: 'The kitchen [is] not much larger than a Tunbridge kitchen, and smokes and stinks the house infernally. The only way of letting the smoke out, for none goes out of the chimney, is through the window, which lets it in again at the window above it.'

In spite of these drawbacks, the villa Dennis bought and subsequently lived in was a smart place. In the basement were a housekeeper's room, kitchen, scullery, butler's pantry, ice-house, servants' hall, dairy and larder, with cellars for wine, beer and coal. The ground floor contained a library, a breakfast parlour, a dining room, a grand saloon of forty-five feet by twenty-one feet, a drawing room, a stone hall and a stone staircase. There were six bedchambers and a dressing room on the first floor, and a further six bedchambers, for servants, on the attic storey. Today, this house is part of the North London Collegiate School for girls.

Dennis was slowing down, without mellowing. The company he kept at Cannons was 'more select' than that of his former days, consisting of 'people of the first class of his own sex' as well as 'unexceptionable' female friends. He was demanding and difficult with his brother Philip, and he berated his nephew, Andrew, for the kind of behaviour in which he himself, when younger, had specialized. His friends had to endure boorish joshing. With one, O'Rourke, Dennis would bang on monothematically about how he possessed the superior Irish lineage;[120] the *Genuine Memoirs* said

[120] The descent of the clan O'Kelly from Milesius (after whom Dennis named one of Eclipse's sons), the King of the Celts in the sixth century BC, may be apocryphal; but there is a more certifiable line from Cellagh, an Irish chief living in the ninth century AD. The O'Kellys ruled for seven hundred years over a kingdom corresponding roughly with what we know as Connaught.

that O'Rourke ('whose soul was made of fire!') put up with it.

On the racecourse, Dennis's energy was undiminished. In 1786, his racer Dungannon, who had come second in the Derby three years earlier, narrowly defeated the Prince of Wales's Rockingham in a valuable Newmarket match, made more valuable still by the heavy betting on the outcome. The losers, reported *The Times* (then the *Daily Universal Register*), complained about the rough tactics, or 'cross and jostling', of Dungannon's rider. There was a rematch the following spring, when Rockingham was in the ownership of a man called Bullock (the Prince, suffering one of his periodic financial crises, had sold his stable), in a race that also featured the Duke of Grafton's Oberon and Sir Charles Bunbury's Fox. *The Times* contributed to the build-up: 'The grand sweepstakes on Tuesday comprehends more first-rate horses than ever ran together before. Vast sums are depending on this extraordinary contest, and the odds are perpetually fluctuating. Dungannon was the favourite, but the tide is turned towards Rockingham.'

On the eve of the race, Dennis withdrew Dungannon. It was not a popular move. *The Times* said, 'The Duke of Bedford was 1200 [guineas] minus on account of O'Kelly's Dungannon not starting on Tuesday, and the minor betters, who had laid their money play or pay, suffered in proportion. Illness was pleaded, and the horse ordered into the stable. Turf speculation daily becoming more and more precarious, since occasional indisposition is as readily admitted at Newmarket as on the stage.'

Very few racegoers believed in Dungannon's 'indisposition', was the implication. It is the charge that the writer John Lawrence was also to make: that the well-being of Dennis O'Kelly's horses tended to reflect the financial interests of their owner. The Duke of Bedford and others had lost the money they had bet, and others – not named by *The Times* – must have gained. 'Whatever bears the name of Rockingham seems somehow or other to have *dupery* inseparable from it,' the paper observed, casting aspersions both on the horse and on a former Prime Minister, the late Marquis of

Rockingham (who had died in 1782). Yet the paper also reported that Dennis had lost at least one bet on the race, having predicted, incorrectly, that Rockingham would not be able to lead from start to finish. Moreover, he lost money overall at the meeting: 'In the last week's business of Newmarket, according to public report, the Duke of Bedford was minus, Lord Egremont was minus, Mr O'Kelly was minus, even the Duke of Queensberry was a little minus. We should be glad, therefore, to know, who was major on the occasion; – or is it on the turf, as we know it often happens in a gaming table, that when £10,000 have been lost in an evening, not a single person is to be found who has won a guinea?' We should treat this report with a little scepticism – *The Times*'s next mention of the affair certainly indicates that its reporting was fallible: 'The report of O'Kelly's being expelled the Jockey Club, in consequence of not suffering Dungannon to start after being led to the post, is not true. O'Kelly, for a number of years past, has been an example to the turf for fair play, and punctuality in payments.'

The comments on Dennis's character were questionable (if they were not meant ironically), and the implication that he was a Jockey Club member was wrong. Later, the paper suggested that Dennis, plagued by ill health, was planning to quit the Turf. But, controversial to the end, he carried on racing. In 1787, thirteen horses ran in his colours. His colt Gunpowder came second in the Derby, and his filly Augusta, bought at the Prince of Wales's dispersal sale, came second in the Oaks. In October, he and the Duke of Bedford made an unsuccessful bid for the colt that had beaten Gunpowder at Epsom, Lord Derby's Sir Peter Teazle.

Dennis's affliction, which was no doubt the reason why this once vigorous man was beaten up so badly by Dick England, was gout. In this, at least, he joined the upper crust: gout, a.k.a. the 'English malady', was 'the distemper of a gentleman whereas the rheumatism is the distemper of a hackney coachman', in the view of the patrician Lord Chesterfield. Perhaps that observation gave solace to Dennis as he endured his agonies. Gout is an accretion of uric acid that forms crystals in joints, particularly in the feet, so that the slightest movement or touch produces excruciating pain. One pictures Dennis, his swaddled feet resting on a stool, extravagantly complaining of his lot and, frustrated at his immobility, furiously shouting at his family and servants. Only Charlotte got kind treatment.

We are inclined to be callous about gout, and to laugh at the bibulous old man with the inflamed extremities. Like a hangover, gout is a joke ailment, a comic comeuppance for high living. Evidence about its causes certainly suggests a link with the extraordinary indulgences of the eighteenth-century lifestyle. A typical dinner of the time was, in the words of historian Liza Picard, 'a nightmare of meat and poultry', with course upon course of beef, pork, chicken, hare, pheasant and snipe; interludes of seafood such as crayfish and turbot; and heavy puddings to follow. Then there was the drink. One bottle of wine was an almost teetotal quantity. William Hickey, inviting some good-time girls to an evening party at an inn, selected them on the basis that 'each . . . could with composure carry off her three bottles'.[121] Six bottles, of wine that was sometimes fortified with spirits, was not an unusual portion. The wine might be kept in lead casks or sweetened with lead sugar, which probably triggered various illnesses, gout among them.

The eighteenth-century sufferer could console himself with the thought that not only was gout classy, it was also, according to medical theory of the time, a guard against other diseases. This was

---

[121] Pris Vincent, one of the women, performed her party piece at the end of the evening: urinating from distance at a target. For the particular amusement of another guest, Lord Fielding, she stood on one side of the table, and appointed Hickey to hold a champagne bottle at the other side. Lifting her petticoats, she aimed a stream of piss so accurately 'that at least one-third actually entered the bottle', Hickey admiringly reported. He added, 'Lord Fielding was near suffocation, so excessively did it excite his mirth'.

a sad illusion, particularly in cases of overweight people such as Dennis. Always bulky, Dennis ballooned in later years, although he may not quite have weighed in at the twenty stone that the *Whitehall Evening Post* assigned to him. Obesity would have brought with it additional problems such as diabetes, high blood pressure, and heart trouble.

Shortly after the October 1787 meeting at Newmarket, Dennis's illness attacked him 'with determined violence', the *Genuine Memoirs* said. He repaired to his house in Half Moon Street, Piccadilly, where a physician called Dr Warren attended to him. Warren would have intervened little up to now, prescribing simply oils for the inflamed areas of Dennis's anatomy and recommending that Dennis limit his alcohol intake – to the trifling amount, say, of a pint of wine a day. Now, more drastic measures were called for: bleeding to realign Dennis's humours, quinine to steady the nerves, laudanum to ease the pain, and perhaps some bespoke herbal medicines.

Unsurprisingly, these treatments did not effect an improvement. Dennis sank into a lethargic state, and, showing little apparent discomfort, slipped towards death. He passed away on 28 December. The *Genuine Memoirs* concluded, 'As his career was a lesson of wonder, so was his death an example of imitation.'

15

The 14lb Heart

DENNIS O'KELLY – ROGUE, madam's companion, and Jockey Club reject – got a distinguished send-off. He was buried with 'great funeral pomp' on 7 January 1788 in the vault of the Cannons church, Whitchurch, where he still lies. Officers of the Westminster Regiment of the Middlesex Militia attended, along with eminent neighbours, who all enjoyed a slap-up dinner afterwards, with a liberal supply of wine.

The farewell from the public prints was, as Dennis might have expected, mixed. Under the heading 'O'Kelly is dead', the *Whitehall Evening Post* announced that it had received two unprintable obituaries, the first overly eulogistic, the second overly hostile. The paper's own verdict leaned towards the second position. One could not expect a man who had made his fortune on the Turf, the paper pronounced, to be morally scrupulous; but one might have hoped that a colonel in the militia would have observed the behaviour of a gentleman. Disaster could not soften Dennis O'Kelly, 'nor prosperity sublime'. He was, though, a generous, undiscriminating host, 'as unambitious in his company, as easily contented, as if he had ended life as he began it – as a chairman in the streets'. On the subject of Charlotte, the *Whitehall Evening Post* held its nose: 'Had [O'Kelly] left the [Fleet] prison a better man than he found it, virtue might have thought it something – but it was not so, unless a man is better by such an addition as Charlotte Hayes.'

The *World Fashionable Advertiser* chose the period of mourning to remind readers of Dennis's embarrassing incident with Miss Swinburne at Blewitt's Inn, York. It had another colourful anecdote to share: that one room of Dennis's villa at Clay Hill was full of portraits of young ladies, 'the most remarkable for their faces and manners – in the seminary which Charlotte Hayes once kept for religious education'.

The Times[122] could not make up its mind. Dennis offered to the poor an example of how they must never despair of gaining wealth, was the paper's conclusion a few days following his death. He had bought Cannons, and then a further portion of the estate, without requiring a mortgage. There, Charlotte Hayes could enjoy 'her pious age'. However, any dissector of Dennis's corpse would find 'all inflammation, all corruption'. On the Turf, where success was synonymous with criminality, Dennis was 'as Sir Isaac Newton was among the philosophers – at the head of his science'.

Then the journalist wrote something puzzling: 'That O'Kelly was a chairman, and afterwards a marker at a billiard table, has been reputed under a very orthodox sanction; but we have every reason to believe that such an assertion is altogether heterodox, though it is to be found in a piece of biography written by myself.'

The claim that stories of Dennis O'Kelly's early life were mythical is not shocking. But was the author saying that he had already written *The Genuine Memoirs of Dennis O'Kelly* (which were certainly published some time that year, 1788)? It would have been fast work – although hacks were expected to turn round such opportunistic books with great speed. The exuberant, cynical tone of the *Genuine Memoirs* tallied with the journalist's cheerful admission in Dennis's obituary that he had reproduced unreliable accounts of our hero's life.

[122] Newly christened; the paper had begun publishing as the *Daily Universal Register* in 1785.

Later, *The Times* decided that it was Dennis O'Kelly's sup-
porter. Referring to the scurrilous stories about Dennis in the
World Fashionable Advertiser, it lambasted 'A certain affected morning print, remarkable for its incautious, groundless and
calumniating assertions', and thundered, 'THE WORLD is a lying
WORLD!' 'Is it possible,' *The Times* asked, forgetting its earlier
portrait of Dennis, 'that in a country, nay in an age like this, it
should be necessary to revive the ancient adage, De mortuis nil
nisi bonum [One should not speak ill of the dead]?'

The *Genuine Memoirs* were both satirical and adulatory, both
scurrilous and discreet. The anonymous hack commissioned to
churn them out may well have haunted the Covent Garden milieu
of Dennis, Charlotte and their associates. While offering plenty of
evidence of Dennis's bad behaviour, he summarized him as a
paragon. While revelling in Dennis's crudities, he advised his
tender readers that he had omitted 'uninteresting coffee-house
anecdotes; attempts at wit; nocturnal broils; and, the indecent
intrigues of public and private brothels. A life so variegated as was
that of Colonel O'Kelly, must have abounded with the common
occurrences of such scenes; but we hold it highly improper that
they should be presented to the general eye. They are fit only for
the depraved contemplation of sensual and dissipated minds, and
are in our opinion more injurious to virtue and society in general,
than even the example of practical immorality.'

All the newspapers were intrigued by Dennis's will. It was a
document (dated 11 October 1786) that proved his devotion to
Charlotte Hayes. He wanted her to be secure, and comfortable.
'Into the proper hands of Charlotte Hayes, called Mrs O'Kelly
[the phrasing is another hint that there was no formal marriage],
who now lives and resides with me', Dennis bequeathed an annuity of £400, secured against the rents at Cannons, where Charlotte
could live if she wished. He ordered that she should have the run
of Cannons, and – suspecting that her parties might be boisterous?
– specified that she should not be liable for any damage to the

furniture. He left her various personal effects: a large diamond ring and other jewellery, as well as a silver tea pot and a coffee pot, along with silver plates and two silver candlesticks. He gave her his carriage and carriage horses too. Charlotte also inherited, with Dennis's brother Philip and nephew Andrew, Dennis's most valuable possession of all: Eclipse. They were to share the stud fees, as well as any fees generated by the stallions Dungannon, Volunteer and Vertumnus; if these horses were not to enjoy stud careers, they were to be sold, to Charlotte's, Philip's and Andrew's benefit. Philip got the broodmares, with the bonus that ten of them could be covered by the O'Kelly stallions free of charge, after which he would have to pay the market rate.

Dennis's will confirmed the stories that, disillusioned by the refusal of the Turf aristocracy to admit him to their inner circles, he had fallen out of love with racing. He ordered that all his racehorses be sold; moreover, he specified – this detail was widely reported – that if either Philip or Andrew should bet on horses, make matches, train horses or race them, 'or be engaged or concerned in any such matters in any shape or manner or upon any account or pretence whatsoever, then . . . they shall forfeit and pay unto my executors[123] and trustees the sum of £500 of lawful British money to be by them deducted and retained for their own use and benefit out of the property'. Andrew ignored this clause, with impunity.

The dispersal sale, on 11 February 1788, was the final proof that Dennis could match anyone in management of Turf affairs, if not in social acceptability. Conducted by the bloodstock auctioneers Tattersalls, it fetched in excess of £8,000 – some thousand pounds more than had changed hands at the sale of the Prince of Wales's stud the previous year. The Prince, having come to a new financial arrangement with his father George III and wasting no

---

[123] They were William Atkinson of Pall Mall, an apothecary, and Thomas Birch of Bond Street, a banker.

time in returning to the Turf, was among the buyers. He spent as extravagantly as he had before his enforced disposal, paying 1,400 guineas and 750 guineas for two sons of Eclipse, Gunpowder and King Heremon; he also bought the Eclipse fillies Scota (550 guineas) and Augusta (150 guineas).[124] According to Theodore Cook (in *Eclipse and O'Kelly*), there was not to be a racing sale of comparable influence for another seventy years.

The sale was supposed to clear Dennis's debts. But he had not been as flush as he thought.

By now, Eclipse was feeling his age. Like his gout-afflicted late master, he was having trouble with his feet: his coffin bones (they are in the hooves) were 'very much rounded and diminished'.[125] When Andrew decided to transfer the O'Kelly stud from Clay Hill to Cannons, Eclipse was too disabled to make the fifty-mile walk, and became the first horse in Britain to travel by means of others' efforts. Philip O'Kelly devised for him a prototype horsebox, a four-wheeled carriage with two horses to draw it. John Oakley, who had ridden Eclipse on his racecourse debut at Epsom, is reputed to have accompanied his charge; 'and when (like other travellers) he chose to take a glass of gin or aniseed for himself, he was directed to furnish his old friend Eclipse with a lock of hay, and a drop of the pail'.[126]

One of the prints carried a twee account of the move in the form of an epistle from Eclipse to his son, King Fergus:

> I set out last week from Epsom, and am safe arrived in my new
> stables at this place. My situation may serve as a lesson to man: I
> was once the fleetest horse in the world, but old age has come

---

[124] Augusta travelled to and fro bewilderingly. Bred by O'Kelly, she was sold to the Prince, bought back, and sold at the dispersal sale; but she ended up at the O'Kelly stud at Cannons.

[125] From *A Short History of the Celebrated Race-horse Eclipse* by Bracy Clark.

[126] From William Pick's *The Turf Register and Sportsman and Breeder's Stud Book.*

upon me, and wonder not, King Fergus, when I tell thee, I was drawn in a carriage from Epsom to Cannons, being unable to walk even so short a journey. Every horse, as well as every dog, has his day; and I have had mine. I have outlived two worthy masters, the late Duke of Cumberland, that bred me, and the Colonel, with whom I have spent my best days; but I must not repine, I am now caressed, not so much for what I can do, but for what I have done.

I am glad to hear, my grandson, Honest Tom, performs so well in Ireland, and trust that he, and the rest of my progeny, will do honour to the name of their grandsire,

Eclipse

Cannons, Middlesex

P.S. Myself, Dungannon, Volunteer, and Vertumnus, are all here.

Compliments to the Yorkshire horses.

Andrew saw that Eclipse did not have much time left. In December of that year, 1788, *The Times* reported that 'The French King has sent over an eminent anatomic drawer to Captain O'Kelly's seat at Cannons, in order to make a minute and complete figure of the celebrated horse Eclipse. He is now there, where it is intended he shall remain a fortnight.' This man may have been Charles Vial de Sainbel,[127] a thirty-five-year-old veterinarian who had been a victim of political machinations at the Royal Veterinary College in Paris.

It was Sainbel – now living in a London house once occupied by Sir Isaac Newton – whom Andrew hastened to fetch just two months later when, on the morning of 25 February 1789, Eclipse fell ill with colic. This intestinal affliction often causes terrible pain for horses, and can be fatal. On arrival at Cannons, Sainbel gave the suffering Eclipse laudanum, and tried the generic treatment of bleeding. He would have punctured a vein in the horse's neck, and

---

[127] This was how the English styled his surname, St Bel. He wrote later that he had made studies of Eclipse when alive. See chapter 21 for more on Sainbel.

allowed up to five pints of blood to drain out. Despite this attention (possibly because of it), Eclipse continued to decline, and died
on 27 February, at seven o'clock in the evening.[128]

Sainbel performed a post-mortem, and satisfied himself that
Eclipse had been beyond the reach of medicine. 'I infer that the
reins [kidneys] performed their functions in a very imperfect
manner, and that the animal died in consequence of the affections
of these viscera, and of a violent inflammation of the bowels,' he
wrote later. Eclipse had a large heart, Sainbel noticed. He weighed
it: it tipped the scales at 14lb. This unusual size, a good five pounds
heavier than standard, has been taken as one explanation for
Eclipse's stamina. But Sainbel and Andrew wanted further explanations, and they agreed to offer a detailed anatomical study. The
first ever work of its kind, it would confirm Eclipse's status as the
paragon of the breed, and it would fix that status for posterity.

So it was a funeral of the flesh only when Eclipse was
interred at Cannons. 'A large assembly' enjoyed cakes and ale as
they paid tribute to the horse. Eclipse, like his father, received a
poetic eulogy. The last line was a dig at Eclipse's rival stallions, and
no doubt at Richard Tattersall, owner of Herod's son Highflyer and
author of the taunt a few years earlier that Eclipse 'had had his
day'.

> Praise to departed worth! Illustrious steed,
> Not the fam'd Phrenicus of Pindar's ode,[129]

---

[128] He was nearly if not actually twenty-five (though his contemporaries would
have said that he had not reached his twenty-fifth birthday, which they
assigned to 1 May). That was a pretty good innings. Herod died at twenty-two,
and Highflyer at twenty. Eclipse's long-lived contemporaries included his
father, Marske, who survived to twenty-nine, and Matchem, who achieved the
great age of thirty-three. Among more recent champions, Nijinsky lived to
Eclipse's age of twenty-five, while Secretariat died at nineteen.

[129] Pindar's first Olympic ode refers to this horse, with which Hiero of
Syracuse won an Olympic crown.

O'er thee, Eclipse, possessed transcendent speed
When by a keen Newmarket jockey rode.

Tho' from the hoof of Pegasus arose
Inspiring Hippocrene, a fount divine!
A richer stream superior merit shows,
Thy matchless foot produced O'Kelly's wine.

True, o'er the tomb in which this fav'rite lies
No vaunting boast appears of lineage good;
Yet the Turf Register's bright page defies
The race of Herod to show better blood.

Eclipse sired 344 sons and daughters who were winners on the racecourse; their victories totalled 862, and their earnings exceeded £158,000. Their prizes put him second in the sires' championship for eleven consecutive years, from 1777 to 1788. While he was never leading sire, he was certainly the most profitable sire of the time. Dennis O'Kelly boasted that Eclipse had earned him £25,000 – and he may not have exaggerated grossly.[130] The press reported that Matchem – who was the most celebrated stallion when Eclipse started his career, and who eventually commanded a fee of fifty guineas – had earned stud fees of £17,000.

Eclipse was to surpass Matchem subsequently, too. For the next fifty years, their male lines were of similar importance to breeders, with Matchem's, if anything, slightly favoured. But that changed, and is a historical curiosity now. Matchem is not the tail male (male line) ancestor of any of the current top thirty sires in Europe; and of only one, Tiznow, in the US list. The only sire in either list with a male-line descent from Herod is Inchinor. The fifty-eight others all descend from Eclipse.

[130] A back-of-the-envelope calculation, based on Eclipse's advertised stud fees and numbers of coverings, gives a career total of about £22,000.

16

The Litigant

ANDREW DENNIS O'KELLY, the guardian of the O'Kelly and Eclipse legacy, was an altogether more refined figure than his uncle Dennis. A portrait from 1784, when Andrew was in his early twenties, shows an urbane young man who has benefited from the education that Dennis, and Philip his father, lacked: fine of feature and of dress, he gazes assuredly at the viewer with almond-shaped eyes.

Unlike his uncle too, he became a figure of the establishment. The Jockey Club, as if compounding the snub to Dennis, accepted Andrew into membership after Dennis's death, and the Jockey Club ruler Sir Charles Bunbury, who had owned only one racehorse sired by Eclipse, sent mares to the O'Kelly stallion Dungannon. Other leading men of the Turf to use the stud included the Duke of Grafton, the Duke of Bedford, Lord Grosvenor, Earl Strathmore and the Prince of Wales. Andrew was a confidant of the Prince's, and had influential political friends. He had cultural interests: he was among the subscribers to a printing of the complete works of Handel, and he held a concert at Cannons with Nancy Storace – who had sung Susanna in the first performances of Mozart's *The Marriage of Figaro* – among the soloists.

Yet Andrew could not cast off the O'Kelly talent for controversy, and he spent a good part of his life enmeshed in disputes and legal complications. One of his earliest tangles with the law concerned his behaviour in the Middlesex Militia, the county force in which Dennis had risen, with the help of patronage and of his wallet, to the rank of lieutenant colonel. Andrew joined the militia's Westminster Regiment too, and was a captain when Dennis died. In 1793, an officer called Thomas Gordon agreed to transfer his lieutenant colonelcy in the regiment to Andrew for £200; Andrew was to pay Gordon a further fifty guineas should the regiment remain embodied a year later. Such clauses were typical of the time. Most sales agreements involved caveats and bonuses of various sorts – the purchase of a horse might require an extra payment if the horse won a particular race, for example. It is no wonder that the Georgians were such a litigious bunch.

Andrew enjoyed his rank for only three years until, in 1796, he faced a court martial. The charge, heard at Horse Guards in St James's, was that, while billeted in Winchelsea, he and fellow soldiers – among them his cousin, Philip Whitfield Harvey[131] – had appropriated government coal from the barracks for the house where Andrew was staying. Andrew's companions swore before the court that they had not realized that the coal was unaccounted for; that they had not realized that the coal was assigned to the men in barracks; that the quantity of coal they had taken was small; and that Andrew was absent for three of the five months when the offences were alleged to have taken place. This testimony did not impress the court. It found Andrew guilty, ruled that he should be dismissed from the regiment, and fined him £100, reserving judgment only on how much compensation he should pay for the coal. A letter from Charles Morgan, writing on behalf of the King, softened the sentence but not the essential blow:

[131] The son of Dennis and Philip's sister, Mary O'Kelly, from her marriage to Whitfield Harvey.

I take the earliest opportunity of acquainting you, that His
Majesty, graciously taking into consideration all the circumstances
of the case, and noticing, moreover, that of 18 articles of charge
preferred against you, only one had been established to the satisfaction of the Court Martial, that very slender evidence had been
offered in support of others; and that several had been entirely
abandoned, did not think it necessary that the said sentence
should be carried into execution; but his Majesty at the same time
judging that it will not consist with the upholding of discipline in
the said regiment, or tend to promote a respectful attraction from
the men towards their Officers, that you should retain your
Commission of Lieutenant Colonel in the corps, was pleased to
express his Royal intention of giving direction, through his
Majesty's Secretary of State, to the Lord Lieutenant of the County
of Middlesex, for displacing you from the Westminster regiment
of Militia.

I am, Sir, your most obedient, and very humble servant,
Charles Morgan.

It was a lofty, conclusive dismissal. But, while the court martial
was reported in *The Times*, it made no dent in Andrew's reputation.
Ejection from the regular forces was shameful; ejection from a
county militia was not so grave.

Another incident shows that Andrew's talent for plunging
himself into disputes was not always accompanied by sound
insight. He intervened on the road from Epsom to London when
he came across a stalled coach in which one of the passengers, a
guards officer, was shouting at the coachman. Andrew took up a
position on one side of the coach, with a companion on the other,
and whipped the coachman and his horses on towards town –
actions that resulted, predictably, in the coach's careering into a
ditch, with injuries to both the coachman and the officer's female
companion. When the coachman sued, the court heard that the
guards officer had taken the young woman, Miss Williams, to

the races, had got drunk, and on the journey home had become abusive, charging the coachman with being in league with highwaymen. The judge, ruling that the officer's behaviour had been 'barbarous', fined him £100. Andrew escaped censure.

His behaviour may have been barbarous, but the guards officer's fear of highwaymen was not exaggerated. If you travelled regularly in the eighteenth century, you had to accept that there was a high chance of getting robbed. 'One is forced to travel, even at noon, as if one was going to battle,' Horace Walpole wrote. His friend Lady Browne observed, 'We English always carry two purses on our journeys, a small one for the robbers and a large one for ourselves.' Andrew himself, a regular commuter between Cannons and his late uncle's house in Piccadilly, became a victim when his chaise was stopped by two footpads, uttering 'violent imprecations'. Andrew defied them, drawing his sword. One of the thieves tried to shoot him, missed, and the pair ran off. By the time Andrew had roused help at the next turnpike, the thieves had got away.

That was in 1793. Seven years later, at eight o'clock on the evening of 3 December 1800, it happened again, but with three attackers. Having held up the carriage, Robert Nutts stood by the two horses, while James Riley opened the chaise door and threatened to blow Andrew's brains out unless he handed over his money. Andrew thought better of raising his sword this time, and gave up some cash. The thieves, dissatisfied with the modest sum, suspected that he was carrying – as recommended by Lady Browne – a larger purse as well, so Nutts came back and searched him, joined by the third thief, who extracted £50 in banknotes from Andrew's breeches. With that, the footpads made their escape. But a constable, Nibbs, had witnessed the robbery, and ran to the nearby Adam and Eve pub, where he enlisted four men to help. Nibbs and his posse caught up with Nutts and Riley, who ineffectually fired their pistols before being arrested. Their companion, who was never identified, got away. Nutts and Riley were convicted of highway robbery, and hanged at Newgate on 24 June 1801.

As the 1790s progressed, the complications in Andrew's life multiplied, bequeathing us a collection of family papers peppered with convoluted references to financial and legal disputes. Correspondents claim not to have been paid, or send impenetrable reports of their transactions. Every O'Kelly property is subject to complex mortgage and leasing arrangements; every deal includes conditions or provisos or insurance clauses. Bailiffs arrive to remove furniture; a tenant charges that Andrew intercepted him on the road and taunted him with the words, 'The bailiffs are coming, the bailiffs are coming.' At one time, Cannons had liabilities attached to it of some £30,000. Andrew aroused distrust and made enemies, such as an anonymous correspondent who wrote to Andrew's friend, Lady Anna Donegall: 'Beware, O'Kelly is not the man he appears. Duplicity is the chief part of his composition. His first aim is to have the reputation of receiving your favours; his second, to continue to pay his expenses from your husband's pocket. Before the death of Lord Donegall's father he and his family were in the greatest distress. Charlotte Hayes was in the Fleet. I thus have cautioned you, wishing to protect innocence, beauty and virtue.' Lady Donegall paid no attention to this warning, and remained on warm terms with Andrew. So, according to the evidence in the files, did Lord Donegall – a baffling show of loyalty, as the two men spent most of their adult lives suing each other. However, contrary to what the anonymous letter writer implied, it seems to have been Andrew who was the financial loser.

George Augustus Chichester, second Marquess of Donegall, was an inveterate spendthrift and gambler. He first did business with the O'Kellys in 1794, when, aged twenty-five and carrying the title Lord Belfast, he visited Cannons and picked out some horses. Already, he had a significant flaw as a business partner: he was an inmate of the Fleet debtors' prison, though allowed out under the day rules.[132] The contract he struck with Andrew's father Philip involved a post-obit: a commitment to pay a sum on the death of his father, the Marquess. Five years later, the Marquess obligingly died, and his son took possession of his title, along with a substantial chunk of what is now Northern Ireland. It would be a long time, however, before he paid his O'Kelly debts.

Within a few years of meeting, Andrew and the newly created Marquess – whose conduct, according to one of Dennis's friends, was 'most atrocious' – were in disagreement about their finances, while continuing to operate as a team. They may have tried to use the partnership to circumvent authority, as for instance in the case of a horse called Wrangler, listed in the *Racing Calendar* for 1801 under Andrew's name. Two Middlesex sheriffs, Perring and Cadell, seized Wrangler while he was on his way to Newmarket, in execution against the chronically indebted Donegall. Andrew protested that Wrangler was his, and sued, with Sir Charles Bunbury turning up at court to swear that he had sold the horse to him. Donegall, who had leased Cannons from Andrew earlier that year, testified from the stand that Wrangler was not his, but Andrew's. Another witness supported this statement by saying that he had observed Andrew making a match for Wrangler, at a race meeting where Donegall had 'damned [Wrangler] for a bolter,[133] and said he would have nothing to do with him'. So far, so good; but then Andrew's case collapsed embarrassingly. A groom confessed that although he had been paid by Andrew, Wrangler was stabled with other horses belonging to Donegall; and another groom, asked to name Wrangler's owner, replied, 'The Marquess of Donegall.' One would like to have seen Andrew's and Donegall's faces when those words were uttered. Before a crowded court, the judge dismissed the case – which had

[132] Which, just over thirty years earlier, Dennis O'Kelly had also enjoyed.
[133] I.e., he was uncontrollable.

surely been a ruse to reclaim a horse that Andrew and Donegall had owned jointly.

Over the next eighteen years, Andrew and Donegall were in and out of court, lobbing claims and counter-claims at each other, all the while offering assurances that it was nothing personal. In 1814, Andrew wrote to Donegall, who was then in Ireland, to remonstrate with him about reports that he and his father Philip had taken 'improper advantage of your lordship'. Donegall replied, 'I beg leave to say that I never fabricated such reports and that they are altogether void of truth, as to the bills filed in chancery against your father and yourself . . . they were contrary to my approbation and without my consent, having always lived on the most intimate footing with you and conceiving you to be a man of the strictest honour and integrity and which was the general opinion of the world when I first had the pleasure of your acquaintance.' This was courteous. The fact was, however, that Donegall owed Andrew some £37,000, from total debts amounting to an eye-watering £617,524 — about £33 million in today's money. Among financial profligates of the era, only the Prince of Wales could rival him. Eventually, Donegall acknowledged the sums he owed Andrew, although whether he followed up the acknowledgement with any cash is not clear. Certainly, in 1819, Andrew's cousin Philip Whitfield Harvey wrote to Andrew from Dublin: 'Lord Donegall is in great distress for even £100. Lady D, that was, is determined to proceed to London immediately without a guinea or even a carriage. She will not allow her noble spouse to quit her apron strings, fearing that he might tie himself to some more deserving object.'[134]

Whether or not the author of the warning letter to Lady Donegall gave a fair report of Andrew's character, he was well informed about Andrew's finances. Dennis's will had implied greater wealth than he really possessed, and his estate turned out

---

[134] Donegall remained deep in the red until his death in 1844.

to be insufficient to pay his debts and legacies. To compensate, Andrew borrowed money, took out mortgages, and rented properties. But the late eighteenth century was not a good time to stretch your finances. There was revolution in France, followed by European war, and soon everyone was feeling the pinch. From 1787, the year of Dennis's death, to 1800, Philip and Andrew advertised regularly in the *Racing Calendar* that all the thirty-plus mares at Cannons, with their foals, were up for sale. Many of the foals found buyers; but, in those straitened times, no one wanted to pay the high prices that the O'Kellys were asking for the mares.[135] Meanwhile, the value of the O'Kelly stallions was falling. By the turn of the century, Dungannon and Volunteer were covering mares at a modest ten guineas each – fees suggesting that there was not a great deal of confidence in their ability to get outstanding racers.

Charlotte Hayes was another encumbrance on Andrew. She was as scattily profligate as ever, and in 1798 she got herself committed again to the Fleet debtors' prison.[136] Andrew's subventions to her at this time included the hefty sum of £728 to satisfy a debt to one Thomas Pilton, a Piccadilly upholsterer, and £105 to buy her the right to the Fleet day rules, allowing her to live outside the prison walls. The next spring, when Charlotte was released, she satisfied further debts, to Thomas and Mary Potts (£48 15s), and to John Thomas (£235 14s). She and Dennis's brother Philip had already agreed that, in the light of the money that Andrew had raised following Dennis's death, Andrew should be granted sole right to property worth that sum. Now Charlotte signed, in her scratchy hand, a document releasing to Andrew all her portion of the estate, with the exception of her £400 annuity. The good news for her was that she would no longer be responsible for the upkeep

---

[135] There is no record of what happened to the horses in the end. Perhaps Donegall bought them – and never paid for them.
[136] She had been in the Fleet from 1758 to 1761, and in the Marshalsea in 1776.

of the horses – though no doubt she had never assumed that responsibility anyway.

The only transfer that had taken place before this was of 'a very extraordinary and rare bird called Parrot gifted with extraordinary powers of speech and song'. But Polley was to live for only another few years. In October 1802, Philip O'Kelly had sombre news to give to his son, in a letter (original spelling preserved) hinting that Charlotte was a constant worry: 'Polley was taking ill on Saturday night last with a purging and bloody flox and all things that was fit for her was got. She died on Sunday morning. Dr Kennedy go her to have her stuffd so she is no more. Charlett is in the same state as ever.' The death, which sounds unpleasant, was a traumatic family event. A family servant, signing herself E. Wilson, wrote to Andrew: 'My trouble was so great at the death of the bird and I did not know what I was doing, the loss of my children never afflicted me more. I am truly sorry and surprised to hear you attribute to my neglect or want of care her death, as it was impossible if my life was at stake to be more attentive than I was. I could not keep her alive no more than I can my good self when it shall please God to call me.'

Polley got the tribute, surely rare for a bird, of an obituary in the *Gentleman's Magazine*, which reminded readers of her skills: 'Died, at the house of Colonel O'Kelly, in Half-moon-Street, Piccadilly, his wonderful parrot, who had been in his family 30 years, having been purchased at Bristol out of a West-India ship. It sang, with the greatest clearness and precision, the 114th Psalm, "The Banks of the Dee", "God Save the King!" and other favourite songs; and, if it blundered in any one, instantly began again, till it had the tune complete. One hundred guineas had been refused for it in London.' The magazine made the double mistake of announcing that Polley would be interred alongside Eclipse at Cannons. In fact, as Philip wrote, she was stuffed, and continued to reside at Half Moon Street; and Eclipse's skeleton at this time was at a small, private museum in Mayfair.

Charlotte appears to have been willing to give up the annuity bequeathed to her by Dennis as well. Lawyers raised objections, however. One told Andrew, who was hoping to sell Cannons, that any deal should be subject to the £400 yearly charge, 'as [Charlotte] has very much encumbered it and may create some difficulties in the title'. A man called Brockbank held the same view, to Charlotte's dismay – which she expressed to Andrew in one sprawling, minimally punctuated (and, again, idiosyncratically spelled) sentence constituting the only letter of hers we have.

February, 1801
My dear Colonel, I am very sorry to find that Mr Brockbank
makes any objection to my giving you the releace for my annuiteis
and the acknowledgement of the other sums mentioned in it that
you and your father have paid and secured to be paid for me but I
am not surprised at aney thing that such a man as Mr Brockbank
should say or do after the manner he has conducted himself
towards me and you – unjust advantage he is attempting to take of
you against my wishes or concent – if you or any other person has
the smallest doubtes of the justness of what is contained in the
releace I shall be ready at any time to com forward and make an
affidavit of those circumstances which Mr Brockbank must be perfectly well acquainted with as I have at different times stated to
him monies that you have paid for me and I have give him money
to keep the transactions of my selling my annuities from your
knowledg and am my dear colonel yours sincerely C. O'Kelly.

The annuity was still attached to Cannons when Andrew at last sold the estate, to Sir Thomas Plumer, in 1811. Charlotte is described in one document as a 'spinster' (another hint that she never married, although the term may be applied loosely) 'who is now advanced in years'; in another, she is living on the Cannons estate (though not in the mansion house) and 'aged about 85 years'. Plumer, who was the solicitor general, indemnified himself against paying her any money. Cannons cost him £55,000.

It is not certain how many further payments Charlotte claimed. E. J. Burford stated that she died in 1813, though on unclear evidence. She does not appear in the Middlesex burial records that contain Dennis O'Kelly, Philip (who died in 1806) and Andrew; and I could not find her in the Westminster archives either. Her death is as obscure as her birth. But this is not the obscurity of poverty and disease that a huge majority of her fellow prostitutes suffered. Surviving into at least her mid-eighties, and doing so, in spite of her various setbacks, in comfort, Charlotte Hayes achieved an impressive transcendence of her background – thanks to her business flair, and thanks as well to Dennis O'Kelly and Eclipse.

Andrew Dennis O'Kelly died, suddenly, in 1820. He left a mystery surrounding his personal life: did he ever marry? In notes about the family left in the O'Kelly archive, Mary O'Kelly Harvey stated that he did, while Theodore Cook, author of *Eclipse and O'Kelly*, disagreed. Cook found references to a son, Charles, and to a daughter, Eliza, and he quoted a letter from Charles to Andrew dealing with the usual O'Kelly themes of bust-ups over rents and mortgages. ('Mr Michell went down to Grosvenor Place and discovered that Walton the broker was in the act of taking away all the furniture and yours with the rest . . . W Stacpoole says he will bring an action against you and he has no doubt but that he will be able to saddle you with all the taxes and rent of the house since Mr Stacpoole left England.') But Cook did not spot any references to this family in Andrew's will (dated 1820), and assumed that they had all died.

It seems that Eliza had. However, Cook disregarded a bequest to one Charles Andrews, a student in Aberdeen to whom Andrew gave an annuity of £200, with the provision that he must pursue his studies satisfactorily and observe morality in his conduct. In the National Archives, there is a will dated 1826 by one Charles Andrew O'Kelly. The brief document states that the author was described as Charles Andrews 'in the will of my late father Lt Colonel Andrew Dennis O'Kelly', and leaves everything to Charles's mother, named Susanna and with an illegible surname, about which one can be sure only that it is not O'Kelly.

The obvious conclusion to be drawn from this will and from Andrew's, which makes no mention of Charles's status as a member of the family, is that Andrew was unmarried, and that Charles was illegitimate. Andrew's will contains no reference, either, to a wife.

One of Andrew's principal legatees was his cousin, Philip Whitfield Harvey. The two were close: they had been in the Middlesex Militia together, and Andrew introduced Philip to the Prince of Wales and his circle. What is not clear is whether Andrew and Philip were involved in more clandestine activities. Philip's wife, Frances, inherited an Irish newspaper called the *Freeman's Journal* from a man called Francis Higgins, who had risen to newspaper proprietorship from an unpromising early career doing odd jobs for a felon in Newgate prison. In his will, Higgins also left Andrew £300, declaring that 'if I did not know that he, my friend, was in great affluence, I would have freely bequeathed him any property I might be possessed of'. Andrew's connection with Higgins, alleged W. J. Fitzpatrick in *Secret Service Under Pitt* (1892), was shady, and Andrew's role was as a conduit between the British government and various secret agents, among them Higgins (the 'Sham Squire'), who used his position at the *Freeman's Journal* to undermine the cause of Catholic emancipation.[137] If that was the case, Andrew may have approached Philip on behalf of the government too. In the family papers, Mary O'Kelly Harvey – daughter of Philip and Frances – is at pains to emphasize her

---

[137] Though as Fitzpatrick thought that Andrew and 'Count' O'Kelly (Dennis) were the same person, he may not be the most reliable guide.

father's distance from the government, and says that he turned down money to write anti-Catholic propaganda, suffering discrimination as a result.[138]

Andrew certainly did make himself politically useful. In 1813, we find him investigating the conduct of the Prince's – now the Prince Regent's – estranged wife, Caroline of Brunswick. George Augustus had married Caroline, his cousin, under pressure from his father. His first meeting with her, just a few days before the wedding in 1795, was a shock: he found her revolting, and later described her as 'the vilest wretch this world was ever cursed with'. The Prince, seriously overweight, was far from gorgeous himself; but the unfailing willingness of glamorous women to become his mistresses may have blinded him to that realization. He sought refuge in alcohol on the happy day, and by the evening was so drunk that he collapsed into the fireplace of the bridal chamber, remaining there insensible until the morning. Nevertheless, the union was at some point consummated, and a daughter produced, before the couple separated. The Prince conducted further affairs. Caroline, it was rumoured, took lovers too – a treasonable offence, and one, if proved, that would have given a convenient justification for dispatching her and any descendants to outer darkness. As part of what was known as the 'delicate investigation', Andrew went to Caroline's house and interviewed her servants, but found no incriminating evidence. In 1821, when George Augustus succeeded to the throne, Caroline arrived at Westminster Abbey for the coronation, but was turned away at the doors.

Andrew was also an ally of the Prince in his racing interests. In that role, he got involved in the Escape Affair.

---

[138] The Act of Union of Great Britain and Ireland came into effect in 1801.

*A target for caricaturists when he was Prince of Wales, George IV is
portrayed more respectfully here, in an Ascot scene by John Doyle.*

17

The Decline of the Jontleman

GEORGE AUGUSTUS FREDERICK, the Prince of Wales, was clever and before he expanded to seventeen and a half stone in weight – handsome. He was also vain, extravagant and self-indulgent. His secret marriage to the Catholic widow Mrs Fitzherbert, his numerous affairs, his Whig sympathies, and his girth all made him a target for satirists. 'Let us enquire who are the chosen companions and confidential intimates of the Prince of Wales. They are the very lees of society: creatures, with whom a person of morality, or even common decency could not associate,' wrote Charles Pigott in his widely circulated lampoon *The Jockey Club: Or a Sketch of the Manners of the Age*.[139] '[George Augustus] was, however, genuinely fond of racing,' says the *Biographical Encyclopaedia of British Flat Racing*, as if pointing out the one trait that excuses everything.[140] One might point also in mitigation to the architectural splendours – among them the streets, terraces and other buildings of John Nash[141]

---

[139] For writing this attack on many of his fellow members, Pigott, you may recall, was invited by the actual Jockey Club to withdraw.

[140] Much as racing enthusiasts say of the Duke of Cumberland, in effect: 'Yes, he butchered a great many Scots; but he did breed Eclipse and Herod.'

[141] Whose best-known achievements include Regent's Park and Regent Street, as well as the remodelling of the Royal Pavilion in Brighton.

– that are the legacy of the Prince's extravagant patronage.

George Augustus ('Prinny') had his first runners on the racecourse – the jockeys wearing the royal colours of purple jacket with gold lace, scarlet sleeves and black cap – in 1784. By 1785, he already had eighteen horses in training, the winners including Eclipse's son (and former Derby winner) Saltram, Rockingham (later to be a rival to Dennis O'Kelly's Dungannon), and Rosaletta, who in one race finished second to Dennis's Soldier. The two owners – from absolutely contrasting backgrounds, but each frowned upon by certain sections of the establishment – were social acquaintances, and Dennis, had he still been alive when Pigott wrote *The Jockey Club*, would no doubt have got a mention alongside other representatives of the 'lees of society'. Prinny was a regular among the guests at Clay Hill when Dennis entertained during the Epsom spring meeting, and they appear together among the crowd of gesticulating and shouting gamblers in Rowlandson's caricature *The Betting Post*.[142]

By 1786, Prinny had twenty-six horses in training. Naturally, he also had huge debts, and because he got no help in clearing them from his father, he was forced to offload the entire stable. Not going to market from a position of strength, he could not command premium prices. The stud, reported the *St James's Chronicle*, 'was not sold but given away', to purchasers who in some cases sold on their horses immediately, for double what they had paid. Two of the fillies, Annette and Augusta, were to finish first and second in the 1787 Oaks – Augusta in the ownership of Dennis O'Kelly. Another lot, a Highflyer yearling, went to a Mr Franco. Later, the yearling kicked out in his box and got his foot stuck between the wooden boards, until the grooms managed to free him uninjured. He got the name Escape.

A year later, Parliament cleared Prinny's debts. Immediately,

---

[142] See chapter 18 and colour section.

he splashed out on racehorses again, buying back some of those he had sold, Escape among them. As the disapproving Charles Pigott wrote, 'No sooner had parliament voted this money, than decency was set at defiance, public opinion scorned, the turf establishment revived in a more ruinous style than ever, the wide field of dissipation and extravagance enlarged, fresh debts contracted to an enormous amount, which it is neither in his own, or the nation's power to discharge, and strong doubts entertained that the money voted by parliament was not applied to the purpose for which it was granted.'

In 1788, Prinny became the first royal winner of the Derby, with his colt Sir Thomas. He had thirty-five horses in training in 1789, and the following year he hired the leading jockey of the day, Sam Chifney, famous for the 'Chifney rush': a perfectly timed finishing burst after a quiet ride at the back of the field

A portrait of Chifney gives him the roughened features of a minor member of Britain's gangland. But he was a dandy. His jockey's attire featured ruffs and frills, and he cultivated 'love locks' that hung down below his jockey's cap. He was also conceited. In his autobiography, to which he gave the frank title *Genius Genuine*, he claimed that 'In 1773 [when he was 18], I could ride horses in a better manner in a race to beat others, than any person I ever knew in my time; and in 1775, I could train horses for running better than any person I yet saw.' He was, in short, an upstart. Riding grooms then were merely promoted stable lads, and were considered to be, essentially, servants. Here was one assuming the trappings of celebrity. Moreover, Chifney did not appear to be honest. Those waiting tactics: were they not a ploy to lose races that he should be winning? Chifney was the kind of person that authorities are only too delighted to punish.

On 20 October 1791, at Newmarket, Prinny's horse Escape started as the hot, 1-2 favourite for a two-mile race worth sixty guineas. He finished last of four. The next day, he turned out again, for a four-mile race over the Beacon Course. Chifney, who had not backed him[143] in the first race, did so this time, at odds of 5-1; so did the Prince. Escape romped home, ahead of a field including two of the horses who had finished in front of him the day before.

As soon as he passed the post, the rumblings of suspicion and discontent started up. Here, surely, was a blatant scam, not only on the part of Chifney, but of the Prince as well, to get better odds in the second race. A Rowlandson caricature, *How to Escape Winning*, shows Chifney pulling Escape's reins and holding his whip in his mouth, while in the foreground Prinny, with a sly look at the viewer, taps his nose. Agitated, Prinny wrote to Sir Charles Bunbury:

> Dear Bunbury, I found on my arrival in London so many infamous and rascally lies fabricated relative to the affair that happened at Newmarket by republican scribblers and studiously circulating the country that I now find it absolutely necessary that these calumnies should be contradicted in the most authentic manner. After having consulted with many of my friends I leave what happened and the manner of contradiction to be discussed between you and my friend Sheridan[144] who has been so good as to undertake the management of this matter. P.s. If you think that any enquiries are necessary respecting Chifney I only beg you will see such steps taken as you think proper – I am very sincerely yours, G.R.

Bunbury did take what he thought were the proper steps. He hauled up Chifney to testify before him and his fellow Jockey Club stewards Ralph Dutton and Thomas Panton. Chifney, in his affidavit, swore that he had bet only twenty guineas on the race that Escape won; that he had not stopped Escape in the first

---

[143] Allowing jockeys to bet invites suspicion at best and corruption at worst. The Jockey Club eventually banned the practice in 1879.
[144] The politician and playwright Richard Brinsley Sheridan, author of *The Rivals* and *The School for Scandal*.

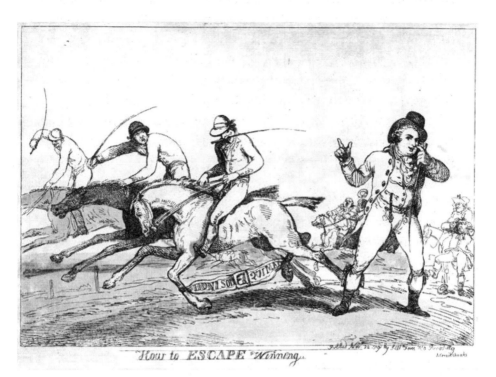

'How to ESCAPE Winning.'

Thomas Rowlandson's view of the Escape affair, How to Escape
Winning *(1791). Sam Chifney, Escape's jockey, pulls the horse, who is
further hampered by a banner saying, 'Honi soit qui mal'* (a motto that
also appears in A Late Unfortunate Adventure at York — page 106).
The Prince of Wales taps his nose knowingly at the viewer.

race; and that he had never profited from the defeat of a horse he had ridden or trained. The stewards were unimpressed. Bunbury paid a visit to Prinny and told him that 'if Chifney were suffered to ride the Prince's horses, no gentleman would start against him'.

Here, in summary, was the new dispensation on the Turf. Just over a century earlier, Charles II had governed at Newmarket; now, the heir to the throne was being put in his place.

Prinny did not like it, and the next year he placed his stud on the market again. There are conflicting reports about whether he did so entirely because of Escape (his debts were again serious, and Escape's was not the only controversial race involving one of his horses); what is clear is that, while he was to return to the Turf once more and to race horses at Newmarket, he shunned the town until at least 1805, and probably thereafter as well, in spite of this letter from Bunbury and the Earl of Darlington:

Sir, We humbly beg leave to represent to your Royal Highness that we are deputed in our official situations as stewards of Newmarket to convey to you the unanimous wish of all gentlemen of the turf now present at Brighton, which we respectfully submit to your consideration.

From serious misconceptions or differences of opinion which arose relative to a race, in which your royal highness was concerned, we greatly regret that we have never been honoured with your presence there since that period. But experiencing as we constantly do, the singular marks of your condescension and favour, and considering the essential benefit not only that the Turf will generally derive, but also the great satisfaction that we all must individually feel from the honour of your presence, we humbly request that your Royal Highness will bury in oblivion any past unfortunate occurrences at Newmarket and you will again be pleased to honour us there with your countenance and support.

Reading the riot act to the Prince was one thing, but alienating him irrevocably was another.

Chifney, by contrast, was dispensable. Possibly the jockey had not always been honest in his riding, but on this occasion he looks like the victim of a miscarriage of justice. Everyone knows that jockeys sometimes stop horses, and that trainers leave horses unfit, or run them over inappropriate distances. However, when you look in detail at alleged incidents of these practices, you rarely find unambiguous evidence. The contemporary counterpart of Sam Chifney, certainly in respect of his unpopularity with the authorities, is the Irish-born jockey Kieren Fallon. In spring 1995, Fallon rode a beaten favourite, Top Cees, in a Newmarket handicap. Three weeks later, he rode Top Cees to an easy victory in the valuable Chester Cup, at the rewarding odds of 8-1. The *Sporting Life*[145] accused Fallon, along with Top Cees' trainer Lynda Ramsden and her husband Jack, of cheating. Fallon and the Ramsdens sued; the paper failed to prove its case, and was forced to pay £195,000 in damages, as well as costs. More recently, Fallon was the most prominent defendant in a race-fixing trial arising from an expensive investigation by the City of London police. The prosecution's evidence had many flaws – among them that, for the races under investigation, Fallon's winning percentage was actually higher than normal. The case collapsed.

In *Genius Genuine*, Chifney recalled that Escape was a 'stuffy' horse – one who needed plenty of exercise – and that the first race had toughened him up for the second. Escape was capable of putting in disappointing runs, and Chifney had shown himself a good judge of when they would take place. In the Oatlands handicap that year, he had chosen to ride Baronet, the eventual winner, instead. There was a horses for courses factor too: Escape had run some of his best races over the Beacon Course. At worst, it appears that Escape's connections were guilty of failing to

---

[145] Later merged with the *Racing Post*.

communicate to the betting public that their horse might not be at his best for the first, 20 October race.

The Prince, albeit after telling Bunbury to deal with Chifney 'as you think proper', stuck by the jockey. According to Chifney, Prinny's words were: 'Chifney, I am perfectly well satisfied with your conduct since you have rode for me, and I believe you have discharged your duty like an honest, faithful servant, and although I shall have no further occasion for you, having ordered all my horses to be sold, I have directed my treasurer to continue during my life to pay you your present salary of two hundred [guineas] a year.' Having received this verbal and financial tribute, Chifney concluded that the Prince was, no matter what others may have been saying, a great man. 'Language cannot describe my feelings on hearing this generous communication. I bowed and retired in silence, beseeching at the same time in my heart the Almighty to pour down his choicest blessings on a Prince whose magnanimity and goodness of heart induced him graciously to condescend to give protection and support to an unfortunate injured man, who but for this act of benevolence must otherwise have starved with his wife and children and who with them are bound to pray for such a generous benefactor.'

Chifney did not conduct his life thereafter with the humility that this encomium implies. Two hundred guineas was a sizeable professional's salary, and Chifney could carry on working as well, because the Jockey Club did not have the power, which it would later assume, to eject ('warn off') miscreants from racing altogether. Unfortunately, Chifney had an extravagant nature, and descended into debt. In about 1800, about nine years after the Escape scandal, he asked for and received permission from the Prince to sell the annuity. This was when Andrew Dennis O'Kelly became involved in the affair.

You will have noticed that, despite the stipulation in his uncle's will that he should abandon racing, Andrew continued to take part in the sport. He was never as serious about it as Dennis had been, but he raced up to seven horses during various seasons in the 1790s, and he also owned horses in partnerships – with the Marquess of Donegall, and with the Prince of Wales.[146] One of the mementoes of their continuing relationship is an 1801 letter from Andrew to George Augustus's equerry: 'I have endeavoured to select some venison out of my park at Cannons which I hope will prove worthy the Prince's acceptance. I have sent it by this day's coach directed to you and request you will do me the favour to present it with my most respectful duty to His Royal Highness.'

In 1800, Donegall took on Chifney as a groom. When Chifney sold his annuity to Joseph Sparkes for 1,200 guineas, someone had to offer security that Sparkes would get his yearly payments in return. Donegall said that he, being a marquess, could not do it, and asked Andrew to underwrite the sum instead. What followed was inevitable. The money went to Sparkes for a few years before drying up, and the annuity became another subject for litigation. In 1813, Andrew wrote that 'the holder of the annuity wishes to resume proceedings against me in the Court of Common Pleas'. Two years later, Andrew settled a sum on George Sparkes (to whom Joseph had assigned the annuity); a year after that, he deposed that the annuity was among Donegall's debts. It was another Donegall/O'Kelly mess.

The lump sum of 1,200 guineas gave Chifney only temporary relief. Defaulting on a payment of £350 to a saddler called Latchford, he was sent to the Fleet, where he died in 1807, aged fifty-three. He left behind the design for the 'Chifney bit', ignored by the Jockey Club at the time but later to become standard equipment in racing stables. Aimed at controlling highly strung horses, the bit gives handlers a firm control of the horse's jaw.

---

[146] A typically complicated arrangement concerned a mare called Scota. Jointly owned by Andrew and Prinny, Scota went to stud on the understanding that Prinny, paying an annuity for the privilege, would breed from her. When he sold his racing interests, he asked for her back.

*

It was apparent to the press at the time that the 1792 sale of the Prince of Wales's stud marked the end of an era. In its 13 March issue, *The Times* observed:

> This was a melancholy sight to the whole kennel of black legs. Here end the hopes of royal plunder. Not even so much as a foal is to remain in his Highness's possession. The Turf is to be considered as a spot no longer tenable; and deserted by the Prince, it will soon be abandoned by every other gentleman in the kingdom.
>
> Indeed, of late years, so much roguery has been practised, that there was no dependance to be placed on the horse or his rider – a pill of compounds given on the morning of running – a jockey purposely losing his weight, and many other tricks which lie in the power of the groom and the rider, without the possibility of detection, laid gentlemen so much at the mercy of their menial servants, that nothing short of ruin could be the consequences of a man of fortune attaching himself to Newmarket. The sale of the Prince's stud, it is therefore to be hoped, will be a good precedent for many more of a similar nature.
>
> The Duke of York [Prinny's brother] was there, and bid for several of the horses. The public, no doubt, would naturally have hoped with us, that at a time when the Prince of Wales had seen the imprudence of keeping up a very large Turf establishment, the Duke of York would have followed his example; especially at a time when the friends of his Highness allege in Parliament that £37,000 a year, added to his other revenues, is not sufficient.

Trends are hard to spot as they begin, but *The Times* was prescient here. The era of Eclipse and O'Kelly – the era when Dennis and the likes of Lord Egremont and the Prince of Wales could be rogues together on the Turf – was over. A new era, of structured and regulated racing, was arriving. That does not mean that skulduggery disappeared. As we shall see, it got worse: more professional, and more vicious. It made one nostalgic for Dennis, the *jontleman* rogue.

In 1793, a *Sporting Magazine* correspondent (probably John Lawrence) was nostalgic already:

> The zenith of racing popularity, when the laurel of victory was disputed, and in eternal competition, among a Duke of Cumberland, a Captain O'Kelly, a Shafto, and a Stroud. There are, tis true, now in health and hilarity, some few of the sportsmen who then graced the turf with their presence and their possessions; they well know how gradually the turf has been declining from the splendour of those days, to its present state of unprecedented sterility. Racing, like cocking, seems to have had its day (at least for the present generation).
>
> Of the late D. O'Kelly, Esq, it may be very justly acknowledged, we shall never see a more zealous, or a more generous promoter of the turf, a fairer sportsman in the field, or at the gaming table. In his domestic transactions he was indulgently liberal, without being ridiculously profuse; and he was the last man living to offer an intentional insult unprovoked, so he was never known to receive one with impunity. In short . . . he was not in the fashion now extant.

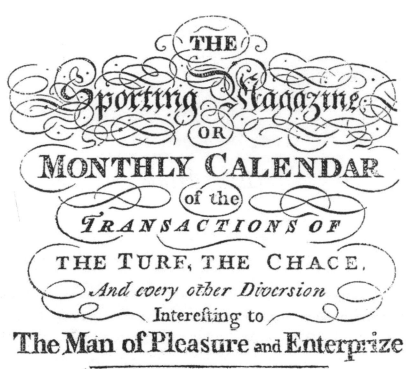

THE
Sporting Magazine,
OR
MONTHLY CALENDAR
of the
TRANSACTIONS OF
THE TURF, THE CHACE,
And every other Diversion
Interefting to
The Man of Pleasure and Enterprize

VOLUME THE FIRST.

LONDON.

Printed for the PROPRIETORS, and Sold by J. WHEBLE;
No. 18. Warwick Square, Warwick Lane, near St. Paul's.
MDCCXCIII.

The Sporting Magazine, *which contained many anecdotes about Eclipse, Dennis O'Kelly and their contemporaries.*

18

Artists' Models

THERE WAS ANOTHER COMMON interest in the lives of the O'Kelly family and the Prince of Wales: the painter George Stubbs (1724–1806). It may have brought them together as agents behind a puzzling episode in Stubbs's later career.

Some time after 1790, a 'gentleman' – his identity as mysterious as that of the anonymous nobleman who commissioned Mozart's *Requiem* – called on Stubbs with a proposal. It was to paint, in the words of the prospectus that appeared in *The Sporting Magazine*, 'a series of pictures [portraits] from the Godolphin Arabian to the most distinguished horse of the present time, a general chronological history of the Turf specifying the races and matches and particular anecdotes and properties of each horse, with a view to their being first exhibited and then engraven and published in numbers'. The gentleman, identified to the public only as 'Turf', said that he had deposited with a banker the sum of £9,000, on which Stubbs could draw as required.

Stubbs was approaching his seventieth birthday. Born the son of a currier (someone who dresses leather) in Liverpool, he had largely taught himself his artistic techniques, a process that had included dissecting horses for eighteen months in

Lincolnshire. He rented a cottage in the village of Horkstow, where, assisted by his very tolerant common-law wife Mary Spencer, he anatomized a series of equine corpses. He bought each specimen alive, bled the horse to death, injected the arteries and veins with wax or tallow, suspended the body from an iron bar, and dissected and drew it for six or seven weeks, until it was so cut up and putrefied that he needed to move on to the next one. His first biographer, Ozias Humphry, gave an example of Stubbs's technique: 'He first began by dissecting and designing the muscles of the abdomen – proceeding through five different layers of muscles till he came to the peritoneum and the pleura through which appeared the lungs and the intestines – after which the bowels were taken out, and cast away.' Airless, noisome, and thick with bluebottles, that room would have displeased today's health and safety inspectorate.

When Stubbs arrived in London, towards the end of the 1750s, he quickly made his mark. His fine portraits, and his peerless paintings of horses and other animals – far in advance of previous works in the genre – put him in great demand among wealthy patrons. But interest in his work declined towards the end of the 1780s; and Stubbs, who was uncompromising and prickly, had a difficult relationship with the recently established but influential Royal Academy. The offer from 'Turf' of £9,000, attractive in itself, came with the bonus of an opportunity to promote the career of Stubbs's son, George Townly Stubbs.

An advertisement for the *Review of the Turf* appeared in *The Sporting Magazine* of January 1794. Dedicated 'by permission to His Royal Highness, the Prince of Wales', the *Review* would be

an accurate account of the performance of every horse of note
that has started from the year 1750 to the present time; together
with the pedigrees; interspersed with various anecdotes of the
most remarkable races; the whole embellished with upwards of
145 prints, engraved in the best manner, from original portraits of

Detail from Stubbs's great painting of Hambletonian (Eclipse's grandson)
after the horse's gruelling match with Diamond.

Right: a bookmaker and his client at Newmarket, at a time when bets were struck on an ad hoc basis.

Below: in the foreground, two men make a deal over a horse; with his back to us, Dennis O'Kelly instructs (to win or lose?) a jockey.

A race meeting at a country course, where the spectators find their own vantage points, by Rowlandson.

Rowlandson's *The Betting Post*, with the Prince of Wales (pointing) on the left, and Dennis O'Kelly (blue coat and crutches) on the right.

Left: the bloodstock auctioneer Tattersalls was at this time based near Hyde Park Corner in London.

Main picture: Rowlandson's caricature shows Dennis O'Kelly (in the portrait on the right wall) as the presiding genius over the scene of intrigue and despair at the subscription club room at Tattersalls, where bets were struck.

Below: Richard Tattersall, standing before a portrait of his beloved Highflyer.

CULATION OF THE CHANCES AT *HAZARD*.
4. that you are *ruined and undone*
1. that you *Rob on the Highway*
2. that you are *Hang'd or Sent to Botany Bay*

BSCRIPTION   CLUB ROOM

STOLEN
A BAY
MARE

CAPT O KELLY

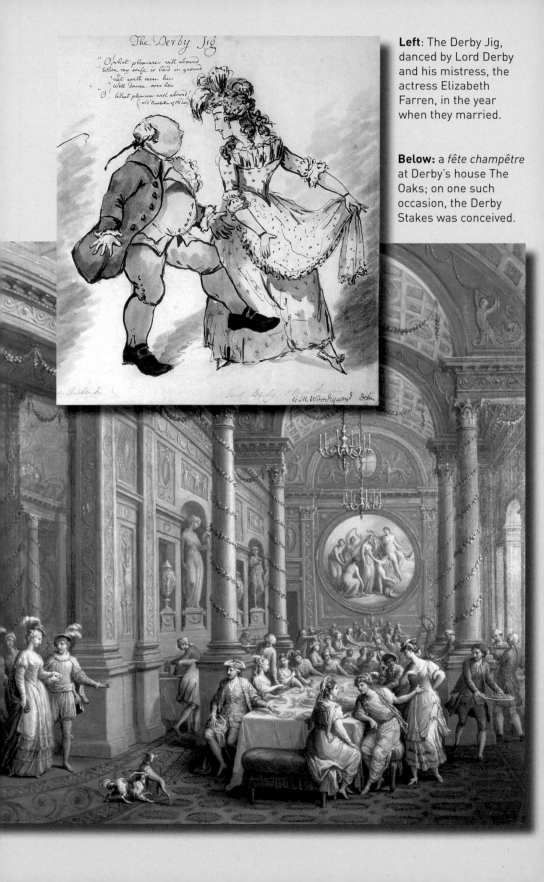

The Derby Jig

"O! what pleasures will abound
"When my wife is laid in ground
"Let earth cover her
"O! We'll dance over her
"O! What pleasures will abound!
(vid Brabston of the day)

G M Woodward delin

Left: The Derby Jig, danced by Lord Derby and his mistress, the actress Elizabeth Farren, in the year when they married.

Below: a *fête champêtre* at Derby's house The Oaks; on one such occasion, the Derby Stakes was conceived.

J. N. Sartorius's painting of the Derby in the 1790s, before it became the race that stopped the nation.

DERBY DAY

ECLIPSE

Buses from Morden Station
to the Course
Every 30 Seconds   Fare 8d

Left: Vera Willoughby's 1932 poster advertises the bus service of one's dreams.

Below: a scene that might be from Evelyn Waugh or P. G. Wodehouse, at Tattenham Corner in the 1920s.

NEWMARKET CHALLENGE WHIP

THIS PIECE OF PLATE with THE HOOF OF ECLIPSE was presented by HIS MOST GRACIOUS MAJESTY William the Fourth to the JOCKEY CLUB May 1832.

ECLIPSE

Eclipse relics (**clockwise from top**): the Jockey Club whip, reputedly containing hair from Eclipse's tail; a framed portion of his chestnut hide; three details of his hoof; and his skeleton. The skeleton is at the Royal Veterinary College, and the other bits of his anatomy are at the Jockey Club Rooms.

From The Anatomy of the Horse *(1766) by George Stubbs. Stubbs paid greater attention than had any previous artist to horse anatomy. However, not all experts believe his representations to have been consistently accurate (page 276).*

the most famous racers, painted by G. Stubbs, RA, at an immense
expense, and solely for this work.

The whole to be published in numbers, each containing three
capital prints, 20 inches by 16, in addition to three smaller,
engraved from the same subject.

An elegant house is open in a central situation, under the title
of the Turf Gallery, to which subscribers have a free admission.

Stubbs would produce the 145 or more paintings, to be exhibited
at a gallery in Conduit Street, off Hanover Square. George Townly
would make engravings from them for prints to be exhibited
alongside the paintings, and to be available for purchase. The prints
would also appear, in large and small sizes and three at a time, in
successive numbers – a partwork, we would call it – of the *Review
of the Turf*.

Stubbs and his anonymous backer knew all about segment-
ing the market. They offered various methods of purchase: you
could buy the whole lot of pictures in advance, or you could buy
single numbers, or single prints. At the time of the advertisement,
there were already sixteen paintings on show in the gallery. One
of them was of Eclipse, and another of his sire Marske. There
were, however, never any more than those sixteen paintings, and
just one number of the *Review of the Turf* appeared. Perhaps the subscription figures were disappointing? In any event, the £9,000
promised to Stubbs did not materialize.

The Prince of Wales and Andrew Dennis O'Kelly have both
been associated with the *Review of the Turf*. The Prince was already
a patron of Stubbs's work. Among his commissions was a portrait,
showing him on horseback, with two terriers running ahead, by
the Serpentine in Hyde Park. According to Stubbs's biographer
Robin Blake, Prinny's obesity is 'carefully concealed'. Judy
Egerton, in her magnificent *Catalogue Raisonné* of Stubbs's works,
viewed the portrait differently, brusquely summarizing it as 'an
overweight bully riding a long-suffering horse'. The two Stubbs

experts arrived at varying conclusions too (though amicably) about the funding of the *Review of the Turf*. Blake agreed with the suggestion, advanced by others before him, that 'Turf' was George Augustus, the Prince of Wales; hence the reticence – shown both by Ozias Humphry and by 'T.N.', Stubbs's obituarist in *The Sporting Magazine* – over the patron's identity. The Prince would have wanted to be discreet about his association with a business venture, and following the Escape affair, in which he had been accused of setting up a betting coup,[147] he was not enjoying high esteem among the racing set who would be Stubbs's main customers. His indebtedness would also explain the non-appearance of the funding.

Holders of this theory, Judy Egerton suggested, may have fallen into the '*Great Expectations* fallacy' – the belief that a mysterious benefactor must be a grand personage. She advanced a different notion, with support from David Oldrey, former deputy senior steward of the Jockey Club: that 'Turf' was Andrew Dennis O'Kelly, in a surreptitious ploy to hype his stallions. Oldrey's principal evidence is that Dungannon, Volunteer and Anvil, the three contemporary stallions in the first *Review of the Turf* exhibition, all stood at the O'Kelly stud. Dungannon may have been worthy of an appearance in the *Review* (though eventually his record as a sire was disappointing), but Volunteer and Anvil were unproven, and sat oddly in a collection that also featured indisputable Thoroughbred giants such as the Godolphin Arabian, Marske and Eclipse. Of Anvil, the catalogue copy said that he 'may be ranked amongst the best stallions of the present day, and from the cross of the Eclipse mares in Mr O'Kelly's stud, with the blood of King Herod, much may be expected from this horse'. This was hype, and Andrew, and his father Philip, would have been embarrassed to be revealed as the authors of it.

To back up this view, Egerton pointed out the unlikelihood

---

[147] See chapter 17.

of the Prince of Wales, with business to transact with Stubbs, leaving his apartments in Carlton House to visit the painter in Somerset Street: he would have issued a summons instead. True; but the Prince could have commissioned an associate – perhaps Sheridan, who acted for him during the Escape affair – to pay the visit on his behalf. In response to Egerton's second argument, that Prinny was in no position to offer advances of up to £9,000, one might point out that an inability to match his expenditure to his financial circumstances was Prinny's regular failing. His racing interests were also represented in the first group of paintings and prints: Anvil had run under his colours; and there was also Stubbs's *Baronet at Speed with Samuel Chifney Up*, portraying the horse and jockey who had won for the Prince the 1791 Oatlands Handicap.

The O'Kelly papers do not help us, so we fall back on speculation. We have seen enough of the O'Kelly way of doing business to suggest a compromise solution to the *Review of the Turf* mystery: that there was a partnership of some kind between the Prince of Wales and Andrew. The arrangements would have been exceptionally complicated, involving breeding rights at the O'Kelly stud and various other considerations. However, subsequent events intervened. The Prince, engulfed in scandal and debt, sold his racehorses; the O'Kellys found that they could not offload the mares at their stud; the outbreak of war with France caused an atmosphere of financial uncertainty. The ambitious project collapsed. Andrew continued to acquire work by Stubbs nonetheless, and by 1809 he owned, according to John Lawrence, one of the largest collections of the artist's work.

Stubbs's portrait of Eclipse for the *Review of the Turf* is a copy of his 1770 *Eclipse at Newmarket, with a Groom and Jockey*, which hangs now in the Jockey Club Rooms in Newmarket. (The 1770 original is in private hands.) In Judy Egerton's expert view, while Eclipse is 'finely modelled' in the later version, 'the handling of the groom and jockey is more awkward', and the paint surface is 'thin'. In *The Sporting Magazine*, the two human figures were described as 'the boy who looked after [Eclipse], and Samuel Merrit, who generally rode him'. Whether the jockey really was Samuel Merriott is discussed elsewhere.[148] The labelling of the adult-looking groom as 'the boy' was a mark of the status of stable staff; today, they remain 'lads' and 'lasses'.

A print of this picture (see this book's colour section) hangs above my desk as I write. Eclipse, saddled, stands before a square brick building with a pitched roof of yellowish tiles. We know, from a landscape study by Stubbs of the same scene, that the building is the four-miles stables rubbing-house at the start of the Newmarket Beacon Course, and can therefore speculate that the scene is the prelude to what may have been Eclipse's toughest race, his match of 17 April 1770 against Bucephalus.[149] Eclipse has a cropped tail and a plaited mane. Light makes gleaming patterns on his chestnut coat. His body is long; he has an athletic elegance. Behind him, the Newmarket heath stretches towards a modest row of trees. The horizon is a quarter way up the picture, and the big sky above is springlike, with massing white and dark clouds.

The 'boy', smartly dressed in a black coat, holds Eclipse's reins, and looks over his shoulder, with what may be apprehension, at the jockey. This groom has had to get Eclipse to Newmarket, keep him fed and watered and healthy and happy, and present him in perfect condition on the day. Now he transfers the responsibility, and all he can do is wait and watch. Eclipse is looking at the jockey too; and Merriott – if it is he – returns the look, calmly. Without that calm, he could not do his job – no matter how good his horse may be. He wears the red colours with a black cap that Dennis O'Kelly had appropriated from William Wildman on buying Eclipse; he carries a whip, but as if reassuring the horse

---

[148] See chapter 8 and Appendix 1.

[149] Eclipse's other race on the Beacon Course took place later that year, on 3 October, against Sir Charles Bunbury's Corsican.

he will not use it, and he does not wear spurs on his boots, reminding us that Eclipse 'never had a whip flourished over him, or felt the tickling of a spur'.[150]

As so often in Stubbs's work, what we witness here is a quiet, contemplative moment apart from the action. Every element of the scene is beautifully placed, so that, in spite of Merriott's striding posture, the painting conveys stillness. The horse and his rider are about to offer a demonstration of greatness, in front of cheering crowds. But Stubbs does not show these jubilant events, either in this or in any other of his paintings. When he does show a race, in his portrait of Gimcrack at Newmarket, the contest is only a trial, climaxing in front of a shuttered stand; it has taken place in the past, and is in the background of the picture, while the foreground has Gimcrack with his stable staff at the rubbing-house. There is in Stubbs's paintings a very British mix, apparent too in the poetry of Tennyson and the music of Elgar, of grandeur and melancholy.

The portrait of Eclipse borrows from a study Stubbs made of the horse, with a plain background behind. The study, donated by the late American collector (and owner of the great horse Mill Reef) Paul Mellon, hangs now in the Royal Veterinary College, facing Eclipse's skeleton.

Stubbs had also used this study for *Eclipse with William Wildman and His Sons John and James* (see colour section). This affectingly informal portrait places Wildman and his sons with Eclipse beneath a giant, forked oak tree. The Surrey downs fall away behind them. Wildman, seated on the trunk of the tree, is pointing – perhaps to his sons, perhaps to the horse. The boys wear tricorn hats as he does, and are finely dressed in blue coats, waistcoats and breeches. The older holds Eclipse's reins; the younger leans casually against the tree, with his hand on the shoulder of his

---

[150] From John Lawrence's *The History and Delineation of the Horse* (1809).

brother, who turns back to say something to him. They look affectionate, and happy, and proud of their horse.[151]

Stubbs's painting stayed in the Wildman family until the early twentieth century, and after various transactions crossed the Atlantic, to be bought in 1929 by William Woodward, chairman of the American Jockey Club. At about this time a clumsy restoration job was done on it. Having since received more skilled attention, it hangs in the Baltimore Museum of Art.

The intimate atmosphere of *Eclipse with William Wildman and His Sons* suggests a close relationship between painter and owner. Wildman may also appear in a series of four Stubbs paintings showing two gentlemen on a day's shooting expedition on the Duke of Portland's estate. Robert Fountain and Judy Egerton discussed the possible identification, though with caveats; the brown-coated man who may be Wildman does not bear a very close resemblance to the figure in the Eclipse portrait. But Wildman did own this series. Other Stubbs works in his collection – at that time, the largest aside from the Prince of Wales's – included portraits of Marske, Gimcrack and Euston; further portraits of horses, grooms and gamekeepers; a painting of a horse frightened by a lioness; and various dogs.

If you cannot afford Stubbs, one collector of the time advised his friend, try George Garrard. Certainly, Garrard (1760–1826) fills the runner-up spot among contemporary painters of Eclipse. His portrait, dated to 1788 (see colour section), shows

---

[151] It is possible that one or both of these boys did not survive William Wildman. The nomenclature and the dates are confusing. Robert Fountain, author of *William Wildman and George Stubbs*, said that the elder son was called William. (Perhaps he was called John William, or William John.) Unable to find any records for William, he speculated that the boy died before his father did (in 1784). Fountain also said that James died in 1827, at the age of fifty-four; so James could not have appeared in *William Wildman and His Sons*, if Stubbs painted it before Wildman sold Eclipse in 1770. See chapter 11.

Eclipse the stallion, with a typically muscly, powerful neck, and a high crest. The horse stands against a background of thick woods – near the ones, we may conjecture, in which he was rumoured to have roamed in his younger days, when his rider Ellers would take him poaching. Garrard's painting is cruder than Stubbs's work, but in compensation conveys Eclipse's strength and power.

The kinds of early representations of the Thoroughbred that one has come to think of as typical of the era are the portraits in which Francis Sartorius (1734–1804) and his son John Nost Sartorius (1759–1828) specialized. Their horses have spindly frames, with long and oddly curved necks; they gallop like rocking horses, with all four legs splayed out at once. The absurdity of this stride was not the painters' fault: no artists then understood how horses moved, because they could not distinguish the motions of the legs with the naked eye. Stubbs may have sensed that something was wrong with the traditional way of representing horses at the gallop, and for that reason – and because he was not an enthusiast for the sport – rarely depicted racing scenes. Of one of the rare exceptions, *Baronet at Speed with Samuel Chifney Up*, a contemporary critic commented, 'There is something very singular in this picture, the horse's legs are all off the ground, at that moment when raised by muscular strength – a bold attempt, and as yet well perfected, this attitude has never been yet described but by Mr Stubbs.'

Stubbs was only half right. A horse *is* airborne briefly during a gallop. But, as the photographer Eadweard Muybridge was to demonstrate some eighty years later, this moment occurs when the legs are tucked under the body. Muybridge's photographic sequence, *The Horse in Motion*, showed that when the legs extended, one rear leg and one foreleg hit the ground first (though not at the same time), and that the others (the 'lead' legs) followed, extending further. For a moment, one leg and then two support half a ton of animal.[152]

---

[152] A 'rotary' motion, or 'cross-cantering', involves different front and rear leads. For dogs, a rotary motion when running is normal.

Clearly, Francis Sartorius had no inkling of these mechanics when he attempted to paint Eclipse at full speed. While the result is, in the words of Theodore Cook,[153] 'somewhat impossible', it does at least convey the horse's huge stride, and reveals a distinctive, and rather ungainly, head carriage, level with his body. The title of one picture names the jockey in the red and black as John Oakley, adding to our doubts about whether Oakley or Merriott – named by Stubbs – was Eclipse's usual partner. A further Sartorius is a rare depiction of a walkover: Eclipse and his jockey are making their leisurely way towards a King's Plate. The course, narrow and climbing and marked with white posts, seems better suited to cross-country runs than to horse races.

John Nost made use of his father's studies, in one instance placing copies of Francis's portraits of Eclipse and of the stallion Shakespeare side by side in a single composition. Why he did so is not clear. Perhaps he believed the rumours that Shakespeare, rather than Marske, was Eclipse's sire. It may be relevant that John Nost lived in Carshalton, near to the O'Kelly stud at Epsom and to the farm where Shakespeare had stood for a while. Although Shakespeare's owners – if they commissioned the portrait – could gain no commercial advantage from it (their horse being dead by the time of composition in the 1780s), they may have wanted it for sentimental reasons.

The Sartoriuses were simply in business to give sporting patrons what they wanted, and their paintings reflect no greater ambition than that. Stubbs had to satisfy patrons too, but he created work with a more ambiguous tone. The nobility of his animals is inscrutable, and vulnerable; the humans merely associate with it. A contemporary artist who has recast that ambiguity in more blatant terms is Mark Wallinger, winner of the 2007 Turner Prize. Wallinger invokes Eclipse in his series entitled *Race, Class, Sex,*

[153] In *Eclipse and O'Kelly*.

paintings of four of Eclipse's male-line descendants. The portraits are life-size, in a hyper-realist style, and set against white backgrounds. According to copy in a catalogue of Wallinger's work, they are a 'recasting of a historical painting genre in terms of the rhetoric of the stud book'. Moreover, they 'can be read in terms of a discourse on representation itself'. The only radical quality of these themes is the jargon accompanying them: Stubbs managed all of this, and more.

Like Eclipse, Dennis O'Kelly was immortalized by one of the greatest artists of the day. There is no record of Dennis's acquaintanceship with Thomas Rowlandson (1756–1827), though his presence in a series of Rowlandson prints is a clue that the two were familiar.

Educated at the Royal Academy, Rowlandson started out as a serious painter, but turned to more immediately remunerative caricatures after squandering a £7,000 inheritance – some of it going to Dennis, perhaps – at the gaming tables of London. With a relish for teeming, anarchic scenes, he excelled at depicting racecourses, with their shady gambling booths, riotous beer tents, lecherous men, loose women and conspiring punters.

The dating of these pictures places them after Dennis's death. Dennis appears shabbily dressed, with stomach bulging above his breeches, wearing a tricorn hat containing some sort of leafy arrangement,[154] and – no doubt because of his gout – carrying a crutch. In *The Betting Post* (see colour section), he is weighing down a small, rotund pony. The Prince of Wales, already at this young age (he must be in his early twenties) showing signs of corpulence, is also on horseback, and has his arm outstretched, striking a bet. The tightly grouped pack of men are all clamouring and gesticulating; only Dennis, who sits slightly detached from the crowd, makes no movement. The implication may be that he is

---

[154] It may be, as a badge of the land of his birth, clover.

the knowing one, the man with a sure grasp of how this race will turn out.

In *The Mount*, Dennis stands before a jockey being helped into his riding gear, and gives instructions with an emphatic gesture of his hand. In *The Course*, he is a figure in the boisterous crowd; he is walking on his crutch and holding a hand to his head, as if in despair at some loss. *Colonel Dennis O'Kelly Making a Deal* (shown in this book's colour section) again shows Dennis, this time with his back to us, giving instructions to a jockey. Why is that 'making a deal'? Perhaps there was a case of mistaken identity when the picture was named, and Dennis was taken for one of the gentlemen examining a horse in the foreground. Or perhaps Dennis's deal with the jockey is somewhat shady.

Dennis may also be the gambler in military uniform in Rowlandson's *A Kick-up at a Hazard Table*, published in 1787, the year Dennis died. He has an empty pocket book, and with a pointed pistol is accusing the man opposite him of cheating. The man brandishes his own pistol – less convincingly – in return, clutches his winnings, and cowers. There is a great hubbub round the table: a spectator holds a chair aloft, and is about to bring it down on Dennis's arm; another is about to tackle Dennis's opponent; some gamblers reach for their swords, while others attempt to get out of the way. Joseph Grego, an early authority on Rowlandson's caricatures, said that the incident that inspired this print took place at the Royal Chocolate House in St James's, and was broken up by guardsmen, 'who were compelled to knock the parties down with the butt ends of their muskets'.

An earlier caricature of Dennis, by an artist called Mansergh, is entitled *The Eclipse Macarony*. A macarony (or macaroni) was a dandy – a word that evokes a young, slender, foppish figure. But Dennis, perched on a horse at the betting post and again wearing a hat with a leafy motif, is gross. His rounded chin juts out over floppy jowls. A substantial, collared coat emphasizes his bulk.

Thus, in their contrasting styles, Rowlandson and Stubbs paid tributes to Dennis and Eclipse: the burly rogue and the gracious equine athlete. It would be pleasing to claim that Eclipse, the greatest racer Stubbs painted, inspired his greatest work. But, superb though the three pictures are, they yield to a still greater portrait that Stubbs was to paint, at the age of seventy-five, of Eclipse's grandson – Hambletonian.

19

Eclipse's Legacy – the Eighteenth and Nineteenth Centuries

THIS CHAPTER AND THE next are about the extraordinary influence that Eclipse has exerted, through his male line, on the development of racing. It tells the stories of the Eclipse descendants who have been at the centre of some of the most significant or dramatic events in the sport. They include the inspirer of the greatest equine painting; the Derby winner that never was; the Derby winner that avenged Waterloo; and the Derby winner that broke a gambler's heart. There is the colt who did not run in the Derby, or in any other Classic, but who became the Eclipse of the nineteenth century. There are two of the fastest fillies on the Turf. There is the supreme steeplechaser, nicknamed simply 'Himself'. There is the colt who was the last winner of the English Triple Crown, but who could not give of his best in the race that was supposed to confirm his greatness. There is the American champion who, in the final leg of the Triple Crown, left the rest nowhere. I might have included many others: the great Italian champion Ribot; Sea Bird, an even greater horse than Secretariat, according to some; Red Rum, the triple Grand National winner; Shergar, winner of the Epsom Derby by a record margin. Through them all, the Eclipse bloodline helped shape racing as it is today. But the horses that follow seem to me to have played important parts in Turf history.

The focus on the male line may appear to be a sexist approach. Certainly, there have been famous horses, such as Seabiscuit, who were not Eclipse's tail male descendants.[155] Some of the horses in the following pages did nothing to perpetuate the line: Running Rein, having given his name to an impostor, disappeared; Arkle was a gelding. The justification for concentrating on the male line is as mentioned earlier: that, as it continues, it multiplies, saturating pedigrees. A successful stallion sires hundreds of sons (and daughters), sometimes thousands. If a few of the sons become successful stallions, continuing the male line, they will have hundreds of sons (and daughters) too. A few generations later, these descendants will cross: multiplication upon multiplication.

According to my count, there are eighty-one instances of Eclipse in the pedigree of St Simon (born in 1881, just under a hundred years after Eclipse's death). Thanks to St Simon's successes as a sire, the increase in that number in succeeding generations was exponential. The Eclipse line thus became the most significant genetic factor in the history of horseracing.

Hambletonian (born in 1792)

Eclipse − King Fergus − Hambletonian

The greatest of all horseracing paintings is a tribute to the Thoroughbred, but not to the Turf. It shows the nobility of a magnificent horse; and it shows us, the spectators, to be exploiters of that nobility.

Hambletonian, stabled in Yorkshire, was a winner of the St Leger, and undefeated in races he had completed (he had once, at York, veered off the course). He was owned by a hard-drinking,

---

[155] Seabiscuit, the American folk hero of the 1930s, descended on the side of his sire, Hard Tack, from the Godolphin Arabian and Matchem − although his dam, Swing On, was from the Eclipse line.

hard-gambling baronet of twenty-eight, Sir Harry Vane-Tempest. In 1798, Vane-Tempest's horse Shuttle lost a 1,000-guineas match to Joseph Cookson's Diamond, the Newmarket champion. Seeking revenge, Vane-Tempest challenged Cookson to race Diamond against Hambletonian, this time for 3,000 guineas. The match would take place on 25 March 1799 (Easter Monday) over the four miles-plus of the Beacon Course at Newmarket, and Hambletonian would carry 8st 3lb, while Diamond would carry eight stone.

The quality of the horses, and the north versus south element of the contest, brought a huge crowd – 'the greatest concourse of people that ever was seen' – to Newmarket. Inns for miles around were packed. Hundreds of thousands of pounds were bet; Hambletonian was the favourite, and went off at 5-4 on. Vane-Tempest, a man of quick and excitable passions, found the tension on race day almost too hard to bear, confessing to Frank Buckle, as the famously unflappable jockey mounted Hambletonian, 'By God, I'd give the whole stake to be half as calm as you!'

At the off, Buckle allowed Hambletonian to settle in behind Diamond. He kicked on ahead after a mile and a quarter, before they reached the dog-leg right turn that took them in the direction of town, towards the finishing post. Hambletonian led by about two lengths, until Dennis Fitzpatrick, Diamond's jockey, spurred his mount forward to challenge. The two, with their riders driving them brutally, charged side by side to the line, Hambletonian just warding off his rival and getting home by 'half a neck'. 'Both horses were much cut with the whip, and severely goaded with the spur, but particularly Hambletonian; he was shockingly goaded.'[156]

[156] From *The Sporting Magazine*, quoted by Judy Egerton in *George Stubbs, Painter*. Different standards of behaviour towards the horse prevailed then. Today, there are no spurs of course, and jockeys get punished for excessive use of the whip.

Vane-Tempest was as exultant after the race as he had been nervous before. He commissioned George Stubbs to paint two pictures recording Hambletonian's triumph, and advertised in *The Sporting Magazine* that 'No artist whatever, except Mr Stubbs, has had my permission to take any likeness of Hambletonian since he was in my possession.' Of this claim, the editor of the magazine sniffed that it 'partakes too much of PUFF for a gentleman's signature to accompany'. Vane-Tempest's puff was evanescent, and he certainly did not behave like a gentleman. He refused to pay Stubbs, went to court to defend himself against the painter's claim for 300 guineas, and lost. One of Stubbs's paintings, of Hambletonian as he won the race, never went beyond the drawing stage, and has since disappeared. That left John Nost Sartorius to portray the scene in traditional fashion: elongated horses stretching for the winning post; gentlemen in top hats in pursuit; roaring crowds.

What we have from Stubbs is *Hambletonian, Rubbing Down* (see colour section). The crowds have gone. Dominating the frame, Hambletonian jerks and twists – improbably balanced on his two left legs – in nervous exhaustion. A squat, dour groom stands at his head, holding the reins; a stable lad rests one hand on the horse's withers, and has a rubbing cloth in the other. Both figures look at us impassively. You have had your fun, they seem to imply; you are intruding now, and it is we whose concern is this battered horse. It is a long way from the celebratory scene that Vane-Tempest thought he had ordered, and one can see why he was disappointed. At the heart of racing are blood, sweat and mystery, never more powerfully depicted than in this masterpiece.

Hambletonian recovered, won more races, and retired to stud. He sired more than 140 winners, and continued an Eclipse line that descended to and beyond the greatest racehorse of the nineteenth century, St Simon.

Whalebone (b. 1807)

Eclipse – Pot8os – Waxy – Whalebone

As well as breeding Eclipse, the Duke of Cumberland owned another great horse, Herod. It was the cross of Eclipse and Herod lines – male and female descendants of Eclipse mating with female and male descendants of Herod – that was 'the strongest single factor in the successful transformation of the Thoroughbred from a typical eighteenth-century weight carrier over long distances to the nineteenth-century carrier of weights over short distances'.[157] Among the first demonstrators of this transformation were the early Derby winners Waxy and his son Whalebone, and they passed on the Eclipse/Herod genius to future generations.

Waxy, whose dam was a daughter of Herod called Maria, was one of six sons of Pot8os among the thirteen runners in the Derby of 1793. He was only fourth favourite in the betting, at 12-1, but he came home with half a length to spare over the odds-on shot Gohanna; and after he and Gohanna had fought a tremendous series of rematches, he spent most of his well-earned retirement at the Duke of Grafton's stud at Euston Hall, Norfolk. Grafton – the undistinguished Prime Minister in the 1760s and the scandalous consorter with the prostitute Nancy Parsons – once ordered that an avenue of trees, through which he might drive to the races, be planted between Euston Hall and Newmarket, twenty miles away. The planters had to stop with six miles to go, when they came up against – Grafton had not considered this obstacle – someone else's land.

The Duke bred Waxy's greatest son by putting Waxy to his mare Penelope. Their offspring, Whalebone, was no looker. He was just over fifteen hands tall – a standard height in Eclipse's day but one that now, just forty years later, was considered modest. A stud groom described him as 'the lowest and longest and most

---

[157] From the *Biographical Encyclopaedia of British Flat Racing*.

double-jointed horse, with the best legs and the worst feet I have ever seen'. Later, the racing writer 'The Druid' (Henry Hall Dixon), who had named Waxy 'the modern ace of trumps in the Stud Book', summed up Whalebone as 'shabby'. In training, The Druid added, Whalebone's chief occupation 'was to rear and knock his hooves together like a pair of castanets'.

Despite these dubious traits, Whalebone went off the 2-1 favourite for the 1810 Derby, and he justified the odds easily, leading all the way. But his subsequent career on the racecourse was chequered, and his initial covering fee on retiring to stud was a modest ten guineas. His performance as a stallion proved that valuation wrong. The line through his son Camel produced numerous champions, among them the great 1930s winner Hyperion. Through another son, Sir Hercules, descend the most valuable horses in bloodstock breeding today. The historian Roger Mortimer wrote of Whalebone, 'A very high proportion . . . of the great horses in racing history include his name in their pedigree.'

Running Rein (b. 1841)

Eclipse — Pot8os — Waxy — Whalebone — Waverly — The Saddler — Running Rein

The judge called Running Rein the winner of the 1844 Derby. The only problem was that Running Rein was somewhere else at the time. Another contestant in the race was also an impostor. A further was pulled by his jockey; yet another was nobbled, and then pulled as well. It was an event of almost farcical corruption.

Turf morals, never impeccable, were at their lowest in the first half of the nineteenth century. In the early 1800s, bookmakers had arrived on racecourses, quoting odds about every horse in a race rather than, as gamblers had done in Dennis O'Kelly's day, striking bets individually ('Eclipse first, and the rest nowhere'). It was during this period too that Tattersalls, the bloodstock auctioneer, opened its subscription rooms, and book-makers who settled bets there formed themselves into a group known as the Ring.[158] Many of them were, in the historian Roger Longrigg's haughtily contemptuous phrase, 'deplorable little men'. They corrupted stable staff and jockeys, and in notorious incidents at Doncaster and Newmarket poisoned horse troughs. One of the most feared was 'Ludlow' Bond, who used to be seen mounted on a grey on Newmarket Heath and who was known as 'death on a pale horse'. Then there was Crockford, 'the second most evil man on the 19th-century Turf' in Longrigg's view[159] and someone of extreme lack of physical attractiveness: 'His cheeks,' the writer Sylvanus wrote, 'appeared whitened and flabby . . . His hands were entirely *without knuckles*, soft as raw veal, and as white as paper, whilst his large, flexible mouth was stuffed with "dead men's bones" – his teeth being all false.' You did not want to meet an angry Crockford. You did not want to meet him cheerful either: his laugh was 'hideous'.

Crockford enjoyed his most rewarding coup when he bribed the starter to ensure that the 1827 St Leger favourite, on whom he had taken many bets, lost. In the Running Rein Derby of 1844, he was the owner of the second favourite, Ratan. Someone got to the horse on the night before the race, however, and next morn-ing Ratan's coat 'was standing like quills upon the fretful porcupine, his eyes were dilated, and he shivered like a man with ague'.[160] The colt nevertheless started for the race; to make doubly certain that he could not win, his jockey, Sam Rogers, pulled him. Crockford, devastated at being done to as he was in the habit of doing to others, died two days later. Gamblers who had bet with him on the Oaks propped him up in an armchair at his club, to

---

[158] The enclosures that house betting rings on racecourses are often known as Tattersalls, or 'Tatts'.

[159] Longrigg's candidate for the top spot is Henry Padwick. See the essay on Hermit, coming up.

[160] Quoted in *Derby Day 200* (1979).

ensure that he appeared to be alive until after the race – that way, their bets remained valid. Corpse-like in life, Crockford passed for a living person when dead.

The man who set about tackling this corruption was Lord George Bentinck. Sir Charles Bunbury had been the first Dictator of the Turf;[161] Bentinck was the second. Bunbury was a rigid man of integrity; Bentinck was an arrogant, impulsive and not always scrupulous gambler. In 1840, he made £60,000 backing his filly Crucifix, who won the 2,000 Guineas, 1,000 Guineas and Oaks; and then, knowing that she had broken down, he dishonestly made more money by laying against her for the St Leger. Later, he got into a duel with the best shot in England, George Osbaldeston, after he had accused Osbaldeston of cheating over a bet and had paid his £200 of losses to him slowly, note by note, asking, 'Can you count?' – to which Osbaldeston replied, 'I could at Eton.' Osbaldeston challenged Bentinck and was determined to kill him, but on the intercession of friends he settled for firing his bullet through his opponent's hat. Bentinck survived to reform the starting system, introducing flag starts to replace the previously chaotic procedure in which a man simply shouted 'Go!', and in particular to pursue corrupt gamblers and their associates. The Running Rein affair was his most notable success.

Running Rein was bought as a yearling by Goodman Levy ('Mr Goodman'), a gambler, and entered for his first race, at Newmarket, the following year. But, instead of Running Rein, the horse that ran at Newmarket was Maccabaeus, a three-year-old. What had happened to Running Rein is not recorded: you fear that it was not pleasant. Maccabaeus was backed down from 10-1 to 3-1, won the race, and made Goodman a fair deal of money. The Duke of Rutland, owner of the runner-up, protested against the

[161] Some historians say that he was the third. The first, by their count, was Charles II, and the second was Tregonwell Frampton, the eccentric 'Keeper of the running horses at Newmarket' under William III, Queen Anne, George I and George II.

Lord George Bentinck, who successfully pursued the chief fraudsters at 'the dirtiest Derby in history'.

result without effect. The case – in which Rutland had Bentinck's support – came to trial, but collapsed when a stable lad (for reasons at which we can only guess) swore that the winning horse really was Running Rein.

'Running Rein' (that is, Maccabaeus) was entered for the following year's Derby,[162] before which Bentinck, who had been gathering evidence over the winter, got up a petition against the colt's taking part. But the Epsom stewards made the odd decision to allow him to race, with the proviso that there would be an inquiry if he won. He did win, by three parts of a length.[163] Enter m'learned friends.

'Produce the horse! Produce the horse!' the judge demanded at the trial – the true age of 'Running Rein' could have been determined by an examination of his teeth. But Goodman and his associates did not produce the horse. Rather, they withdrew from the case, and fled the country. 'If gentlemen would associate with gentlemen, and race with gentlemen, we should have no such practices. But if gentlemen will condescend to race with blackguards, they must expect to be cheated,' the judge concluded.

The cheating in the 1844 Derby had not stopped at Maccabaeus and Ratan. The rider of the favourite, Ugly Buck, like Sam Rogers on board Ratan, pulled on his reins to make sure that his mount could not win. The stewards grew suspicious about the appearance of a horse called Leander, and when Leander had to be put down because Maccabaeus had struck into him and broken his leg, they ordered that his jaw be cut off and examined. The vets announced that Leander was a four-year-old. Leander's owners,

---

[162] The Derby is for three-year-old colts and fillies. Goodman's cheat was not unprecedented. The trainer for five-times Derby winner Lord Egremont admitted that he had twice won the race with four-year-olds.

[163] A four-year-old competing against three-year-olds at this time of year would normally carry 11lb more on his back, to compensate for his greater maturity.

German brothers called Lichtwald, were warned off English race-courses for life. They took it badly, one of them declaring that the English were liars – Leander was not four, but six!

After all that, the winner of the 1844 Derby was announced as Orlando. His owner was Colonel Peel, brother of the Tory Prime Minister Sir Robert Peel and, unfashionably, an honest sportsman.

Bentinck's lifelong ambition was to win the Derby. Two years later, he sold his racing stud in order to commit himself to politics. One of the yearlings in the sale was called Surplice. In 1848, Surplice won the Derby – for his new owner, Lord Clifden. Bentinck's despair was recorded by his friend Benjamin Disraeli, who had come across him a day or two later in the House of Commons Library.

> [Bentinck] gave a sort of superb groan. 'All my life I have been trying for this, and for what have I sacrificed it?' he murmured. It was in vain to offer solace. 'You do not know what the Derby is,' he moaned out.
>
> 'Yes, I do, it is the Blue Ribbon of the Turf.'
>
> 'It is the Blue Ribbon of the Turf,' he slowly repeated to himself, and sitting down, he buried himself in a folio of statistics.

A few months later, Bentinck died of a heart attack. He was forty-six.

Gladiateur (b. 1862)

Eclipse – Pot8os – Waxy – Whalebone – Defence – The Emperor – Monarque – Gladiateur

By the mid-nineteenth century, England had been exporting Thoroughbreds, to Europe and to the New World, for more than a hundred years. Racehorses went to Ireland, France, Italy, Germany, Austria, Hungary, Russia, Switzerland, the Netherlands and Scandinavia; they went to North and South America; they went to South Africa, Australia and New Zealand. In 1730, Bulle Rock, a son of the Darley Arabian, emigrated to Virginia, and similarly bred racers followed him across the Atlantic, among them the first Derby winner Diomed, who had a grandson called American Eclipse. Sons and daughters of Whalebone, in the Eclipse male line, also made the journey. In France, the Société d'Encouragement pour l'Amélioration des Races de Chevaux en France (Society for the Improvement of French Bloodstock) promoted the importation of English stock, and the French Stud Book referred to the Thoroughbred as the *Pur-Sang Anglais* (Pureblooded English). The English, meanwhile, continued to assume that their bloodstock was the best. Gladiateur, 'The Avenger of Waterloo', shattered that illusion.

The one claim that the English could make of Gladiateur was that an Englishman, Tom Jennings of Newmarket, trained him. Jennings did a skilful job, because Gladiateur suffered from navicular disease, an inflammation of the bones in one of his front feet, and was often unsound. He was unfit when he raced for the 2,000 Guineas, but won, at odds of 7-1. For the Derby, he was in much better shape, and he came from behind – he was in tenth place as the field rounded Tattenham Corner – to pass the post in front by two lengths. It was a sensational result, and a French newspaper played up the Anglo-French rivalry, reporting that Gladiateur had required protection from six hundred hired bouncers, and that there had been a plot by the English to seize his jockey, Harry Grimshaw, and bleed him, so that he would be too weak to perform at his best.

In fact, Gladiateur's triumph was popular, as triumphs by favourites tend to be. The colt next crossed the Channel to his homeland, and in front of 150,000 spectators won the Grand Prix de Paris. After two victories at Goodwood came the St Leger, the third leg (after the 2,000 Guineas and the Derby) of the Triple Crown, won previously only by West Australian (in 1853). Two days before the race, Gladiateur was lame. But he defied his infirmity to defeat the Oaks winner, Regalia. His only defeat that year came when Grimshaw, who was short-sighted, allowed him to get too far behind the leaders in the Cambridgeshire handicap, in which he was unplaced.

Though increasingly unsound, Gladiateur won all his six races the following season, his greatest victory coming in the Ascot Gold Cup. It was another race in which Harry Grimshaw allowed his rivals – there were just two, Regalia and Breadalbane – to get away from him, and at halfway he was some three hundred yards in arrears. Then he gave Gladiateur his head. The colt, oblivious to the effect on his suspect foreleg of pounding over the bone-hard ground, swallowed up the others' lead, overtook them before the turn into the straight, and passed the post forty lengths clear. Regalia finished exhausted, and Breadalbane was pulled up. 'The Vigilant', writing in *The Sportsman*, described it as 'the most remarkable race I have ever seen, or ever expect to see . . . The style in which the great horse closed up the gap when he was at last allowed to stride along was simply incredible.'

Some great racehorses – Eclipse, Highflyer, St Simon – become great sires. Some racehorses below that rank – Phalaris, Sadler's Wells, Storm Cat – also become great sires. And some great racehorses – Sea Bird, Brigadier Gerard, Secretariat – do not become great sires. Gladiateur, who retired to stud at the end of the 1866 season, fell into this last category. He has, nevertheless, an immortal place in racing history, as the most notable tribute to him, a life-size statue at the entrance to Longchamp racecourse, recognizes.

The erosion of the status of the English as breeders and owners of the best racing stock did nothing but accelerate thereafter. In the next twelve years, there were four further French winners of the Ascot Gold Cup, and French colts and fillies had won five more English Classics by 1880. During the twentieth century, champions came from all over. By common consent, the three greatest horses of the century were Sea Bird, Secretariat and Ribot – respectively, French, American and Italian. The last winner of the English Triple Crown was Nijinsky (in 1970): bred in Canada, owned by an American, and trained in Ireland.

Other racing powers arose. Japan sent over El Condor Pasa to finish second to Montjeu in the 1999 Prix de l'Arc de Triomphe. In 2006, five thousand Japanese fans converged on Paris to cheer on their hero, Deep Impact, in the Arc; they bet on him so enthusiastically that at one stage his price was 10-1 *on*. In a race that was not run to suit him, he finished only third, although he was arguably the best horse in the field.

Today, the two most influential owners on the British Turf are not British. They are Coolmore, the Irish bloodstock operation run by John Magnier, and Darley, owned by Sheikh Mohammed bin Rashid Al Maktoum, ruler of Dubai.

Hermit (b. 1864)

Eclipse – Pot8os – Waxy – Whalebone – Camel – Touchstone – Newminster – Hermit

Henry Weysford Charles Plantagenet Rawdon Hastings, fourth Marquess of Hastings, was a wastrel, and he knew it. 'Money with me oozes away; in fact, it positively melts,' he observed. Unable to be contented, he could divert himself only with the fleeting thrills of gambling and drinking, and of making off with Florence Paget, the belle of her day and the fiancée of Hastings's contemporary Henry Chaplin.

The jilted Chaplin consoled himself by purchasing racehorses. Among them was Breadalbane, left trailing by Gladiateur in the 1865 Derby and the 1866 Ascot Gold Cup; and a chestnut yearling, later named Hermit. After a promising season as a two-year-old, Hermit emerged as one of the favourites for the Derby of 1867.

Whatever infatuation Hastings may have felt for Florence

Paget did not last long. A revealing photograph shows him lying on a chaise longue, languidly perusing a book, while by his side Florence bends her head over some embroidery; in another, Florence is seated, while Hastings lies at her feet, facing away from her, with a newspaper. Neither image conveys marital bliss. Florence was soon sending little notes to Chaplin, and Hastings developed an obsession with inflicting a further defeat on his rival. He bet against Hermit as if, Florence noted in alarm, the colt 'were dead'.

From a week before the race until a few moments before it reached its climax, Hastings appeared certain to collect. On 15 May, Hermit broke a blood vessel on the gallops, and his jockey switched to another colt, with a less celebrated rider taking the mount in his place. Confidence in his chances deteriorated further on the atrociously cold Derby Day, 22 May, when amid a collection of forlorn horses parading in the paddock before the race, Hermit looked the most forlorn of all. You could back him at the desperate price of 66-1. Hail pelted down as the runners and riders prepared to race, and they endured ten false starts before getting underway. As they came round Tattenham Corner into the home straight, the leaders were Marksman, Van Amburgh, and the 6-4 favourite Vauban. With just under a furlong to go, the 10-1 shot Marksman gained a clear lead; then Hermit, coming from way back, swooped, catching Marksman a few strides from the line to win by a neck.

At the unsaddling enclosure, Hastings gave the victorious Hermit a pat. He had lost £120,000 on the race, £20,000 of it to Henry Chaplin.

Hastings's fortunes never recovered. He sold his Scottish estates, and soon fell into the clutches of Henry Padwick, a moneylender dubbed by Roger Longrigg as 'the most evil man of the 19th-century Turf'. Padwick's speciality was destroying the lives of his clients. He and his bookmaking associate Harry Hill, having laid heavily against Hastings's colt The Earl for the 1868 Derby, ensured that the bets would come good by getting Hastings to withdraw The Earl from the race. No matter, Hastings thought. I still have the favourite, the filly Lady Elizabeth. What he did not know was that, because he had over-raced Lady Elizabeth in an effort to claw back his debts, he had ruined her as a top-class racer. She ran unplaced. She ran again, also unsuccessfully, in the Oaks a few days later, when Hastings was hissed by the crowd for putting her through this gruelling schedule. Demonstrating the mistake into which Hastings had been led, The Earl went on to win the Grand Prix de Paris, as well as three races at Royal Ascot. Had he taken part in the Derby and run to that form, he would almost certainly have won.

It was at this stage that the third Dictator of the Turf, Admiral Henry John Rous (1791–1877), entered the story. Rous was vigorous, enthusiastic, opinionated and inflexible. He was the first public handicapper, devising a new weight-for-age scale (under which young horses received weight from older rivals) and assessing the merits of racers with the aid of his notebook and old naval telescope. He was enraged by The Earl and Lady Elizabeth affair, feeling certain that Padwick and John Day (trainer of both horses) had, for their own gain, misled Hastings about the horses' well-being. Without stopping to think about his evidence, Rous wrote to *The Times* to allege that 'Lord Hastings has been shamefully deceived', and, explaining Hastings's compliance, asked the rhetorical question, 'What can the poor fly demand from the spider in whose web he is enveloped?' Hastings denied that he had been deceived, or that he had acted under influence, and Day sued. But the case did not get to court. Rous withdrew his letter, because the principal witness died.

Hastings, aged only twenty-six, suffered a drastic deterioration in health in autumn 1867. At the St Leger, he was walking with crutches. It is not known exactly what was wrong with him; only that he was a broken man. He met his end, like fellow Old Etonian Captain Hook, while reflecting on Good Form. 'Hermit's Derby broke my heart,' he said. 'But I didn't show it, did I?'

St Simon (b. 1881)

Eclipse – King Fergus – Hambletonian –Whitelock – Blacklock –Voltaire –Voltigeur –Vedette – Galopin – St Simon

Like Eclipse, St Simon was effortlessly superior to his rivals on the racecourse, and was never extended; he became a great sire; he was higher at his croup (his rump) than at his withers; and he had a difficult temperament. One day, in an effort to calm him down, his handlers introduced him to a cat. But this was not to be a love affair such as the one between the Godolphin Arabian and Grimalkin.[164] Rather, it was like introducing a mouse to a rattlesnake. St Simon picked up the cat and threw it against the roof of his box; the impact was fatal.

Towards the end of St Simon's two-year-old career, his experienced trainer, Matthew Dawson, predicted that he would 'probably make the best racehorse that has ever run on the Turf'. His jockey, Fred Archer, was similarly impressed. Riding him in a training exercise on an April morning, Archer decided that the colt was performing a little sluggishly, and gave him a touch with his spur. St Simon took off; Archer regained control of him only as they neared the entrance to Newmarket High Street. 'He's not a horse,' the shaken jockey reported. 'He's a steam engine.'

Under the rules of racing, St Simon could not compete in the Classics, because of the death of the Hungarian-born Prince Batthyany, who had bred him and made the entries. Instead, he proved his greatness most vividly in the Ascot Gold Cup. With the field nearing the home turn, St Simon was cantering behind the leader, Tristan (winner of the race the previous year). His jockey, on this day Charlie Wood, merely had to shake the reins for St Simon to sail past; he won by twenty lengths, and kept galloping for a further mile. The next day, Tristan won the Hardwicke Stakes. St Simon went on to win races at Newcastle and

---

[164] See chapter 6.

Goodwood, the latter again by twenty lengths, before retiring to stud.

Fred Archer (1857–1886) won greater fame than has been accorded to any other English jockey. Sir Charles Bunbury and other men of the Turf of Eclipse's day, when jockeys were 'boys' and when the upstart Sam Chifney got his comeuppance, would not have approved of this adulation, and Admiral Rous would have regretted it too. Rous 'was courteous and considerate to jockeys, but nothing would have induced him to invite one to his dinner table'.[165] This, though, was a new era, of mass communication; an era that nurtured celebrity. Horseracing, which had featured only patchily in the public prints until the mid-nineteenth century, was widely reported, and jockeys were the public faces of the sport. Archer was the finest of them, a man of unmatchable talent and willpower. Only Gordon Richards, in the first half of the twentieth century, and Lester Piggott, in the second half, have come close to achieving the same level of public recognition. 'Archer's up!' people would say, to indicate that all was well with the world.

All, however, was not well with Archer. He was obsessively determined, as top jockeys must be, and he earned the nickname 'The Tinman' owing to his relish for making money. In his seventeen seasons, he rode a third of his eight thousand mounts to victory; he won the Derby five times, the Oaks four times, and the St Leger six times. But he put himself through some terrible punishment to gain these successes. A tall man, he could keep himself under nine stone only by restricting his lunch to a biscuit and a small glass of champagne, sometimes resorting also to a fierce purgative known as 'Archer's Mixture'. When, in autumn 1886, he contracted a fever after wasting down to 8st 7lb to ride in the Cambridgeshire handicap, he lacked the physical resources to fight the illness. Delirium compounded the depression he had suffered

---

[165] From the *Biographical Encyclopaedia of British Flat Racing*.

since the recent death of his young wife, and on 8 November he shot himself.

St Simon sired Persimmon, the best horse to be raced by a member of the British royal family. When Albert Edward ('Bertie'), the Prince of Wales, led in the victorious Persimmon after the 1896 Derby, top hats filled the air, and the cheering echoed round the Epsom Downs. A film of the finish of the race was projected in London theatres to thrilled audiences, who demanded several repeats and sang 'God bless the Prince of Wales'. Persimmon went on to win the St Leger, and the following season won the Ascot Gold Cup as well as a new, prestigious race: the Eclipse Stakes. Fabergé later modelled him in silver.

This was the moment at which the supremacy of the Eclipse line was ensured. '[St Simon] and his descendants,' the Thoroughbred Heritage website asserts, '[dominated] global racing at the turn of the 20th century and for decades after.' St Simon's greatness confirmed Eclipse as the greatest sire of all.

Eclipse's Legacy — the Twentieth and Twenty-first Centuries

LISTS OF THE GREATEST horses in history are male-dominated. Does that mean that fillies and mares are not as good? Overall, yes it does. But five fillies have, albeit with weight allowances, beaten the colts to win the Derby. Sixteen fillies, most recently the outstanding Zarkava, have won Europe's richest race, the Prix de l'Arc de Triomphe. Three fillies have won the Kentucky Derby. In 2007, the filly Rags to Riches won the Belmont Stakes, defeating Curlin — and Curlin went on to win the world's two richest races. Fillies and mares are certainly as popular as their male counterparts, and often more so: racing fans tend to ascribe special qualities of pluck and fortitude to females doing battle with male rivals.

Sceptre (born in 1899)

Eclipse — King Fergus — Hambletonian — Whitelock — Blacklock — Voltaire — Voltigeur — Vedette — Galopin — St Simon — Persimmon — Sceptre

Pretty Polly (b. 1901)

Eclipse — Pot8os — Waxy — Whalebone — Sir Hercules — Birdcatcher — Oxford — Sterling — Isonomy — Gallinule — Pretty Polly

Two of the best and most popular female racehorses raced in the early years of the twentieth century. Sceptre won four Classics, but may be best known for a race she lost. Pretty Polly acquired such a formidable reputation that she started favourite for twenty-three of her twenty-four races, and in twenty-one of them was at odds-on.

Sceptre needed a big supply of pluck and fortitude, because she had an owner, a gambler called Robert Sievier, who put her through an exceptionally gruelling schedule. From April to June 1902, she ran in the 2,000 Guineas, 1,000 Guineas, Derby, Oaks, Grand Prix de Paris, and two races at Royal Ascot. In the autumn, she cemented her position as 'the country's sweetheart' with victory in the St Leger. But Sievier, on a winning streak as a punter when he bought Sceptre, hit a losing one that her exploits could not offset, and he sold her the following spring. Under new ownership, she lined up in July 1903 for the ten-furlong Eclipse Stakes at Sandown. Over the next ninety-seven years, only a few contests would challenge this one for the title of race of the century.

The owners of Sandown Park had wanted to stage a race to make a mark with their recently established course. With backing from Leopold de Rothschild, they offered a huge purse of £10,000 (double the prize that went to the winner of the Derby), and appropriated the most prestigious of racing names: Eclipse. The Eclipse Stakes, inaugurated in 1886, was the first contest of the year in which older horses met the Classic generation of three-year-olds. Sceptre's main rivals in 1903 were Ard Patrick, winner of the previous year's Derby – the only one of the five Classics that Sceptre had missed out on; and Rock Sand, winner of that year's 2,000 Guineas and Derby. 'All the rings were packed to suffocation, and everybody was keyed up to the highest pitch of excitement,' a contemporary report noted, and the three rivals lived up to the occasion by staging an epic. Turning into the home straight, Ard Patrick hit the front, and was immediately challenged by Sceptre, with Rock Sand drawing alongside. With two furlongs to go, Rock Sand started to lose touch, and Sceptre edged ahead; but, as the crowd bellowed encouragement at the filly, Ard Patrick timed a last effort to get back up on the line and win by a neck. (In the autumn, Sceptre again defeated Rock Sand – who by then had completed the Triple Crown by winning the St Leger.)

While Sceptre and Pretty Polly had overlapping careers, they did not meet on the racecourse. Pretty Polly won the 'Fillies' Triple Crown' (1,000 Guineas, Oaks, St Leger), and suffered only two defeats – the second, to the consternation of the Ascot crowd, in the last race of her career, the Ascot Gold Cup. Unfashionably bred, she appeared not to be a success at stud, and was not a solicitous mother. Only later did it become apparent that her descendants included an impressive number of outstanding racers.

Phar Lap (b. 1926)

Eclipse – Pot8os – Waxy – Whalebone – Sir Hercules – Birdcatcher – The Baron – Stockwell – Doncaster – Bend Or – Radium – Night Raid – Phar Lap

Like Seabiscuit (who was not an Eclipse male-line descendant), Phar Lap was a hero of the Depression. His tremendous exploits lit up a bleak time, and made him the most famous racer in New Zealand and Australian history. This fame inspired people, as Eclipse's fame had done, to take more than usual interest in his anatomy, their findings offering an interesting theory about the Eclipse legacy.

Phar Lap's story, again like Seabiscuit's, has been well documented in print and on film. Phar Lap – the name derives from a Thai word for lightning – was foaled in Timaru, New Zealand, and was sold for just 160 guineas. He grew into a giant chestnut, standing at over seventeen hands. Probably needing to mature into his frame, he began his career moderately, before running up a tremendous sequence of races, including fourteen in a row without defeat. In Australia's most prestigious horserace, the Melbourne Cup, Phar Lap was third in 1929, first in 1930 (carrying 9st 12lb) and unplaced in 1931 when asked to carry the impossible burden of 10st 10lb. After that, Phar Lap travelled to Mexico for the Agua Caliente Handicap, the richest prize ever given in North American racing. He won, in track record time. Two weeks later he was dead, for reasons about which there is still debate. Some suspect poisoning.

At autopsy, Phar Lap was discovered to have an abnormally large heart – the same weight, 14lb, as Eclipse's. The theory is that it was an inheritance – not through the male side of his pedigree, but through a daughter of Eclipse called Everlasting (and tracing back to a stallion called Hautboy). The large heart characteristic, so the theory goes, is carried by a gene on the X chromosome, which a father can transmit only to a daughter.[166] But this is just a theory. Understanding what the approximately 2.7 billion base pairs of horse genomic DNA do, how they interact with one another, how they are passed on by mare and stallion during reproduction, and how they are expressed in the resulting foal, is going to be the work of the next several decades.

Phar Lap's remains, like Eclipse's, were preserved. His heart is at the National Museum of Australia in Canberra; his hide is at the National Museum of Victoria in Melbourne; and his skeleton is at the National Museum of New Zealand in Wellington.

Arkle (b. 1957)

Eclipse – Pot8os – Waxy – Whalebone – Sir Hercules – Birdcatcher – The Baron – Stockwell – Doncaster – Bend Or – Bona Vista – Cyllene – Polymelus – Phalaris – Pharos – Nearco – Archive – Arkle

---

[166] If a male passes on his X rather than his Y chromosome, his offspring is female. So Eclipse's daughters – according to the 'X factor' theory – got the chromosome with the gene that expressed a large heart. Some of his sons were pretty good racers – but not because of that characteristic, unless they had inherited it from their mothers.

As we have seen, Eclipse exerted an unparalleled influence on the development of horseracing, around the world. His two principal contributions – speedier, more precocious Thoroughbreds and, indirectly, an industrialized bloodstock industry – are mostly phenomena of Flat racing. But Eclipse's name is all over National Hunt pedigrees too. The line from him through the stallions Phalaris and Nearco that resulted in Nijinsky also produced the greatest horse in the history of steeplechasing.

Steeplechasing has its origins in matches over the countryside towards some landmark, such as a steeple. In the early nineteenth century, aficionados bred greater speed into these contests by mating their stout mares with Thoroughbred racers.[167] Cheltenham, which is to jump racing what Newmarket is to the Flat, first staged its Grand Annual Steeplechase – still a feature of the Cheltenham Festival – in 1834, despite the antipathy of the Rev. (later Dean) F. C. Close, who had deplored the atmosphere of the town during race week. 'It is scarcely possible to turn our steps in any direction without hearing the voice of the blasphemous, or meeting the reeling drunkard, or witnessing scenes of the lowest profligacy,' he expostulated.

Yes, Cheltenham's contemporary inhabitants might agree, that sounds familiar.

The first official Grand National, at Aintree in Liverpool, took place in 1839,[168] when Captain Becher, on Conrad, fell into one of the brooks; he remounted, and on the second circuit fell into it again. Ever after, it was Becher's Brook. Our enduring image of poor Becher, one of the crack jockeys of the day, is of a man lying dazed in a stream while his rivals jump over him.

For many years, the Grand National was the most important

[167] They still do. National Hunt horses do not further the breed, because almost all of them are, like Arkle, geldings. Sometimes, Flat-bred racers turn out to excel at steeplechasing; among them was Red Rum, winner of three Grand Nationals.
[168] Some racing historians argue that the first Grand National was in 1836.

race in the National Hunt (the name indicates the roots of the sport) calendar. But, gradually, the Cheltenham Gold Cup gained recognition as the blue riband event. The race that fixed the Gold Cup in the public consciousness as the Derby of steeplechasing was another candidate for race of the century: the 1964 show-down between the hero of Ireland, Arkle, and the defending champion from England, Mill House.

When Mill House won the Gold Cup in 1963, the English thought that they had a horse who would dominate the event for many years. But the Irish were sure that they had an even better one. Mill House and Arkle first met later that year, in the Hennessy Gold Cup at Newbury, when Arkle slipped on landing three fences from home, and Mill House came out on top. The Irish still said their horse was superior. At Cheltenham the follow-ing spring, the rivals met again, in what was virtually a match: there were only two other horses in the race, and they were left a long way behind. It was what everyone wanted to see: Arkle and Mill House turning for home together, head to head. Then Arkle pulled clear, jumped the last, and accelerated up the Cheltenham hill to the finishing post. 'This is the champion,' Peter O'Sullevan, the commentator, called. 'This is the best we've seen for a long time.'

O'Sullevan was right. The connections of Mill House tried to refute his verdict, but in three subsequent meetings, Arkle gave their horse ever more severe drubbings. Arkle won two more Gold Cups, and put up astonishing weight-carrying performances in handicaps, winning an Irish Grand National, two Hennessy Gold Cups and a Whitbread Gold Cup with up to 12st 7lb on his back.

Arkle ran his last race, the King George VI Chase, at Kempton Park on 27 December 1966.[169] Aged nine, I was there.

[169] The King George is usually held on Boxing Day, but had been delayed because of frost and snow.

It was the first time I had seen the already legendary steeplechaser in the flesh. I had ridden a horse once in my life, I had spent no time with horses, but I could tell, as Arkle appeared in front of the stands before the race, that this was the animal at the centre of the day's events: in his deportment, in his alertness, in what one can sum up only as his presence, he stood out from the rest. It was a bearing that the *Irish Times* had described as exhibiting 'the dignity, the look of supreme assurance that marks a President de Gaulle'. In Ireland, Arkle was and still is 'Himself'. He was almost unbeatable, and he was 9-2 on. I thought that I was there to see an exhibition.

I, and my cousin and his girlfriend, were standing by the rails on the inside of the course, near the last fence. We could not see much from there, but we were, briefly, very close to the action. As the field passed a few feet away at the end of the first circuit, all seemed well: Arkle was leading, and travelling comfortably. He maintained his lead, though not by far, on the second circuit. He jumped the final fence about five lengths in front of the second horse, who, I was told afterwards, was called Dormant. As they galloped past, I craned my neck over the rails (did someone lift me?). The two horses' receding backsides now appeared to be level. Something was wrong. The crowd noise had that eerie, muted quality you get at a football ground when the away team scores.

Arkle had lost. We learned later what had happened: he had staggered to the line with a broken bone in his foot. It was, for a nine-year-old boy expecting to return home aglow with the memory of a triumphant performance, a jolting anti-climax.

Once the disappointment had eased, I learned to accept that defeat for Arkle on that December day at Kempton was immaterial. He had nothing left to prove. He had earned the highest rating any chaser had ever received, or is ever likely to receive, and was so superior to his rivals that the rules of handicapping had to be specially adjusted to accommodate him. He was bombarded with letters and presents, and was the hero of poems and songs. Occasionally, a new champion gets mentioned in the same breath as Arkle, but none challenges his position as, in the words of his biographer Sean Magee, 'the presiding spirit of steeplechasing'.

Nijinsky (b. 1967)

Eclipse – Pot8os – Waxy – Whalebone – Sir Hercules – Birdcatcher – The Baron – Stockwell – Doncaster – Bend Or – Bona Vista – Cyllene – Polymelus – Phalaris – Pharos – Nearco – Nearctic – Northern Dancer – Nijinsky

Eclipse, and his descendant St Simon, seemed to those who saw them to be invincible. They were supreme. However, supremacy is not the only definition of greatness; sometimes, greatness is a quality that comes with flaws. It is a poignant syndrome, recognized ever since Achilles' mother neglected to allow the protective waters of the Styx to soak his ankles. I have always been drawn to sporting figures of brilliant talent who at key moments have been unable to prove their superiority: the Australian distance runner Ron Clarke, who broke numerous world records but never won a gold medal; the graceful tennis player Hana Mandlikova, so often betrayed by nerves on the big occasions; and the racehorse Nijinsky, effortlessly in command in all his races, until he ran in the most valuable race of all.

Nijinsky was the discovery of Vincent O'Brien. Few people in racing would disagree with a *Racing Post* poll that named O'Brien, a man of restrained bearing and uncanny judgement, the outstanding trainer of the twentieth century. In National Hunt racing, he sent out the winners of three consecutive Grand Nationals, three consecutive Gold Cups (four in all), and three Champion Hurdles. Turning to the Flat, and setting up stables at Ballydoyle in Tipperary, he had similar success, and eventually won six Derbies. In 1968, the year of his colt Sir Ivor's Epsom victory, O'Brien spotted the year-old Nijinsky on a farm in Ontario, Canada. 'He really filled my eye,' he explained later. He recommended the colt to Charles Engelhard, a jowly industrialist who was one of the leading racehorse owners of the time.[170]

Nijinsky was the champion two-year-old in 1969, won the following year's 2,000 Guineas, Derby and Irish Derby with ease, and put up his finest performance in the King George VI and Queen Elizabeth Stakes at Ascot, cantering past a classy field of older horses. By this time, there was more public recognition for Nijinsky than any British or Irish Flat racer had gained for many years – and more than any has gained since. He looked magnificent; like Arkle, he radiated class. To add to his charisma, there was the impassive presence on his back of Lester Piggott, the most talented jockey of his generation.[171] Piggott was notoriously laconic, apparently no more excited about winning a Derby than he was about victory in a lowly selling race; but he certainly appreciated Nijinsky. 'That day,' he said about the King George, 'he was the most impressive horse I ever sat on.'

What went wrong with Nijinsky is debatable. A bout of ringworm following the King George cannot have helped: the colt lost nearly all his hair. Nevertheless, Vincent O'Brien got him ready for the St Leger, and in September at Doncaster Nijinsky became the first horse since Bahram in 1935 to win the Triple Crown.[172] He seemed to do it as effortlessly as ever, and Piggott did not push him. Only with the benefit of hindsight did one notice that the horse had no energy to spare.

Three weeks later, Nijinsky stepped on to the Longchamp turf for the contest that O'Brien and Engelhard intended to be the glorious conclusion to his career: the Prix de l'Arc de Triomphe, the most valuable race in Europe. There was a huge crowd, and a

---

[170] Engelhard, who spoke in a gravelly voice produced with almost no movement of the facial muscles, was rumoured to be the model for Ian Fleming's villain Goldfinger.

[171] Liam Ward rode Nijinsky in Ireland. Lester Piggott rode nine Derby winners during his career, a record.

[172] 2,000 Guineas, Derby, St Leger.

good portion of it invaded the Longchamp paddock in an effort to get close to the celebrated horse. Always highly strung, Nijinsky got very worked up; he was sweating and on his toes, and Piggott had a hard job controlling him as they cantered to the start.

Nijinsky was drawn on the outside of the field, a position that forced Piggott, when the race got underway, to drop in behind the other runners. I can still remember Peter O'Sullevan's commentary, my best guide as I watched the race on a tiny black and white television. Nijinsky was near the back of the field, fourth from last; the field was nearing the entrance to the home straight, and still there were only three horses behind him, while a wall of horses was in front. Unable to get an opening, Piggott lost ground and momentum by taking his mount wide. At last Nijinsky got into gear, came charging down the outside, and with the winning post in sight caught the leader, Sassafras, and pushed his nose in front — then he swerved, and the two horses hit the line, seemingly together. The judge called for a photo. The angle of the television cameras at Longchamp, giving a deceptive view of finishes, left viewers uncertain about the result. At the course, O'Brien was surrounded by well-wishers telling him that his horse had won, but he could sense, as we could at home, that the verdict was not going to go the right way. In those days, you had to wait for the photograph to be developed. But soon came the inevitable announcement: Sassafras was the winner, by a head.

Piggott received a lot of stick. He had let Nijinsky get too far behind the leaders; he had waited too long; it was an impossible task to make up that amount of ground in the short Longchamp straight — that was what the critics said, and O'Brien agreed. But even the outstanding trainer of the twentieth century can get things wrong, as O'Brien was immediately to demonstrate. Deciding that Nijinsky was back on form and ready to sign off his career victoriously, he sent over the colt just two weeks later for the Champion Stakes at Newmarket.

'The moment I saw Nijinsky in the parade ring,' Piggott

said, 'I could tell that he had not got over the Arc experience: he was a nervous wreck, and the huge crowd which had turned out to bid him farewell just made matters worse.' Nijinsky ran sluggishly, and finished second again,[173] a performance offering strong evidence that he had been past his best on Arc day too. The Nijinsky of a few months earlier would have had no trouble in winning at Longchamp, even from his backward position in the field.[174] But what happened to him at Longchamp and Newmarket is a common syndrome: since 1970, numerous fine horses have demonstrated how hard it is to maintain scintillating form throughout a long season.[175]

I had wanted Nijinsky to win the Arc very badly. He was the best horse: he should have won. I still get a pang when I think about it, and I find the video of the race painful to watch. But I think that the defeat strengthened Nijinsky's hold on my imagination. The following year, another exceptional colt, Mill Reef, won the Derby, Eclipse Stakes and the King George, and went on to Longchamp and won the Arc as well. Mill Reef was a more durable horse than Nijinsky, and may have been a better one; but he never excited me as much.[176]

[173] The winner, Lorenzaccio, was, as Piggott said, 'not remotely in the same league as Nijinsky in his prime'. But Lorenzaccio did have some importance as a sire, maintaining one of the rare male lines that endures from the Byerley Turk and Herod.

[174] Dancing Brave's brilliant Arc victory in 1986 showed that it was possible to make up ground in the Longchamp straight.

[175] Among them: Troy (1979 Derby, Irish Derby, King George), third in the Arc; Shergar (1981 Derby, Irish Derby, King George), fourth in the St Leger; Nashwan (1989 2,000 Guineas, Derby, Eclipse, King George), third in the Prix Niel; Generous (1991 Derby, Irish Derby, King George), eighth in the Arc; Authorized (2007 Derby, Juddmonte International), tenth in the Arc.

[176] Mill Reef's owner was Paul Mellon, who endowed the Yale Center for British Art. Mellon's collection of work by Stubbs included the painter's first study of Eclipse; he donated it to the Royal Veterinary College. Mill Reef was trained by Ian Balding, father of Clare, the BBC television and radio presenter.

The story is not really sad. Nijinsky enjoyed a contented life at stud at Claiborne Farm in Kentucky, and sired the Derby winners Golden Fleece, Shahrastani and Lammtarra. Moreover, his racecourse performances had an extraordinary effect. They alerted the world to the ability of his sire Northern Dancer, who at his base on Windfields Farm in Maryland went on to set a record, still unbroken, for the highest covering fee in history. And they inspired the growth of racing and breeding empires whose policy, pursued in a more determined way than anyone had seen before, was to corner the market in the best bloodlines.

Nijinsky was syndicated for $5.5 million, following a common practice among owners of top stallions in the second half of the twentieth century. You have to spread the risk, as you would in any corporate venture. While the valuation of stallions is enormous, their failure rate – and this includes some of the best racers – is frightening. So you distribute the ownership, sharing the costs and the profits among, say, forty partners, each getting the right to send one mare to the stallion a season.

Some stallions, such as Dubai Millennium (see below), die young; a few, like the American champion Cigar, turn out to be infertile; most simply get offspring who do not run very fast. The successful ones, however, are by a huge margin the biggest earners in racing. At six-figure fees for each mare they cover, they perform more than a hundred coverings a season, and they can keep it up for twenty years or longer. What they earned on the racecourse was insignificant by comparison. The point of racing, for the heaviest hitters in the industry, is not the actual sport, but what goes on in the breeding shed. The logical strategy, then, is to do systematically what Vincent O'Brien and Charles Engelhard did with Nijinsky: annex the best bloodlines, spot the potential stallions early, race them, and retire them to stud. Dennis O'Kelly would have been at home in the modern bloodstock world.

Engelhard did not see this policy come to fruition, dying at the age of fifty-four in 1971. O'Brien pursued it with two partners:

his son-in-law John Magnier, and Robert Sangster. Magnier, who ran the Coolmore stud and is now in charge of the entire international business, is a fearsome and laconic operator about whom it has been observed that the softest part of his head is his teeth. Sangster, heir to the Vernons pools business, was (he died of cancer in 2004) exuberant, a generous giver of parties and a lover of the jet-setting life that came with international racehorse ownership. O'Brien himself is modest and courteous. In the 1970s and early 1980s, this unusual threesome would descend on the sales in Keeneland and Saratoga and buy up the best yearlings – offspring of Northern Dancer in particular – they could find. Prices rocketed, and Northern Dancer's stud fee rose to $1 million.

There have been several outcomes of the bloodstock boom of the 1970s and 1980s. One is that Coolmore has grown into the most powerful bloodstock operation in the world. Another, that racing, at the very top level, is no longer a pursuit for aristocrats, unless they engage in it with the ambition and ruthlessness required in big business. The Queen was the leading owner on the British Turf in 1954 and 1957; she is nowhere near that position today, and she last enjoyed success in a Classic in her Silver Jubilee year, 1977.[177] There is of course a third outcome: the boom in breeding Classic colts and fillies, who would go on themselves to breed world-class offspring, strengthened the dominance of the bloodline from Eclipse.

Secretariat (b. 1970)

Eclipse – Pot8os –Waxy –Whalebone – Sir Hercules – Birdcatcher – The Baron – Stockwell – Doncaster – Bend Or – Bona Vista – Cyllene – Polymelus – Phalaris – Pharos – Nearco – Nasrullah – Bold Ruler – Secretariat

With Secretariat, we return to the champion as invincible athlete.

---

[177] The Queen's filly Dunfermline won the 1977 Oaks and St Leger.

Actually, Secretariat was beaten a few times, through bad luck, careless preparation and, once, disqualification. In the races that mattered, though, he was awesome.

The US Triple Crown races take place over five weeks in May and June. They are the Kentucky Derby, over one and a quarter miles at Churchill Downs; the Preakness Stakes, over a mile and one and a half furlongs at Pimlico; and the Belmont Stakes, over one and a half miles at Belmont Park. They are quite unlike the tests that horses face in the English Classics. The course at Newmarket (the 2,000 Guineas) is a straight mile, with a dip and then a rising finish; the contestants at Epsom (the Derby) go on a roller-coaster ride over the Downs; Doncaster (the St Leger) is a park course, but nevertheless has uphill and downhill sections. American tracks are all flat, left-handed ovals, and they have dirt surfaces[178] – turf racing is less important in the US.

Secretariat entered the Kentucky Derby, on the first Saturday in May in 1973, as the favourite, but on the back of a defeat and facing doubts over whether he would stay the distance. When the gates opened, it soon became clear that his stamina would face a proper test, because his jockey, Ron Turcotte, dropped him to the back of the field, from where he was forced to race wide to gain a position. In spite of that disadvantage, the reddish chestnut colt with the blue and white chequered blinkers powered home, in a time that has never been bettered. In the Preakness Stakes, two weeks later, Turcotte again started slowly, and this time drove his mount past the entire field early in the back stretch. Any normal horse would have used up too much energy in that manoeuvre. Secretariat, however, kept on going. His victory margins over the second horse, Sham, and the third, Our Native, were the same as they had been in the Derby. Only the

---

[178] Some tracks, but not the Triple Crown ones, have introduced artificial surfaces such as Polytrack, also in use at the English courses Lingfield, Wolverhampton and Great Leighs.

timing was in dispute: unofficial clockers recorded that Secretariat had broken the Pimlico track record, although the official timing device did not.

Secretariat was by now a national figure, a cover star of *Time* and *Newsweek*. His defining race awaited him, and at Belmont Park on 9 June he and Sham went into battle once more, with Secretariat aiming to become the first Triple Crown winner for twenty-five years. It was brutal: the two colts fought for the lead at an apparently suicidal pace. Before the end of the back stretch Sham dropped away, broken, as Bucephalus had been when trying to match strides with Eclipse. Sham finished last, and never raced again. Secretariat carried on galloping relentlessly. 'He is moving like a tremendous machine!' the commentator yelled. In the home straight, Turcotte looked back; he would have needed binoculars to get a proper view of his nearest pursuer. The rest were nowhere. Secretariat passed the post thirty-one lengths in front. He had set a new world record for twelve furlongs, and as Turcotte[179] tried to pull him up, he passed the thirteen-furlong marker in a new world record as well. 'It is hard to conceive,' Tony Morris and John Randall wrote, 'how any horse in history could have lived with him, at any distance, on that magic afternoon of 9 June 1973.'

In 1972, Secretariat had been the first two-year-old to be named Horse of the Year. This award is the climax of a ceremony staged each January in Beverly Hills to honour the stars of horseracing: it is known as the Eclipse Awards. A Triple Crown winner and American sporting hero, Secretariat was a shoo-in as the 1973 Horse of the Year as well.

Secretariat was another of Eclipse's descendants to boast an unusually large heart. How large we do not know for sure, because it was never weighed; the veterinarian who examined him, Dr

---

[179] Five years later, Turcotte fell from his horse in a race at Belmont, and was left a paraplegic.

Thomas Swerczek, thought that it was at least twice as large as normal. A few years after Secretariat's death, Swerczek weighed the heart of Secretariat's rival Sham, discovered it to be 18lb, and decided that Secretariat's had been a whopping 22lb. If there is anything in the 'X factor' theory, which argues that the large heart gene resides on the X chromosome that a father passes on only to daughters,[180] it may explain why Secretariat, a moderately successful sire of male offspring, was a very successful sire of females.

Dubai Millennium (b. 1996)

Eclipse – Pot8os –Waxy –Whalebone – Sir Hercules – Birdcatcher – The Baron – Stockwell – Doncaster – Bend Or – Bona Vista – Cyllene – Polymelus – Phalaris – Sickle – Unbreakable – Polynesian – Native Dancer – Raise a Native – Mr Prospector – Seeking the Gold   Dubai Millennium

Sheikh Mohammed bin Rashid Al Maktoum and his relatives from the Dubai royal family arrived on the international racing scene in the late 1970s. Flush with oil money, they raised still further the heat in the American sales rings. Some of the deals were staggering, and they illustrated how bloodstock was a pursuit only for those who could afford to take huge, scary gambles. In 1983, Sheikh Mohammed[181] paid a world record $10.2 million to outbid Coolmore, as well as the American partnership of trainer D. Wayne Lukas and self-made tycoon Eugene Klein, for a Northern Dancer colt. The colt, Snaafi Dancer, was shipped over the Atlantic to the stables of John Dunlop in Sussex. Dunlop soon discovered that Snaafi Dancer was too slow to race; 'A nice little horse but no bloody good' was his summary. So Snaafi Dancer, who at least boasted a pedigree that might appeal to breeders, went to stud. He

---

[180] See the essay on Phar Lap.
[181] He became ruler of Dubai in 2006.

was infertile. Goodbye $10.2 million, plus training and stabling fees. Two years later, Coolmore broke the Snaafi Dancer record by paying $13.1 million for Seattle Dancer, a son of Nijinsky. While Seattle Dancer earned some money on the racecourse, he did so only to the tune of about £100,000, and while he was fertile he was nevertheless a moderate stallion.

No doubt Coolmore was bitterly disappointed by this setback, as Sheikh Mohammed had been by the Snaafi Dancer debacle. But they both know that failure is the norm, and that if their judgement is sound – they employ some of the best judges of horseflesh in the business – they will find the rare Thoroughbreds that compensate for the rest. At about the time it bought Seattle Dancer, Coolmore was advertising a young stallion, Sadler's Wells. In spring 2008, Sadler's Wells (another son of Northern Dancer) retired, having broken the record of Eclipse's rival Highflyer to become champion sire fourteen times. If you own Sadler's Wells, you can afford quite a few Seattle Dancers.

Sheikh Mohammed set up his own training operation, Godolphin (named in tribute to the Godolphin Arabian), in 1994. (The overall name of the sheikh's racing empire, Darley Racing, pays tribute to another of the foundation sires, the Darley Arabian – Eclipse's great-great-grandfather. The sheikh's breeding operation is the Darley Stud.) Two years later, he inaugurated the world's richest horse race, the Dubai World Cup, which now has a purse of $6 million. Racing, and other sports including golf and powerboat racing, have been key elements in the sheikh's promotion of Dubai as a glamorous destination for tourism and business. The country's capital is the fastest growing city on the planet.

Dubai Millennium was supposed to be the supreme racing exemplar of Sheikh Mohammed's ambitions. According to the bloodstock writer Rachel Pagones, Sheikh Mohammed 'spent hours alone with Dubai Millennium, going into the colt's box after evening stables to feed him carrots, stroke his shining, sunwarmed coat and simply sit'. Originally called Yaazer, Dubai

Millennium had taken on the burden of high expectation on the day that his trainer told the sheikh that this was the best horse he had ever trained, and got the response, 'In that case I will change his name.'

The colt's new name signified his obvious target as the 2000 running of the Dubai World Cup; but before that, his first big challenge was the 1999 Derby, a race no horse carrying Sheikh Mohammed's colours had won.[182] It went badly. Dubai Millennium, ridden by Frankie Dettori,[183] got worked up in the paddock, pulled too hard, was a spent force by the time the field rounded Tattenham Corner, and finished ninth.

Sent back to trips of a mile, he won three races in a row, climaxing with the Queen Elizabeth II Stakes at Ascot, after which Sheikh Mohammed declared him to be 'the best we have had in Godolphin'. Proving that he had read the script, Dubai Millennium turned up for the World Cup the following March 2000, in stupendous form, pulverizing the field to win by six lengths in record time. 'It is the greatest race in my life,' Sheikh Mohammed said.

Dubai Millennium's next race was at Royal Ascot, where his most dangerous opponent was the French champion Sendawar, owned by the Aga Khan. Sendawar was a very good horse, but the betting market made an insulting mistake in promoting him to favouritism. It was like Bucephalus taking on Eclipse, or Sham taking on Secretariat: Sendawar tried to keep up with Dubai Millennium, was broken, and fell away, leaving Dubai Millennium to win by eight lengths.

Now the racing world wanted to see him face another superstar: Montjeu, winner of the 1999 Prix de l'Arc de Triomphe and

[182] It is still the case. Lammtarra, the 1995 winner, was trained by Godolphin but ran in the colours of Sheikh Mohammed's nephew. In 2008, New Approach raced to victory at Epsom in the colours of the sheikh's wife, Princess Haya – he had given her the horse as a present.

[183] The popular jockey at last broke his Derby duck in 2007, on Authorized.

of the 2000 King George VI and Queen Elizabeth Stakes (in which he had evoked memories of Nijinsky by overtaking the field in a canter). Montjeu was in the ownership of Sheikh Mohammed's great rivals Coolmore, and soon after the Ascot race the Coolmore team challenged Dubai Millennium to come to Ireland, to race against Montjeu in the Irish Champion Stakes. Sheikh Mohammed responded by issuing a counter-challenge, through the *Racing Post*: an old-fashioned match, one on one, $6 million staked by each side. It would have been an early candidate for race of the century, but it was not to be. On the day that the *Post* carried the story, Dubai Millennium broke a leg on the Newmarket gallops, and, after a life-saving operation, retired to stud. He had covered only one book of mares when he contracted grass sickness, an often fatal condition that destroys a horse's nerve endings. He did not survive.

Dubai Millennium's career marked the high point of Sheikh Mohammed's horseracing fortunes. In the first years of this century, Coolmore has gained the upper hand. The Ballydoyle racehorses – now in the care of the boyish-looking, softly spoken Aidan O'Brien (no relation of Vincent) – are dominating Europe's most prestigious races, and the 'Coolmore Mafia' are colonizing the winners' enclosures that had been the regular haunts of the sheikh's Godolphin team. O'Brien seems to produce champions from a conveyor belt.[184]

In breeding, the superiority is even more marked. The leading four sires in Europe in 2007 were all Coolmore's, while the sires from Sheikh Mohammed's Darley Stud were off the pace. Meanwhile, relations between the two operations, for reasons that have been kept extraordinarily well hidden, have broken down, and the rivals have returned to slugging it out in the sales ring.

---

[184] In the past few years alone, they have included Giant's Causeway, Galileo, High Chaparral, Hawk Wing, Rock of Gibraltar, Dylan Thomas, Henrythenavigator and Duke of Marmalade.

Their competing bids pushed up the price of a two-year-old colt, to whom Coolmore later gave the unflattering name The Green Monkey,[185] to $16 million – another world record – while Darley paid $9.7 million for Jalil, a son of leading sire Storm Cat. Both colts conformed to what one might call the Snaafi Dancer syndrome, failing to live up to their valuations.

In the bloodstock world recently, then, it has been John Magnier first, Sheikh Mohammed nowhere, and you get the impression that the sheikh does not find that result acceptable. Recently, he has switched tactics, buying as stallion prospects colts with proven form, such as the 2007 Derby winner Authorized. In 2007, he spent at least $200 million on bloodstock, and he went on to splash out a further $420 million on the Woodlands Stud, the largest stud farm in Australia. Magnier, notwithstanding his estimated personal fortune of £1.3 billion, would be pushed to match those sums.

More than two hundred years after Eclipse's death, the battle to secure the best bloodstock – which one might characterize as the battle over Eclipse's legacy – involves huge egos, business ruthlessness, and national pride. As I said, Dennis O'Kelly was there first.

---

[185] The Green Monkey is a Barbados golf course to which Coolmore has ties.

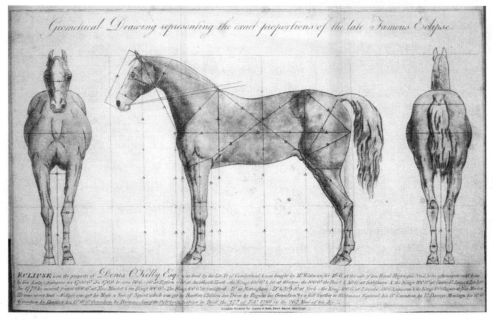

Anatomical drawings of Eclipse from Charles Vial de Sainbel's An Essay on the Proportions of the Celebrated Eclipse — *the work that helped Sainbel to set up the Royal Veterinary College.*

The Skeleton

ECLIPSE STANDS, SKELETALLY, in a glass case in the small museum of the Royal Veterinary College in Hertfordshire. Opposite him, misdated to c.1750 rather than to c.1769, is his portrait, Stubbs's first study of him. Eclipse has had a tortuous and often undignified journey here, and he has survived questions about his identity as well as several attempts at impersonation. Now, he is back in his rightful, starring role; and he is for the second time at the centre of pioneering research.

The first research took place following his death in 1789, when Charles Vial de Sainbel, the French veterinarian, anatomized him. Sainbel, and his English wife, were back in England – where he had earlier failed to set up a veterinary college – escaping from the dangers of revolutionary France. His friends had gone to the guillotine or had emigrated, and his estates had been confiscated. A tall man with a dark complexion and prominent cheekbones, he was amiable, ambitious, egotistical and punctilious. Getting his college off the ground was now a pressing need. Perhaps he made Andrew O'Kelly an offer to examine Eclipse, having seen that the great horse would be the means of furthering his cause.

Sainbel skinned the body and removed the organs. One of his first services to subsequent researchers was the discovery that

Eclipse's heart was abnormally large, at 14lb.[186] Then Sainbel set about measuring the skeleton. This is not a straightforward job. You cannot do it simply with a tape measure, because you do not know how the angles of the joints would have been affected by half a ton of bodyweight. Sainbel's solution was to take the straightforward measurements and to deduce the rest in proportion to them. The results are odd. He gives the length of Eclipse's head as twenty-two inches, which is short, and the horse's height as three times that figure, sixty-six inches, which is exceptionally tall. It translates to 16.2 hands – a good height for a twenty-first-century racehorse but giant by the standards of Eclipse's era. (Racing historians reckon Eclipse's true height to have been about 15.3 hands.) There are dubious details in Sainbel's portrait of Eclipse too. He shows a white blaze extending down Eclipse's face and covering his muzzle, and a white stocking covering his hock, whereas in the Stubbs and Sartorius portraits the blaze is only on the front of Eclipse's head, and the top of the stocking is below the hock. These discrepancies have led to questions about whether Eclipse really was the horse that Sainbel studied.

Sainbel calculated that Eclipse's stride could cover twenty-five feet, that he could complete two and one-third galloping actions a second, and that he could cover four miles in six minutes and two seconds. That all seems somewhat theoretical. More impressive is the vet's account of the mechanics of the gallop: Sainbel described the motions, involving lead legs and brief elevation from the ground, that Muybridge was to photograph some ninety years later. However, despite his hope of offering 'a surer guide to the brush or chisel of the artist, who commonly only employs them in opposition to nature', he failed to influence the conventions of horse painting. Artists, until visual evidence made

---

[186] See chapter 20 for more on the theory that the characteristic was passed on, through female offspring, to great racehorses including Phar Lap and Secretariat.

them change their ways, carried on depicting the 'rocking horse' gallop.

Whatever the flaws in Sainbel's study, it impressed the men he wanted to influence. They approved his proposals and came up with his financing, and the Veterinary College, London,[187] the first British school for veterinarians, welcomed its first students in January 1792. Sainbel was the inaugural professor.

He enjoyed the fruition of his campaign only briefly. In August the following year, Sainbel developed a fever, and died at the age of forty. (His symptoms, of severe shivering, hint that his fatal condition was the infectious disease glanders, which can be transmitted from animals.) Sainbel's testament, and one of the few sources of income for his widow, was *Essays on the Veterinary Art: Containing an Essay on the Proportions of the Celebrated Eclipse*. He had concluded that, while Eclipse had 'never been esteemed handsome', the horse's frame was 'almost perfect'. Even if Eclipse's offspring had made no impression on Thoroughbred history, his role as the figurehead in Sainbel's campaign to further animal welfare would have confirmed him as one of the most important of all Thoroughbreds.

Eclipse's skeleton now began its wanderings. Its first owner was Edmund Bond, who was the O'Kellys' vet and who had attended Sainbel's dissection of the corpse. Bond kept it in his own small museum in Mayfair. When he died, he left behind a debt of £500 to a fellow vet called Bracy Clark, who received payment from Bond's widow in the form of Eclipse.

Bracy Clark, while writing the first attempt at a full account of Eclipse's career as well as other studies of equestrian matters, was a man of varied interests, also assembling an insect cabinet that earned him membership of the Linnaean Society, and founding the first cricket club in Worcester. But he lacked ideal facilities

---

[187] It began styling itself 'Royal' in 1826.

for keeping a skeleton. Eclipse was, literally, Bracy Clark's skeleton in the cupboard – or rather, the limbs were in two adjoining cupboards, with the torso and head stashed on top. At last recognizing that this arrangement was unsatisfactory, he donated Eclipse for display in a cabinet in Egyptian Hall, Piccadilly, where at various times the exhibits also included Egyptian artefacts, a family of Laplanders 'complete with house and reindeer', and a pair of eighteen-year-old Siamese twins.[188] The Royal College of Veterinary Surgeons offered to take the responsibility off his hands for sixty guineas, but got a brusque response – 'a hundred being demanded for this invincible monarch of the racecourse'. Bracy Clark also rebuffed the first rumours ('very ungenerous and ridiculous') that his possession was fake. 'The bones themselves, which are remarkable, would sufficiently evince their genuineness to any person not wilfully blind or prejudiced,' he insisted.

Meanwhile, other parts of Eclipse's anatomy were acquiring the status of religious relics (see colour section). The royal family took possession of a couple of his hooves, and in 1832, at the climax of a grand dinner, William IV presented one of them to the Jockey Club. It was mounted on a salver, and had an inscription carved in gold. The club instituted it as the trophy for an annual race, the Eclipse Foot, staged at Ascot. The hoof is still in the Jockey Club Rooms in Newmarket, along with the Newmarket Challenge Whip – into which are reputed to be woven hairs from Eclipse's mane and tail – and Stubbs's copy[189] of his painting of Eclipse at the Newmarket Beacon Course rubbing-house. So Eclipse has a hallowed place at an institution that never admitted Dennis O'Kelly, his owner.

What happened to the second royal hoof is a mystery. When Theodore Cook was writing *Eclipse and O'Kelly*, he received the following letter: 'Lord Knollys, Balmoral Castle, 1906: Dear Mr Cook, I have submitted your letter to the King, and I find that his

[188] Also known as the London Museum, the hall was demolished in 1905.
[189] Made for the *Review of the Turf*. See chapter 18.

272

Majesty does possess one of Eclipse's hoofs. Yours very truly, Knollys.' However, my enquiries at The Royal Collection drew a blank, with no record showing up on the collection's database – unless for some reason Eclipse's was the unmarked hoof inscribed 'Xmas 1902'. A third hoof, converted into a snuff box, was last recorded in Jamaica. The last report of the fourth placed it in Leicestershire. A William Worley was said to have owned a tie-pin made from material from one of the hooves. In 1910, there was a proposal that the Jockey Club hoof travel to Vienna, so that the Emperor of Austria could take snuff from it at a lunch to mark the opening of a field sports exhibition.[190]

Portions of Eclipse's hide went hither and thither too. Theodore Cook, writing his biography of Eclipse and O'Kelly in 1907, reported that there was a section of chestnut hide, together with a letter saying that it had come from Andrew O'Kelly, at The Durdans, a grand house in Epsom. When the light shone on it, Cook enthused, it produced 'that extraordinary iridescent effect which makes a true chestnut the loveliest colour in the world'. A letter in Cook's possession from a man who was friendly with the son of Thomas Plumer, who had bought Cannons from Andrew, said that the younger Plumer could remember playing with Eclipse's skin in the Cannons loft. Then there was a story that a portion of Eclipse's hide was being kept in pickle at a tanner's in Edgware; another of Cook's correspondents cut off a bit and sent it to him.

In 1860, just three weeks before he died at the age of eighty-nine, Bracy Clark got his 100 guineas. His customer was John Gamgee, who thought that Eclipse would bring lustre to his new veterinary college in Edinburgh. 'The skeleton of Eclipse now in

---

[190] Eclipse's skeleton, notwithstanding a request from Edward VII that it be part of the exhibition, was not entrusted to the journey. The grand lunch was delayed a week, because news of Edward's death came through on the day it had been due to take place. It is not clear whether the hoof was part of the occasion.

our possession, still connected by its ligaments, is proof that Eclipse was a horse of most perfect symmetry,' wrote Gamgee's father, Joseph, in the *Edinburgh Veterinary Review*, while noting that 'some very important errors' had crept into Sainbel's original measurements. Despite this prize attraction, Gamgee struggled to make an impact with his college. He transferred to London, where he called his venture the Albert Veterinary College, but again got into difficulties. Packing it in, and preparing to head off to America in search of better fortune, Gamgee donated the skeleton to the Royal College of Veterinary Surgeons.

Eclipse's new home was the RCVS museum in Red Lion Square. It was not hospitable. In the early 1900s, a member of the RCVS council noted with dismay 'the dirty and dusty state [the skeleton] is in . . . if it is not kept in a clean state there will soon be no skeleton of Eclipse at all'. Another said, 'I was in the museum this morning and I think it more a place to set potatoes in than anything else.' Nevertheless, the college did not take any remedial action until 1920: converting its dark and dusty museum into a library, it handed over the skeleton to the Natural History Museum, which had first put in a request for it eighteen years earlier.

By this time, there was another point of comparison between bits of Eclipse's anatomy and religious relics: they were unfeasibly numerous. In 1907, when Theodore Cook was trying to unravel the story, 'Six "undoubted" skeletons of Eclipse claimed my bewildered attention. No less than nine "authentic" feet were apparently possessed by this extraordinary animal. The "genuine" hair out of his tail would have generously filled the largest arm-chair in the Jockey Club. The "certified" portions of his hide would together have easily carpeted the yard at Tattersalls.'

Lady Wentworth, the dogmatic Thoroughbred historian, doubted the credentials of the skeleton in the Natural History Museum. She noted the conflicting measurements, as well as the differences between Sainbel's portrait and Stubbs's, and she argued that the task of reassembling a skeleton from separate parts, kept by the vets Edmund Bond and Bracy Clark among the remains of other horses, was akin to 'solving a Greek crossword puzzle'.[191] In her view, the bones were those of 'a common cross-bred horse'. The marketable value of the skeleton was an incentive to fraud, Lady Wentworth alleged. 'Eclipse's skeleton, like Caesar's wife, would have to be above suspicion before we could base any theories on it.'

Nevertheless, this skeleton continued to enjoy official status, if not appropriate prominence. In 1972, the racing paper the *Sporting Life* ran a sad story about how 'The Turf's greatest horse lies forgotten in a museum basement.' That neglect ended eleven years later, when Eclipse travelled to Newmarket to join the exhibits at the new National Horseracing Museum, opened by the Queen. He stayed in Newmarket for twenty years, although his ownership changed in 1991, when the Royal College of Veterinary Surgeons – much to the disappointment of the Natural History Museum, which holds the skeletons of other Thoroughbreds including St Simon, and which had come to regard Eclipse as its natural possession – donated it to the Royal Veterinary College as a 200th birthday gift. At the same time, the American collector Paul Mellon gave the college his Stubbs portrait – the one that Stubbs used as a model for *Eclipse with William Wildman and His Sons* and *Eclipse at Newmarket, with a Groom and Jockey* – as well as a bronze statue of Eclipse by James Osborne.[192] Eclipse completed his travelling in 2003, when he moved from Newmarket to join the portrait and statue at the opening – again by the Queen – of the Eclipse Building at the RVC in Hatfield, Hertfordshire.

[191] She does not appear to have had any evidence that the skeleton was in separate bits when in Bond's care. John Orton, writing in 1844, said that Bond exhibited it.

[192] There is a replica of this statue next to the paddock on the Rowley Mile course at Newmarket.

*

I glance up from my computer screen, and I see above my desk my print of Eclipse, as painted by Stubbs, preparing to race against Bucephalus. I click on a folder named 'Pics', and there is Eclipse with William Wildman and his sons, or Eclipse at stud painted by Garrard, or Eclipse by Sartorius walking over the course for the King's Plate. Now, it is time to enter the great horse's physical presence.

I take the train to Potters Bar, and a taxi beyond the suburban streets into the Hertfordshire countryside. We pull up at the Royal Veterinary College's Eclipse Building, and I go into a reception area overlooked, from the floor above, by Eclipse's statue. The RVC receptionist, informing a colleague of my arrival, announces herself as 'Pam in Eclipse'. I look to my left; through an open door, at the opposite end of a modestly sized room, is the skeleton. I go in.

Panels on the wall tell the stories of Eclipse and Sainbel. I turn round; there is the Stubbs painting. It requires a conceptual leap to link skeleton and portrait: the bones, fleshless, appear to be those of a smaller animal than a Thoroughbred. Are they linked? Or is the RVC's proudest possession a fake? Dr Renate Weller, of the RVC's Structure and Motion laboratory, joins me, and we look at the skeleton. This certainly seems to be the skeleton of an animal who stayed constitutionally sound into old age, showing only a fusion of the last thoracic and first lumbar vertebrae, and of the fourth and fifth lumbar vertebrae. But did Sainbel anatomize the horse whom Stubbs painted? We look at the portrait. Dr Weller, who has a nicely sceptical sense of humour, is inclined to dismiss Stubbs, despite his reputation for verisimilitude, as a source of anatomical evidence. She points to the angle of the fetlock, and says that it is too steep; the angle of the shoulder is 'much too steep'; the angle of the tarsus (the joint on the hind leg) 'looks bizarre'; and Eclipse's neck appears to be too short. 'I don't like this picture,' she concludes.

We move to Dr Weller's narrow, shared office, where,

weighing down the papers in a tray on a filing cabinet, are two resin models of Eclipse's humerus (the bone at the top of the fore-limb). She tells me about the RVC's research. The college has examined seven hundred horses, and eighteen horse skeletons. Its aims are to further the understanding of equine anatomy, and to gain insights into the relationship between the conformation of a horse and equine injuries.

Dr Weller and her colleagues in the RVC's Structure and Motion team removed Eclipse's right (off) front leg and put it through a CT scanner, taking care that the metal pins used to mount the skeleton did not overheat the apparatus. They loaded the CT images into a program called Mimics, which reproduced them in 3D; a further piece of software, Magics, combined the images of the individual bones to produce a complete 3D image of the leg. The Mimics file guided a laser to carve a replica of the leg in a tank of resin. Yet another piece of software, which had been developed for such uses as simulating the effect of surgery on children with cerebral palsy, depicted the mechanics of the limb.

The Structure and Motion team's conclusions have a ring of bathos. Eclipse, they found, was by contemporary standards a small, light-framed Thoroughbred, 'with average bone measurements without any outstanding features'. But maybe that was the horse's secret? As Muybridge showed with his photographic sequence of the gallop, a running horse, weighing some 500kg, hits the ground first with just one leg; only briefly are all four legs bearing the half-ton or more. Did Eclipse's averageness keep him sound? Dr Weller and her colleagues have since looked at other skeletons, among them the Natural History Museum's St Simon and Brown Jack. Brown Jack: now there, indisputably, was a sound horse. From 1929, he won six consecutive runnings of Royal Ascot's Queen Alexandra Stakes – at two and three-quarter miles, the longest Flat race in the calendar. Dr Weller, unsentimental about the RVC's Eclipse association, says, 'Brown Jack impressed me more.'

This opinion notwithstanding, Eclipse has a key role in the

RVC's promotional and educational activities. In 2004, the college sent its reproduction leg to the Royal Society Summer Exhibition. The leg is also the star prop in the RVC's educational outreach programme to schools and colleges. Seeing a physical specimen, the RVC says, teaches more about anatomy, and inspires more enthusiasm for the subject, than any number of diagrams and text-book explanations. The college, which is lobbying for the financial support to create an entire replica of Eclipse's skeleton, believes that its Eclipse project can be the prototype for the creation of similar teaching aids. The project may also show the way towards modelling of human subjects, so that replicas can give evidence of the likely outcome of surgery.

Eclipse is also at the heart of advanced genetic research. Matthew Binns of the RVC, Paula Jenkins of the Natural History Museum, and Mim Bower of Cambridge University have been leading a project to explore genetic variations in Thoroughbreds. The horses they have examined include, as well as Eclipse, Hermit, whose Derby victory broke Lord Hastings's heart, and St Simon, the 'steam engine' ridden by Fred Archer. Their findings will give us our fullest understanding yet of these great horses, and may also offer information to help trace horses' genetic weaknesses. One of the great worries for the bloodstock industry is that, in an inbred animal, genetic defects may be perpetuated and become widespread.

The researchers started by encasing in wax a tooth from the Eclipse skull, and drilled it. The genetic material they extracted contained bad news. This tooth did not belong to an animal from what, according to the official records, was Eclipse's matrilineal line.[193]

[193] The researchers examined mitochondrial DNA, which is passed down the distaff line and which can therefore identify Thoroughbred 'families'. (In the bloodstock world, the term 'family' indicates the bottom, female line of a pedigree.) Thoroughbred families were first classified by the nineteenth-century Australian historian Bruce Lowe, who gave them numbers. Eclipse belongs to family number 12.

In the light of the convoluted history of the skeleton, a separation of the body from its proper head, and the replacement of the head with a substitute, are not surprising occurrences. The Natural History Museum, when it possessed the skeleton, displayed it headless, and has in its archives a letter from a man who had heard that Eclipse's head was kept in a grotto – destroyed by fire in 1948 – in Weybridge.

As I write, results of tests on the body are yet to appear, though I am hopeful that they will conform to the accepted pedigree and thus indicate, with near incontrovertibility, that the RVC's skeleton really is Eclipse's. If the tests reveal a different pedigree, however, they will not prove fakery. Rather, I should be inclined to suspect that the pedigree was inaccurate. The skeleton seems to be the one that Sainbel studied. How could he have stripped and anatomized the wrong horse? He knew what Eclipse looked like: he said that he had seen him alive.[194] It is hard to imagine a set of circumstances that could have compelled him, with the O'Kellys' connivance or at their instigation, to pass off a fake as the real thing. I remain convinced that the skeleton in the RVC, or most of it, is Eclipse.

No other racehorse has done this much. Eclipse was a supreme champion, who easily defeated the best racehorses of the day. His bloodline was to dominate the bloodstock industry. In alliance with Herod, his genetic influence transformed racing into a spectacle of thrilling speed, for masses of people to enjoy. He is the icon of the sport, its unquestionable symbol of greatness: its Jesse Owens, or Michael Jordan, or Donald Bradman, or Pele. The Eclipse Stakes and the Eclipse Awards, along with various other

---

[194] Dr Weller does not think that the inconsistency between Stubbs's and Sainbel's portrayals of Eclipse's white markings is significant. 'Since horse passports were introduced, vets have had to draw horse's markings,' she says. 'The differences between what two vets will draw are amazing.'

institutions named after him, are tributes to his status. Not only does he endure as ancestor of every Thoroughbred alive today, but as an inspiration to veterinary research and education.

I mentioned Owens, Jordan, Bradman and Pele. But they are only human. There is something otherworldly, as Stubbs knew, about a great horse; something belonging to the realm of legend.

From the distance over the Downs, a chestnut Thoroughbred appears: galloping with head low, jockey motionless, the rest nowhere.

Sources

Chapter 1

Anon., *The Genuine Memoirs of Dennis O'Kelly, Esq*
Anon., *Nocturnal Revels*
Cook, *Eclipse and O'Kelly*
Gatrell, *City of Laughter*
Hitchcock, *Down and Out in Eighteenth-Century London*
Picard, *Dr Johnson's London*
Porter, *English Society in the 18th Century*
Weinreb and Hibbert (eds), *The London Encyclopaedia*
Williams, *History of the Name O'Kelly*
Town & Country magazine (September 1770)
Fleet prison debtors' schedules, London Metropolitan Archives
Papers of Colonel Andrew Dennis O'Kelly, Brynmor Jones Library, University of Hull

Chapter 2

Anon., *The Genuine Memoirs of Dennis O'Kelly, Esq*
Anon., *Nocturnal Revels*
Archenholz, *A Picture of England*
Brown, *A History of the Fleet Prison, London*
Burford, *Wits, Wenchers and Wantons*
Burford and Wotton *Private Vices — Public Virtues*
Clayton, *The British Museum Hogarth*
Hickey, *Memoirs*
Linnane, *Madams, Bawds and Brothel-Keepers of London*

Porter, *English Society in the 18th Century*
Rubenhold, *The Covent Garden Ladies*
Thompson, *The Meretriciad*
Weinreb and Hibbert (eds), *The London Encyclopaedia*
Fleet prison debtors' schedules, London Metropolitan Archives
Fleet records, National Archives
Noble Collection, Guildhall Library

Chapter 3

Anon., *Nocturnal Revels*
Bloch, *Sexual Life in England*
Blyth, *The High Tide of Pleasure*
Burford and Wotton, *Private Vices – Public Virtues*
Chinn, *Better Betting with a Decent Feller*
Cook, *Eclipse and O'Kelly*
Egan, *Sporting Anecdotes*
Harcourt, *The Gaming Calendar and Annals of Gaming*
Linnane, *Madams, Bawds and Brothel-Keepers of London*
Oxford English Dictionary
Picard, *Dr Johnson's London*
Pick, *An Authentic Historical Racing Calendar*
Porter, *English Society in the 18th Century*
Prior, *Early Records of the Thoroughbred*
Rice, *The History of the British Turf*
Rubenhold, *The Covent Garden Ladies*
Steinmetz, *The Gaming Table, Its Votaries and Victims*
Thompson, *The Meretriciad*
Thompson, *Newmarket*
Thormanby, *Sporting Stories* (1909)
The Sporting Magazine (1792, 1795)

Chapter 4

Cook, *Eclipse and O'Kelly*
Duke of Ancaster's Stud Book (1772–78)
FitzGerald, *Royal Thoroughbreds*
FitzGerald, *Thoroughbreds of the Crown*
Heber, *An Historical List* (1754, 1755, 1756)
Kiste, *King George II and Queen Caroline*

Longrigg, *The History of Horse Racing*
Magee, *Ascot: The History*
Mortimer, *The Jockey Club*
Newmarket Match Book (1754)
Oxford Dictionary of National Biography
Pick, *An Authentic Historical Racing Calendar*
Pond, *Sporting Kalendar* (1754, 1755, 1756)
Rice, *The History of the British Turf*
Seth-Smith, *Bred for the Purple*
Thompson, *Newmarket: From James I to the Present Day*
Walker, *An Historical List* (1769)
Lloyd's Evening Post (1765)
London Chronicle (1765)
London Evening Post (1765)
Pacemaker (October 2007)
St James's Chronicle (1765)
The Thoroughbred Record (1924)

Chapter 5

Blake, *George Stubbs and the Wide Creation*
Church, *Eclipse: The Horse, the Race, the Awards*
Clark, *A Short History of the Celebrated Race-horse Eclipse*
Cook, *Eclipse and O'Kelly*
FitzGerald, *Thoroughbreds of the Crown*
Fountain, *William Wildman and George Stubbs*
Heber, *An Historical List* (1764, 1765, 1768)
Lawrence, *The History and Delineation of the Horse*
Lawrence, *A Philosophical and Practical Treatise on Horses*
Lawrence and Scott, *The Sportsman's Repository*
Longrigg, *The History of Horse Racing*
Mortimer, *The History of the Derby Stakes*
Orchard, *Tattersalls*
Taplin, *The Gentleman's Stable Directory*
Williams, *UK Solar Eclipses from Year 1*
The Field (12 June 1937)
Lloyd's Evening Post (30 March–2 April 1764)
London Chronicle (22–24 March 1764; 3 April 1764)
London Evening Post (3–5 April 1764)
The Sporting Magazine (1814)

Chapter 6

Church, *Three Generations of Leading Sires*
Clark, *A Short History of the Celebrated Race-horse Eclipse*
Cook, *Eclipse and O'Kelly*
FitzGerald, *Royal Thoroughbreds*
Holcroft, *Memoirs of the Late Thomas Holcroft*
Lawrence, *A Philosophical and Practical Treatise on Horses*
Lawrence, *The History and Delineation of the Horse*
Lawrence and Scott, *The Sportsman's Repository*
Longrigg, *The History of Horse Racing*
Markham, *How to Choose, Ride, Train and Diet*
Morris, *Thoroughbred Stallions*
Mortimer, *The Jockey Club*
Prior, *Early Records of the Thoroughbred*
Rice, *The History of the British Turf*
Robertson, 'The Origin of the Thoroughbred'
Taunton, *Famous Horses*
Taunton, *Portraits of Celebrated Race Horses*
Thompson, *Newmarket: From James I to the Present Day*
Trew, *From 'Dawn' to 'Eclipse'*
Wentworth, *Thoroughbred Racing Stock*
Willett, *The Classic Racehorse*
The Field (25 December 1920)
Pedigreequery.com
TBHeritage.com

Chapter 7

Bawtree, *A Few Notes on Banstead Downs*
Church, *Eclipse: The Horse, the Race, the Awards*
Clark, *A Short History of the Celebrated Race-horse Eclipse*
Cook, *Eclipse and O'Kelly*
Curling, *British Racecourses*
Epsom Common
Gill, *Racecourses of Great Britain*
Grosley, *A Tour to London*
Heber, *An Historical List* (1766, 1768)
Home, *Epsom: Its History and Surroundings*
Hunn, *Epsom Racecourse*

Lawrence, *The History and Delineation of the Horse*
Lawrence, *A Philosophical and Practical Treatise on Horses*
Lillywhite, *London Coffee Houses*
Longrigg, *The History of Horse Racing*
O'Brien and Herbert, *Vincent O'Brien*
Pagones, *Dubai Millennium*
Picard, *Dr Johnson's London*
Piggott and Magee, *Lester's Derbys*
Porter, *English Society in the 18th Century*
Pownall, *Some Particulars Relating to the History of Epsom*
Rice, *The History of the British Turf*
Salter, *Epsom Town Downs and Common*
Waller, *1700: Scenes from London Life*
West, *Tavern Anecdotes*
Whyte, *History of the British Turf*
The Times digital archive (1787)
Town & Country (August 1770)
Coolmore.com
Epsom Salt Council website
Measuring Worth website

Chapter 8

Bawtree, *A Few Notes on Banstead Downs*
Church, *Eclipse: The Horse, the Race, the Awards*
Clark, *A Short History of the Celebrated Race-horse Eclipse*
Cook, *Eclipse and O'Kelly*
Egan, *Book of Sports*
Egerton, *George Stubbs, Painter*
Gill, *Racecourses of Great Britain*
Grosley, *A Tour to London*
Lawrence, *The History and Delineation of the Horse*
Lawrence and Scott, *The Sportsman's Repository*
Longrigg, *The History of Horse Racing*
Magee, *Ascot: The History*
Mortimer, *The Jockey Club*
Osbaldiston, *The British Sportsman*
Orton, *Turf Annals*
Pick, *An Authentic Historical Racing Calendar*
Porter, *London: A Social History*

Prior, *Early Records of the Thoroughbred*
Rice, *The History of the British Turf*
Salter, *Epsom Town Downs and Common*
Taunton, *Famous Horses*
Tuting and Fawconer, *The Sporting Calendar* (1769)
Walker, *An Historical List* (1769)
Whyte, *History of the British Turf*
The Sporting Magazine (September 1793; January 1794)

Chapter 9

Anon., *The Genuine Memoirs of Dennis O'Kelly, Esq*
Burford, *Royal St James's*
Church, *Eclipse: The Horse, the Race, the Awards*
Clark, *A Short History of the Celebrated Race-horse Eclipse*
Cook, *Eclipse and O'Kelly*
Egerton, *George Stubbs, Painter*
FitzGerald, *Royal Thoroughbreds*
Lawrence, *The History and Delineation of the Horse*
Longrigg, *The History of Horse Racing*
Orchard, *Tattersalls*
Orton, *Turf Annals*
Pick, *An Authentic Historical Racing Calendar*
Rede, *Anecdotes and Biography*
Rice, *The History of the British Turf*
Seth-Smith, *Bred for the Purple*
Thompson, *Newmarket: From James I to the Present Day*
Tuting and Fawconer, *The Sporting Calendar* (1769, 1770)
Walker, *An Historical List* (1769, 1770)
The Sporting Magazine (September 1793)
Town & Country (August 1770; September 1770)
York Courant (14 August 1770; 2 October 1770)

Chapter 10

Anon., *Nocturnal Revels*
Anon. (Charles Pigott), *The Jockey Club*
Archenholz, *A Picture of England*
Burford, *Royal St James's*
Burford, *Wits, Wenchers and Wantons*

Burford and Wotton, *Private Vices – Public Virtues*
Hickey, *Memoirs*
Linnane, *Madams, Bawds and Brothel-Keepers of London*
'OMIAH: An Ode Addressed to Charlotte Hayes'
Rubenhold, *The Covent Garden Ladies*
Thompson, *The Courtesan*
Thompson, *The Meretriciad*
Weinreb and Hibbert (eds), *The London Encyclopaedia*
Annual Register (1774)
The London Magazine (1772)
The Times (September 1815)
Town & Country (February 1769)

Chapter 11

Black, *The Jockey Club and Its Founders*
Cain, *The Home Run Horse*
Conley, *Stud*
Cook, *Eclipse and O'Kelly*
Egerton, *George Stubbs, Painter*
FitzGerald, *Thoroughbreds of the Crown*
Fountain, *William Wildman and George Stubbs*
Harding, *An Elegy on the Famous Old Horse Marsk*
Lawrence, *The History and Delineation of the Horse*
Lawrence and Scott, *The Sportsman's Repository*
Orchard, *Tattersalls*
Orton, *Turf Annals*
Pick, *An Authentic Historical Racing Calendar*
Randall and Morris, *Guinness Horse Racing: The Records*
Taunton, *Portraits of Celebrated Race Horses*
Tuting and Fawconer, *The Sporting Calendar* (1769, 1770)
Walker, *An Historical List* (1769, 1770)
Willett, *The Classic Racehorse*
Willett, *The Story of Tattersalls*
Racing Calendar
Racing Post Bloodstock Review 2007
The Sporting Magazine (January 1794)
TBHeritage.com

Chapter 12

Black, *The Jockey Club and Its Founders*
Curling, *British Racecourses*
Derby Day 200
Gill, *Racecourses of Great Britain*
Longrigg, *The History of Horse Racing*
Magee, *Ascot: The History*
Mortimer, *The History of the Derby Stakes*
Thompson, *Newmarket: From James I to the Present Day*
Towers, *An Introduction to a General Stud Book*
Tyrrel, *Running Racing*
Willett, *The Classic Racehorse*
Willett, *A History of the General Stud Book*
Guardian (21 March 2006)
Racing Calendar
The Sporting Magazine (June 1814)
British Horseracing Authority website
The Cox Library website
The Jockey Club website
TBHeritage.com
Weatherbys website

Chapter 13

Anon., *The Genuine Memoirs of Dennis O'Kelly, Esq*
Black, *The Jockey Club and Its Founders*
Cook, *Eclipse and O'Kelly*
Egan, *Boxiana*
Egan, *Sporting Anecdotes*
Epsom Common
Harcourt, *The Gaming Calendar and Annals of Gaming*
Lawrence, *The History and Delineation of the Horse*
Lawrence and Scott, *The Sportsman's Repository*
Parsons, Philip, *Newmarket: Or an Essay on the Turf*
Shoemaker, *The London Mob*
Steinmetz, *The Gaming Table, Its Votaries and Victims*
Thormanby, *Sporting Stories*
Waugh, *Will This Do?*
White, *Ancient Epsom*

Annual Register (1775)
Independent on Sunday (February 1998)
The Sporting Magazine (September 1793; June 1814)
The Times (March 1786)
Town & Country (September 1770)
HotBoxingNews.com
Clay Hill papers, Surrey History Centre
Papers of Colonel Andrew Dennis O'Kelly, Brynmor Jones Library, University of Hull

Chapter 14

Anon., *The Genuine Memoirs of Dennis O'Kelly, Esq*
Anon., *The Minor Jockey Club*
Buss, *The North London Collegiate School*
Cook, *Eclipse and O'Kelly*
Fraser, *William Stukely and the Gout*
Harcourt, *The Gaming Calendar and Annals of Gaming*
Hickey, *Memoirs*
Picard, *Dr Johnson's London*
Porter, *English Society in the 18th Century*
Shoemaker, *The London Mob*
Steinmetz, *The Gaming Table, Its Votaries and Victims*
Thormanby, *Sporting Stories*
Williams, *History of the Name O'Kelly*
Gentleman's Magazine (1787, 1802)
Racing Calendar
The Sporting Magazine (October 1792; February 1796; March 1796)
The Times digital archive
Whitehall Evening Post (1 January 1788)
Canons records, North London Collegiate School
Papers of Colonel Andrew Dennis O'Kelly, Brynmor Jones Library, University of Hull
Plumer papers, London Metropolitan Archives

Chapter 15

Church, *Eclipse: The Horse, the Race, the Awards*
Clark, *A Short History of the Celebrated Race-horse Eclipse*

Cook, *Eclipse and O'Kelly*

Egan, *Sporting Anecdotes*

Mortimer, Onslow and Willett, *Biographical Encyclopaedia of British Flat Racing*

Orton, *Turf Annals*

Sainbel, *Elements of Veterinary Art*

Taunton, *Portraits of Celebrated Race Horses*

Trew, *From 'Dawn' to 'Eclipse'*

Gentleman's Magazine (1787 supplement)

Monthly Review (1788)

Racing Calendar

Racing Post Bloodstock Review 2007

The Times digital archive

Whitehall Evening Post (2 January 1788; 7–10 March 1788)

World Fashionable Advertiser (7, 8, 12 January 1788)

Pedigreequery.com

St Lawrence, Little Stanmore, burial records, London Metropolitan Archives

Will of Dennis O'Kelly, National Archives

Chapter 16

Burford and Wotton, *Private Vices – Public Virtues*

Cook, *Eclipse and O'Kelly*

Fitzpatrick, *Secret Service Under Pitt*

Picard, *Dr Johnson's London*

Porter, *English Society in the 18th Century*

Weinreb and Hibbert (eds), *The London Encyclopaedia*

Gentleman's Magazine (1802)

The Newgate Calendar (exclassics.com)

Racing Calendar

The Times digital archive

Traceyclann.com

Fleet prison debtors' schedules, London Metropolitan Archives

Papers of Colonel Andrew Dennis O'Kelly, Brynmor Jones Library, University of Hull

Plumer papers, London Metropolitan Archives

Wills of Andrew Dennis O'Kelly and Charles Andrew O'Kelly, National Archives

Chapter 17

Anon. (Charles Pigott), *The Jockey Club*
Cook, *Eclipse and O'Kelly*
FitzGerald, *Thoroughbreds of the Crown*
Longrigg, *The History of Horse Racing*
Magee, *Ascot: The History*
Mortimer, *The History of the Derby Stakes*
Mortimer, Onslow and Willett, *Biographical Encyclopaedia of British Flat Racing*
Thompson, *Newmarket: From James I to the Present Day*
Tyrrel, *Running Racing*
Whyte, *History of the British Turf*
Racing Calendar
The Sporting Magazine (September 1793)
The Times digital archive
Fitzwilliam/Langdale papers, Public Record Office, Northern Ireland
Papers of Colonel Andrew Dennis O'Kelly, Brynmor Jones Library, University of Hull

Chapter 18

Blake, *George Stubbs and the Wide Creation*
Cook, *Eclipse and O'Kelly*
Egerton, *British Sporting and Animal Paintings*
Egerton, *George Stubbs, Painter*
Grego, *Rowlandson the Caricaturist*
Lawrence, *The History and Delineation of the Horse*
Noakes, *Sportsmen in a Landscape*
The Sporting Magazine (January 1794)

Chapter 19

Blake, *George Stubbs and the Wide Creation*
Derby Day 200
Egerton, *George Stubbs, Painter*
Longrigg, *The History of Horse Racing*
Magee, *Ascot: The History*
Mortimer, *The History of the Derby Stakes*
Mortimer, Onslow and Willett, *Biographical Encyclopaedia of British Flat Racing*

Noakes, *Sportsmen in a Landscape*
Randall and Morris, *A Century of Champions*
Thompson, *Newmarket: From James I to the Present Day*
Willett, *The Classic Racehorse*
Annual Register (1844)
Pedigreequery.com
TBHeritage.com
Victorian-cinema.net

Chapter 20

Church, *Eclipse: The Horse, the Race, the Awards*
Lennox, *Northern Dancer*
Longrigg, *The History of Horse Racing*
Mortimer, Onslow and Willett, *Biographical Encyclopaedia of British Flat Racing*
Pagones, *Dubai Millennium*
Randall and Morris, *A Century of Champions*
Guardian (November 2005)
Observer (October 2005)
Ascot.co.uk
Australian Government Culture and Recreation website/ Melbourne Cup
Horsesonly.com (Mariana Haun, 'The X Factor')
National Museum of Australia website
SportingChronicle.com

Chapter 21

Black, *The Jockey Club and Its Founders*
Church, *Eclipse: The Horse, the Race, the Awards*
Clark, *A Short History of the Celebrated Race-horse Eclipse*
Cook, *Eclipse and O'Kelly*
Hall, 'The Story of a Skeleton: Eclipse'
Sainbel, *Elements of Veterinary Art*
Weinreb and Hibbert (eds), *The London Encyclopaedia*
Wentworth, *Thoroughbred Racing Stock*
The British Racehorse (November 1963)
The Veterinary Record (March 1991)
Royal Veterinary College website

Appendix 1

Eclipse's Racing Career

When details differ, I have given the sources:

* Tuting and Fawconer, *The Sporting Calendar* (1769, 1770)
† B. Walker, *An Historical List of Horse-Matches, Plates and Prizes, Run for in Great Britain and Ireland* (1769, 1770)
‡ Bracy Clark, *A Short History of the Celebrated Race-horse Eclipse* (1835)
§ William Pick, *An Authentic Historical Racing Calendar* (1785)
¶ John Orton, *Turf Annals of York and Doncaster* (1844)

1769

3 May, Epsom. Noblemen and Gentlemen's Plate, for horses that have not won £30 (matches excepted). Four-mile heats. Five-year-olds (Eclipse, Gower, Trial), 8st* (8st 7lb†); six-year-olds (Chance, Plume), 9st 3lb; older horses, 9st 13lb. Winner, £50.
Heat 1: **1st Eclipse** (Mr Wildman); 2nd Gower (Mr Fortescue); 3rd Chance (Mr Castle); 4th Trial (Mr Jennings); 5th Plume (Mr Quick).
Heat 2: **1st Eclipse**; distanced Gower, Chance, Trial, Plume.
Betting: (heat 1) 1-4 Eclipse; (heat 2) 6-4, 5-4, evens Eclipse to distance field.
(Jockey: John Oakley)

29 May, Ascot. Noblemen and Gentlemen's Plate. Two-mile heats. Four-year-olds, 8st 5lb; five-year-olds (Eclipse, Cream de Barbade), 9st 3lb. Winner, £50.

Heat 1: **1st Eclipse** (Mr Wildman); 2nd Cream de Barbade (Mr Fettyplace).
Heat 2: **1st Eclipse**; 2nd Cream de Barbade.
Betting: 1-8 Eclipse.

13 June, Winchester. King's Plate. Four-mile heats. For six-year-olds; 12st (younger horses carry same weight). (Six-year-olds Slouch, Chigger, Juba, Caliban, Clanvil; five-year-old Eclipse.) Winner, 100 guineas.
Heat 1: **1st Eclipse** (Mr Wildman); 2nd Slouch (Mr Turner); 3rd Chigger (Duke of Grafton); 4th Juba (Mr Gott); distanced Caliban (Mr O'Kelly), Clanvil (Mr Bailey).
Heat 2: **1st Eclipse**; 2nd Slouch; 3rd Chigger; 4th Juba.
Betting: (heat 1) 5-4* (evens†) Eclipse; 5-2, 3-1* (2-1†) Caliban; 2-1, 3-1 Chigger; 5-1, 6-1* (4-1†) Slouch; (heat 2) 1-10 Eclipse.

15 June, Winchester. City Plate. Four-mile heats. Five-year-olds (Eclipse) and six-year-olds; 10st; older horses, 10st 7lb. Winner, £50.
1st Eclipse (Mr Wildman) walked over.

28 June, Salisbury. King's Plate. Four-mile heats. For six-year-olds; 12st (younger horses carry same weight). Winner, 100 guineas.
1st Eclipse (Mr Wildman) walked over.

29 June, Salisbury. City Plate. Four-mile heats. 10st. Winner, silver bowl and 30 guineas.
Heat 1: **1st Eclipse** (Mr Wildman); 2nd Sulphur (Mr Fettyplace); distanced Forrester (Mr Taylor).
Heat 2: **1st Eclipse**; 2nd Sulphur.
Betting: 1-10* (1-8†) Eclipse.

25 July, Canterbury. King's Plate. Four-mile heats. For six-year-olds; 12st* (12st 1lb†) (younger horses carry same weight). Winner, 100 guineas.
1st Eclipse (Mr Wildman) walked over.

27 July, Lewes. King's Plate. Four-mile heats. For six-year-olds; 12st (younger horses carry same weight). (Six-year-old Kingston; five-year-old Eclipse.) Winner, 100 guineas.
Heat 1: **1st Eclipse** (Mr Wildman); 2nd Kingston (Mr Strode).
Heat 2: **1st Eclipse**; 2nd Kingston.
(Jockey: John Whiting‡)

19 September, Lichfield. King's Plate. Three-mile heats. For five-year-olds; 8st 7lb. Winner, 100 guineas.
Heat 1: **1st Eclipse** (Mr Wildman); 2nd Tardy (Mr Freeth).
Heat 2: **1st Eclipse**; 2nd Tardy.
Betting: 1-7 Eclipse.

9 races, 9 wins, including 5 King's Plates. Prize money: £706.50.

1770

17 April, Newmarket. Beacon Course (4 miles, 1 furlong, 138 yards). 8st 7lb.
Eclipse (Mr Wildman) beat Bucephalus (Mr Wentworth). Winner, 1,000 guineas (Mr Wildman contributed 400 guineas; Mr Wentworth contributed 600 guineas).

19 April, Newmarket. Round Course. King's Plate. Four-mile heats. For six-year-olds; 12st (younger horses carry same weight). Six-year-olds Diana (mare), Chigger; five-year-olds Eclipse, Pensioner. Winner, 100 guineas.
Heat 1: **1st Eclipse** (Mr O'Kelly); 2nd Diana (Mr Fenwick); 3rd Pensioner (Mr Strode); 4th Chigger (Duke of Grafton). Diana and Chigger withdrawn.
Heat 2: **1st Eclipse**; distanced Pensioner.
Betting: (heat 1) 1-10* (1-15†) Eclipse; (heat 2) 6-4*, 7-4§ Eclipse to distance Pensioner.

5 June, Guildford. King's Plate. Four-mile heats. For six-year-olds; 12st (younger horses carry same weight). Winner, 100 guineas.
1st Eclipse (Mr O'Kelly) walked over.

3 July, Nottingham. King's Plate. Four-mile heats. For six-year-olds; 12st (younger horses carry same weight). Winner, 100 guineas.
1st Eclipse (Mr O'Kelly) walked over.

20 August, York. King's Plate. Four-mile heats. For six-year-olds; 12st (younger horses carry same weight). Winner, 100 guineas.
1st Eclipse (Mr O'Kelly) walked over.
(Jockey: Samuel Merriott¶)

23 August, York. Great Subscription. Four miles. For six-year-olds and upwards. Six-year-old Eclipse (8st 7lb); seven-year-old Bellario (9st); eight-year-old Tortoise (9st). Winner, £319 10s.

1st Eclipse (Mr O'Kelly); 2nd Tortoise (Mr Wentworth); 3rd Bellario (Sir Charles Bunbury).

Betting: 1-20 Eclipse; 4-7 Tortoise to beat Bellario. 1-100 Eclipse in running.

(Jockey: Samuel Merriott¶)

3 September, Lincoln. King's Plate. Four-mile heats. For six-year-olds; 12st (younger horses carry same weight). Winner, 100 guineas.
1st Eclipse (Mr O'Kelly) walked over.

3 October, Newmarket. Beacon Course (4 miles, 1 furlong, 138 yards). For six-year-olds, 8st 10lb (younger horses carry same weight); older horses, 9st 2lb. Six-year-old Eclipse; five-year-old Corsican. Subscription 30 guineas† (O'Kelly paid 100 guineas*‡). Winner, 150 guineas (one quarter of 20 subscriptions of 30 guineas each†).
1st Eclipse (Mr O'Kelly); 2nd Corsican (Sir Charles Bunbury).
Betting: 1-70 Eclipse.

4 October, Newmarket. King's Plate. Four-mile heats. For six-year-olds; 12st (younger horses carry same weight). Winner, 100 guineas.
1st Eclipse (Mr O'Kelly) walked over.

9 races, 9 wins, including 6 King's Plates. Prize money: £2,157.

Overall record: 18 races, 18 wins, including 11 King's Plates. Prize money: £2,863.50.

Jockeys

Details about Eclipse's jockeys are sparse. The earliest report that John Oakley was in the saddle for Eclipse's Epsom debut comes in William Pick's *Authentic Historical Racing Calendar* (1785). John Lawrence, who did not see Eclipse race but did see him at stud, says that 'we believe' that Oakley 'generally, or always rode Eclipse'. But when in 1793 George Stubbs painted a copy of *Eclipse at Newmarket, with a Groom and Jockey* (the original is dated 1770), the exhibition catalogue identified the jockey as 'Samuel Merrit, who generally rode him'; John Orton wrote that Merriott (the more usual spelling) rode Eclipse at York. Bracy Clark, in his record of the 1769 King's

Plate at Lewes, wrote, 'Eyewitnesses say that John Whiting rode him this time; whether Oakley, his constant groom, always rode him is not certain.' The Turf historian James Christie Whyte asserted that '[Dennis] Fitzpatrick and John Oakley rode him in almost all his races'. According to the dates in Orton's *Turf Annals*, however, Fitzpatrick (the first Irish jockey to ride in England) was the same age as Eclipse – in other words, in 1769 he was five.

Bracy Clark's mention of Oakley as Eclipse's 'constant groom' is arresting. In the days before race-riding became a distinct role, grooms usually doubled as race-riders. If Oakley were the groom, he – knowing the headstrong horse best – would have been a good choice of rider for Eclipse's first race.

Is Oakley the groom – or, as the catalogue copy puts it, 'the boy who looked after him' – in Stubbs's painting? Eclipse may have belonged by this time to Dennis O'Kelly, who commissioned Stubbs; we do not know whether the groom would have changed stables with the horse. John Orton, though, described Oakley as a rider, chiefly for Lord Abingdon.

There is a jockey on board Eclipse in the Sartorius picture of Eclipse and Shakespeare. He looks a bit like the jockey in the Stubbs painting; but you could not swear that he is the same person. Another Sartorius painting is entitled *Eclipse with Oakley Up*. John Nost Sartorius was not painting at the time of Eclipse's racing career, but may have copied studies by his father, Francis.

One is inclined to treat all these reports with caution. The earliest ones, identifying Oakley at Epsom (Pick) and Merriott at Newmarket (Stubbs), seem to be the most trustworthy.

Appendix 2

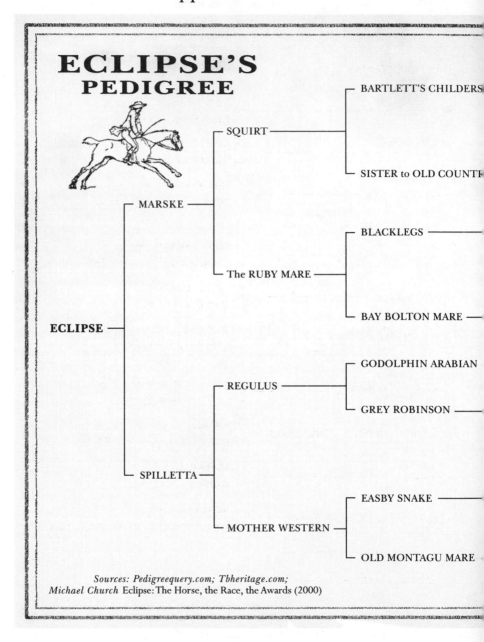

ECLIPSE'S PEDIGREE

- ECLIPSE
  - MARSKE
    - SQUIRT
      - BARTLETT'S CHILDERS
      - SISTER to OLD COUNTR
    - The RUBY MARE
      - BLACKLEGS
      - BAY BOLTON MARE
  - SPILLETTA
    - REGULUS
      - GODOLPHIN ARABIAN
      - GREY ROBINSON
    - MOTHER WESTERN
      - EASBY SNAKE
      - OLD MONTAGU MARE

Sources: Pedigreequery.com; Tbheritage.com;
Michael Church Eclipse: The Horse, the Race, the Awards (2000)

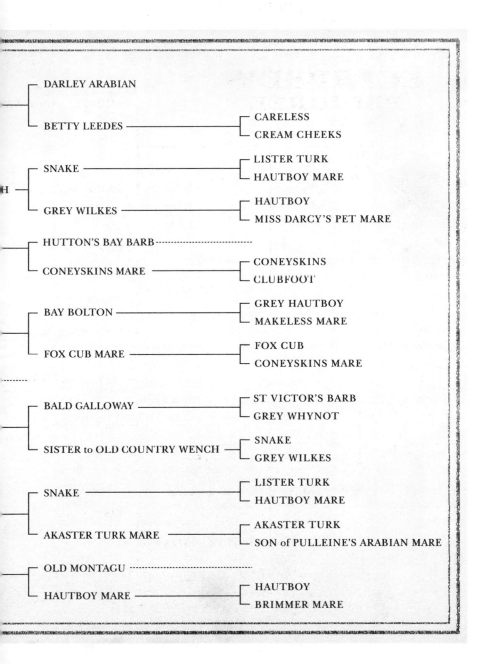

James Weatherby and William Sydney Towers, publisher and author respectively of *An Introduction to a General Stud Book* (1791), did an impressive job of introducing authority to the publication of pedigrees, sorting through previous haphazard compilations. Towers' account of Eclipse's breeding continues to be the one – small updates apart – you will see most commonly reproduced. But doubts, some of them ineradicable, surround the identities of several of the great horse's ancestors. In two instances, the *GSB* version is likely to be wrong.

The Sire's Side
Marske and Shakespeare

Eclipse is a son of Marske, according to all the published pedigrees. But as soon as Eclipse became famous, there was gossip about his paternity. The father was not Marske, some said, but a stallion called Shakespeare, whose claims had been suppressed by conspiracy (see also chapter 5).

These rumours were potentially damaging to William Wildman. Cannily, he had bought Marske as soon as he saw the potential of Eclipse, realizing that Marske's value as a stallion would shoot up once the ability of his son was known. By the time Eclipse had retired from his unbeaten career, Wildman was advertising Marske – whose services, when he was at the Duke of Cumberland's stud, had been considered to be worth no more than half a guinea – at a covering fee of thirty guineas. He had to prevent breeders, hoping to get another Eclipse, from entertaining the idea that they should send their mares to Shakespeare instead. One early attempt to quell the rumours was an advertisement in Tuting and Fawconer's 1771 racing calendar: the ad contained a signed statement by Bernard Smith, the stud groom of the Duke of Cumberland, asserting that Marske was Eclipse's sire. But it did not convince all men of the Turf. The bloodstock auctioneer Richard Tattersall argued, 'for Shakespeare was a large and strong chestnut with white legs and face who got chestnuts and was a good runner. Marske was a bad runner, a brown, who got brown or bay. Mr O'Kelly's groom says Eclipse's dam was covered by both, and first by Shakespeare.'[196]

There are three flaws in Tattersall's reasoning. First, while Shakespeare was the winner of two King's Plates, and while Marske was inconsistent, Marske did win a Jockey Club Plate; his two defeats by the outstanding Snap were no disgrace. Second, fathers do not dictate the hair colouring of their offspring, either in equine or in human breeding; indeed,

[196] Quoted in Theodore Cook's *Eclipse and O'Kelly*.

the same sire and dam may produce variously coloured foals. Marske mated, indisputably, twice more with Eclipse's dam Spilletta: their daughter Proserpine (1766) was bay; their son Garrick (1772) was chestnut. Third, why should Dennis O'Kelly's groom have possessed any authority in the matter? Eclipse was born at the Duke of Cumberland's stud.

William Taplin, in *The Gentleman's Stable Directory* (1791), asserted that the Duke of Cumberland and his groom were uncertain whether Marske or Shakespeare was Eclipse's sire, but resolved the issue by calculating that 'the time of the mare's bringing forth (during the great Eclipse) coming nearest to the day she was booked to have been covered by Marske, to him was attributed the distinguished honour of getting one of the first horses of the known world'. Taplin seems to be saying that Marske's more recent covering of Spilletta is evidence that he was the father. That evidence demonstrates nothing, and perhaps what he means is that Marske covered Spilletta eleven months (a horse's gestation period) before the birth.

This must be the meaning of 'she came to Marske's time' in John Lawrence's account, the fullest summary of this problem. In *The History and Delineation of the Horse* (1809), Lawrence wrote:

> It has always been taken for granted, that he [Eclipse] was a son of Marske, a fact, beyond the power of man to ascertain. Eclipse's dam was covered both by Shakespeare and Marske, and she came to Marske's time, so the honour was awarded to him. If I recollect awright, she had missed by him the previous year. But the circumstance of a mare coming regularly to her time, determines nothing, since they are so uncertain in that respect, in which I have repeatedly known variations from a week or ten days, to two or three weeks. Great stress was laid upon the supposed likeness of Basilius, one of the earliest sons of Eclipse, to old Marske, and indeed the resemblance appeared to me strong; but I could discover no common family resemblance between Eclipse and his presumed full-brother Garrick. On the other hand, I think Eclipse strongly resembled the family of Shakespeare, in colour, in certain particulars of form, and in temper. Nothing can be more unimportant than these speculations, and Eclipse's pedigree would suffer no loss of honour or credit, should Shakespeare be placed at the head of it; which horse had more of the Darley Arabian in him, than Marske, and in all respects, was equally well-bred, and full as good a runner. Shakespeare, like Marske, was a great-grandson of the Darley Arabian, through Hobgoblin and Aleppo, and his dam the little Hartley mare, the dam also of Blank, was a grand-daughter of the same Arabian, and out of the famous Flying Whig. One or two of the sons of

Eclipse, still alive, appear to me strongly to resemble the Shakespeare.

It is necessary, however, to subjoin the late intelligence on this subject, with which I have been favoured by Mr Sandiver, of Newmarket, which goes to assert, on the authority of the stud-groom, that Eclipse's dam really never was covered by Shakespeare. On this I can only observe, that in the year 1778, I was frequently in the habit of visiting Old Eclipse, then at Epsom, on which occasions I often discoursed the subject of the disputed pedigree, with Colonel O'Kelly's then groom, who assured me that the mare was covered by Shakespeare, which account I also had from various other persons, as a well-known fact. And to conceal nothing, it had been reported, that a groom had been bribed to ascribe the get of Eclipse to Marske, there being a strong interest in the reputation of that stallion.

You would have thought that the evidence of a groom at the Duke of Cumberland's stud, where Eclipse had been born, would be more authoritative than that of a groom working for Dennis O'Kelly, who acquired the horse six years later. But Lawrence appears to have given the accounts equal weight. He went on to reproduce the J. N. Sartorius picture – presumably commissioned by someone keen to make a point – of Shakespeare and Eclipse. We, no longer believing that a father invariably stamps his appearance on his children, cannot accept likeness to one sire or lack of likeness to another as evidence of paternity.

In 1763, when Eclipse was conceived, Marske and Spilletta both lived at Cranbourne Lodge, where the Duke of Cumberland had his stud. Shakespeare was standing at Catterick, North Yorkshire. Would Cumberland's staff have sent Spilletta to Yorkshire to be covered by Shakespeare, and then put her to Marske; or have put her to Marske, and then sent her to Shakespeare? Either option seems eccentric. But what convinces me that Marske was Eclipse's father is that the earliest records say he was. The Royal Stud Book at Windsor contains a note of the following entry for Cumberland's 'sucker' (foal) in a match at Newmarket:

Mask [sic], out of Spilletta a chesnut colt, with a bald face, and the off hind leg, white up to the hock. First spring meeting. Match against the Duke of Grafton's colt, by Doctor; Lord Rockingham's colt, by the Godolphin Hunter; Lord Bolingbroke's colt, by Damascus; Lord Gower's colt, by Sweepstakes; Lord Orford's colt, by Feather; Mr Shafto's colt, by his Hunter.

The 1764 *Racing Calendar* also noted the forthcoming match for 'RH the Duke's C. [colt] got by Mask, his dam by Regulus'. Cumberland and his competitors, the entry stated, would each advance 100 guineas for the race, to be run on the Duke's course, with the racers carrying 8st 10lb, during Easter week in 1768.

The next document is the catalogue of the sale of the late Duke of Cumberland's stud on 23 December 1765. Lot number 29 is 'A chesnut colt got by Mask', knocked down to William Wildman for forty-five guineas. Eclipse. There were eighteen broodmares in the sale. Of those covered in 1765, seven had been to Marske. None had been to Shakespeare. There is no record of Cumberland's ever having sent a mare to Shakespeare.

In 1764 and 1765, no one had any reason to tamper with the records. Marske was an unfashionable stallion; his siring of an ungainly chestnut yearling was not going to improve his profile. Only when Eclipse started racing did Marske's value soar. *Then*, his connections had a strong incentive to promote him as Eclipse's sire; but not six years earlier. So the match book entry and sale document are probably truthful.

The Shakespeare rumours did not compromise Marske's career. Sold by Wildman to the Earl of Abingdon, Marske went on to command the extraordinary covering fee of 100 guineas. He was champion sire in 1775 and 1776.

Bartlett's Childers

Marske was a son of Squirt, who was a son of Bartlett's Childers. A full brother (by the Darley Arabian, out of Betty Leedes) to the great Flying Childers, Bartlett's Childers (born in 1716) tended to break blood vessels in hard exercise, and was sometimes known as 'Bleeding Childers'. He never raced. There is a tiny doubt that he ever existed. However, contemporary references to him in the racing calendar of John Cheny and in the stud book of Cuthbert Routh, a Yorkshire breeder, argue in his favour. Cheny wrote that 'many gentlemen of honour' asserted that there were two Childers brothers.

Spanker Mare

Betty Leedes, dam of Bartlett's Childers, appears in the *General Stud Book* as the daughter of Cream Cheeks, and as the granddaughter of the Spanker Mare. Bred by James Darcy (son of Charles II's master of the stud), the Spanker Mare (born in about 1665) was the product of a mating between Spanker and his mother, the Old Morocco Mare. The Spanker Mare thus had the Old Morocco Mare as her mother and grandmother; in the formula of bloodstock breeding, she was inbred to the Old Morocco Mare 2 × 1 (two generations back as well as one generation back). (Spanker was also Betty Leedes's grandfather on her sire's side.)

Some historians find this close inbreeding distasteful, and question whether James Darcy would have indulged in it. The Thoroughbred Heritage website suggests that it is 'more likely' that the Old Morocco Mare mated with a horse called Young Spanker – her grandson. But Lady Wentworth, author of *Thoroughbred Racing Stock*, insisted that the mother/son union accorded with 'the Arab principle' – than which, in her book, there could be no higher.

The Spanker Mare, daughter of the incestuous union, supposedly gave birth to a full sister to Cream Cheeks called Betty Percival. In 2002, researchers at the Department of Genetics at Trinity College, Dublin, published their account of tests of two horses tracing back in the female line to Betty Percival, and of one tracing back in the female line to Cream Cheeks. The DNA of the Cream Cheeks descendant did not match that of the Betty Percival descendants. The finding meant that Cream Cheeks and Betty Percival had different dams.

Which was the daughter of the Spanker Mare? There was already evidence that it was not Cream Cheeks. In *Early Records of the Thoroughbred* (1924), C. M. Prior quoted Cuthbert Routh's claim that Cream Cheeks's dam was 'a famous roan mare of Sir Marmaduke Wyvill's'. Routh and Wyvill were neighbours.

Does this finding remove incest from Eclipse's background? Not necessarily. Another of his ancestors is Charming Jenny, a third daughter of the Leedes Arabian and the Spanker Mare.

The Dam's Side
The Cumberland Dispersal Sale Catalogue

The entry, with original spelling, reads: 'A chesnut Colt, got by Mask, his dam by a full brother to Williams's Squirrel, his great grandam by Lord Darcey's Montague, his great great grandam by Hautboy, his great great great grandam by Brimmer.' You will notice that the grandam's generation is missing. The entry should read: 'his dam by Regulus [or should it? – see below], his *grandam* by a full brother to Williams's Squirrel', etc. The compiler of the catalogue seems to have got the pedigree confused with the similar one of a mare in the sale, Miss Western.

Spilletta (sometimes spelled 'Spiletta')

According to the stud book of her later owner, the Duke of Ancaster, she was a chestnut, not a bay as recorded in the *GSB*.

Born in 1749, Spilletta was officially the daughter of the stallion Regulus, and out of a mare called Mother Western. But in 1754, the year of her unsuccessful racing season, she was listed in Reginald Heber's racing calendar as a daughter of Sedbury. John Pond, in his 1754 racing calendar, hedged his bets, listing her as Sedbury's on one page and as Regulus's on another. Our justification for assigning her to Regulus is that this is the more recent version, and the one that became accepted.

Mother Western

Spilletta's breeder, Sir Robert Eden, certainly did mate Mother Western with Sedbury to get a filly called Miss Western (born in 1746). She was also bought by the Duke of Cumberland; it was her pedigree that got confused with Eclipse's in the dispersal sale catalogue.

Mother Western's sire is officially Easby Snake (or 'Smith's Son of Snake'). But in the earliest records of Miss Western's racing career, her dam (Mother Western) is listed as by 'Sir Marmaduke Wyvill's Scarborough Colt'. This is the version in both Pond's and Heber's 1751 racing calendars; Heber maintains it in 1752, but Pond switches to 'a full brother to Mr Williams's Squirrel' – Easby Snake. Again, the later version became the one that was perpetuated.

In this case, there is a reason to doubt the official version. In the 1748 and 1749 editions of Cheny's racing calendar, there are announcements for races involving two of Sir Robert Eden's colts: the colts are out of mares, or more probably a mare, whose sire is the Scarborough Colt. Sir Robert owned only a few horses. It is possible that this mare is Mother Western. If so, one can only be baffled at why the record of her sire changed. As we have seen, however, this sort of thing happened a lot.

Implications

As I have explained, I do not believe that Shakespeare was Eclipse's sire. But what if he were? Like Marske, he was a great-grandson in the male line of the Darley Arabian; he was also a great-grandson of the Darley Arabian in the female line (i.e., he was inbred to the Darley Arabian 3 × 3). His presence in Eclipse's pedigree would increase significantly the number of strains of the Darley Arabian in modern Thoroughbreds. It would also reduce the number of strains of the Lister Turk, who does not appear in Shakespeare's background.

The removal of the Spanker Mare from Eclipse's pedigree would, disappointingly, delete two strains of Old Bald Peg – the Spanker Mare's great-grandmother on the father's side, and grandmother on the mother's side (3 × 2). (Or the Spanker Mare may – see above – have been the daughter of Young Spanker, in which case the inbreeding to Old Bald Peg would be 4 × 3. Young Spanker appears in only one contemporary record, and not in the *General Stud Book*; we know nothing of his female ancestry.)

Old Bald Peg is an iconic horse for historians of the Thoroughbred. Of pure Eastern blood (the *General Stud Book* describes her as the daughter of an Arabian and a Barb mare), she lived at Helmsley in Yorkshire. She was the property of the Duke of Buckingham and then, when Helmsley was seized by the Commonwealth, of Thomas Fairfax, Oliver Cromwell's commander-in-chief. Later, Buckingham found his way back to Helmsley, thanks to a marriage with Fairfax's daughter. By sending Old Bald Peg's daughter, the Old Morocco Mare (born in about 1655), to the Darcy stud to meet the Yellow Turk, Buckingham bred Spanker, the outstanding racehorse of Charles II's reign.

Old Bald Peg is at the root of what pedigree experts call family number six. The numbering system was the invention of an Australian researcher called Bruce Lowe, who at the end of the nineteenth century traced back the tail female lines of winners of classic races, and numbered the lines to reflect their successes. Tail female descendants of Tregonwell's Natural Barb Mare had won the most classics, and went into family number one; the Burton Barb Mare was at the root of family number two, and so on. (Eclipse descends in tail female from a Royal Mare listed as the tap-root of family number twelve.) The list went down to number forty-three. However, the genetic evidence cited above appears to show that Cream Cheeks, Bartlett's Childers's mother and therefore Eclipse's great-great-great-grandmother, may not have been Old Bald Peg's tail female descendant, and therefore was not a member of family number six. Her removal diminishes the influence of that family, and of Old Bald Peg on pedigrees in general.

If Sedbury, not Regulus, were the sire of Eclipse's dam Spilletta, the Godolphin Arabian would disappear from Eclipse's pedigree. The number of strains of the Godolphin Arabian in contemporary Thoroughbreds would be greatly reduced; and the number of strains of the Byerley Turk would be greatly increased. Regulus was the Godolphin Arabian's son; Sedbury was the Byerley Turk's great-grandson. Sedbury was also a descendant of the Helmsley Turk, an important early sire but one who does not appear in Eclipse's official pedigree. However, I am inclined to believe that Spilletta's sire's name changed from Sedbury to Regulus in the early records as a result of proper correction.

I have doubts, though, about Eclipse's damsire, for reasons stated above. The inclusion of the Scarborough Colt in place of Easby Snake in the pedigree would introduce to it a new name, the Thoulouse Barb. He was the Scarborough Colt's tail male grandfather, and had been imported at the end of the seventeenth century by a Cumberland breeder, Henry Curwen, who had bought him from Louis XIV. The Scarborough Colt was also a descendant – as Easby Snake was not – of Old Bald Peg.

Conclusion

Pedigrees of early racehorses are full of question marks, dead ends and questionable attributions. The names – exotic, homely and bizarre – tantalize. Behind them lie histories that are only fragmentarily apparent. We want to know more about them.

Nothing that we may discover has implications for Eclipse's reputation. Eclipse is Eclipse.

Appendix 3

The O'Kelly Family

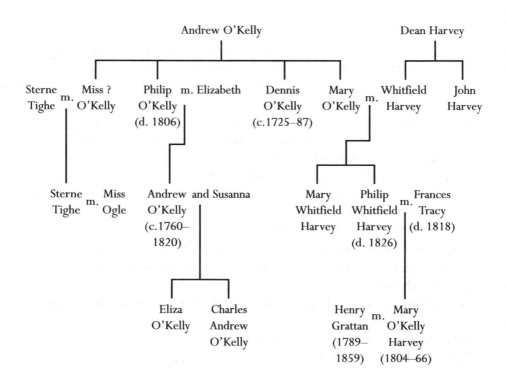

Appendix 4

Racing Terms, Historical and Contemporary

Bay A coppery brown – the most common colour in Thoroughbreds. Other Thoroughbred colours include black, brown (the distinction between black and brown is often fine), chestnut, grey, and roan (grey hairs with a base of a darker colour).

Betting post Where betting transactions took place on a racecourse before the introduction of betting rings. Bets were struck between individuals rather than, as later, between backers and bookmakers.

Black type Victory or a placing in a **Pattern** or Listed race will show in black (bold) type in sales catalogues. It is a valuable qualification for horses seeking a career at stud.

Blackleg A gambler, usually dishonest.

Blinkers A hood with eye-cups that reduces a horse's range of vision. Some horses need them to concentrate. A visor has slits in the cups, allowing a slightly better view.

Breeze-up A sale at which prospective purchasers can watch horses go through their paces.

Broodmare A mare employed for breeding.

By/out of A foal is 'by' its sire, and 'out of' its dam.

Claimer After a claiming race, any runner may be claimed for an advertised sum or more. This sum is reduced if the owner runs the horse with less weight.

Colt A male horse, younger than five.

Conformation The shape and build of a horse.

Cover To impregnate a mare.

Damsire The sire (father) of a dam (mother), or maternal grandfather.
Distance 240 yards. In Eclipse's day, a horse who had not passed the distance post by the time the winner had passed the finishing post was 'distanced'.
Do a tap A jockey dismounting from a horse who has run badly might say, 'He didn't do a tap.' The horse never got going properly.
Dotted up Won easily. Other favourite expressions include 'bolted up', 'hacked up', 'sluiced up', 'won doing handsprings', and 'won with his/her head in his/her chest'.

Each way Two bets: one that the horse will win, the other that the horse will be placed. A £1 each way bet costs £2. To be 'placed' means to finish first or second in races with five to seven runners (but only to finish first in races with four runners or fewer); first, second or third in races with eight to fifteen runners; and first, second, third or fourth in handicaps with sixteen runners or more. The odds with bookmakers are a fifth or (in most handicaps) a quarter of the win odds. Say you place £1 each way on a 10-1 shot in a handicap. The horse wins: you get £10 plus £2.50 (the place return, a quarter of the win return) plus your £2 stake – £14.50. The horse is placed: you get £2.50 plus the £1 of your stake that was the place bet – £3.50.
Exchange A betting exchange is an online version of a betting post: a place where layers and backers find each other to strike individual bets. Exchanges such as Betfair are controversial: critics say that they encourage corruption, allowing people to **lay** horses that they know will not win, or that they have the means of stopping from winning. The earliest indication that a horse is injured before a big race is often when the horse's exchange price lengthens.
Exposed An exposed horse has shown how good he or she is – the implication being, not good enough to win today's race. An unexposed horse may be about to show form in advance of any previously revealed.

Family A horse's ancestors in the **tail female** line. A horse's half brother or half sister has the same mother; having the same sire does not make horses half siblings.
Filly A female horse, younger than five.
Fizzy A fizzy horse is in an excitable state, or inclined to get that way. Also 'buzzy'.

Furlong One-eighth of a mile: 220 yards.

Gelding A castrated male horse. Temperamental horses who are unlikely to become stallions but who might be good racers usually get this treatment; most male horses who race at the age of six and above are gelded. In 2003, the gelding Funny Cide won the Kentucky Derby. Geldings are ineligible for the Epsom Derby.

Giving, receiving It is better to receive than to give. Receiving weight from a rival or rivals means carrying less; giving means carrying more.

Going The state of the ground. On British turf courses, the going descriptions are, in descending order of hardness: hard (a word that clerks of the course use rarely), firm, good to firm, good, good to soft ('soft' is 'yielding' in Ireland), soft, and heavy. It is said of some racehorses that they 'go on any ground', but most have preferences. Horses with economical, daisy-cutter actions usually prefer ground that is fast (on the firm side); those who bend their knees and pound the turf go better on, or perhaps are less disadvantaged by, slow, soft ground.

Greek Same as **blackleg**.

Hand Four inches, a unit of measurement of a horse's height. The measurement is from the ground to the withers – the top of a horse's shoulders. Eclipse is generally agreed to have been about 15.3 hands, which was a good height in the mid-eighteenth century but modest by the standards of Thoroughbreds today.

Handicap A race in which horses carry weights according to ratings allotted by the official handicapper. In theory, they should finish in a dead heat. An example from a handy copy of the *Racing Post*: a five-furlong handicap at Lingfield in which horses rated 72 to 83 took part, won by the 78-rated Zowington. He carried 8st 13lb. A filly called Ocean Blaze finished second; she was rated 76, and therefore carried 2lb less, 8st 11lb.

Handicapper In Britain, the official handicappers work for the British Horseracing Authority, and assign ratings that dictate the weights horses will carry in handicap races. If a horse is a handicapper, he or she specializes in this type of race, not being good enough to run in **Pattern** (Group) or Listed races. In the US, handicappers are racing enthusiasts who study form.

Horse Apart from the obvious, generic definition, the term implies an ungelded male of five years old and above.

Jockey Before it came exclusively to mean 'rider', jockey was a generic term for a racing man.

Lay To lay a horse is to accept the bet of someone backing it. Bookmakers are 'layers'.

Lead (leg) The leg that advances further. (In horses, the side of the lead foreleg and lead rear leg is usually the same.) The other one hits the ground first. A horse may 'change legs' (switching lead legs) while galloping, sometimes when feeling uncomfortable on the ground. Turning left, a horse should lead with the left foreleg; turning right, with the right. A horse turning left but on a right lead is on the 'wrong' leg.

Let down A horse that will not 'let himself down' is reluctant to gallop properly, perhaps because he finds the ground too hard, or too soft.

Maiden A horse who has not won a race. Or a race for horses who have not yet won a race.

Mare A female horse of five years old and above.

Missed out 'He missed out the open ditch.' This expression, which a steeplechase jockey might use, does not mean that the horse ran around the fence to avoid jumping it (a manoeuvre that would result in disqualification), but that he jumped it clumsily.

Nap A tipster's strongest recommendation.

Near/off side A horse's near side is the left; the off side is the right. A rider mounts and dismounts on the near side. Eclipse's white stocking was on his off hind leg.

Nick In breeding, a cross – of, for example, Eclipse with Herod mares, or Eclipse sons or daughters with Herod daughters or sons – that regularly produces good racers.

Nursery A **handicap** for two-year-olds.

Off/not off Primed, or not, to run to full potential.

On the bridle (or bit)/off the bridle (or bit) A horse on the bridle is coasting along, without effort from the jockey; when the horse is off the bridle, the jockey is working away.

Out of the handicap The top weight in the Grand National carries 11st 10lb; the lowest weight a horse can carry in the race is 10st. Let us say that the top weight has a handicap rating of 165. A horse with 10st on his back would, in theory, have a rating of 141 – 24lb (1st 10lb) lower. But what of a horse rated 135? He also carries 10st, but should, to have a chance against the others, carry 9st 8lb. He is 'out of the handicap'.

Pattern The 'Pattern' of racing was introduced in the early 1970s. Pattern races are the most prestigious contests, ranked Group 1, Group 2 and Group 3. Winning or placed form in these races, and in the Listed races that follow them in prestige, shows in **black type** in form guides and sales catalogues.
Pinhooking Buying foals with the aim of selling them on as yearlings.

Rough off To give a horse a holiday from training.
Rubbing-house Where horses in Eclipse's era were saddled, and where they were rubbed down after races or between heats.

Seller After a selling race, the winner is sold at auction, and other runners may also be bought.
Stud A stallion; more commonly, a farm with horses for breeding. A stud may house broodmares only.
Stuffy A stuffy horse needs lots of exercise to get fit.

Tail male, tail female Respectively, the top and bottom lines in pedigrees. The top line ascends through the sire to his sire (the grandsire), and through the grandsire's sire, and so on; the bottom line ascends through the dam to her dam (the granddam), and through the granddam's dam, and so on.
Thoroughbred A horse whose breeding satisfies the criteria of compilers of stud books.
Tote The Tote runs the Totalisator, a pool betting system known in France and the US as the Pari-mutuel. The UK and Ireland are unusual among racing countries in having a tote as well as bookmakers. France, the US, and Japan are among the nations with tote monopolies; Australia has bookmakers on-course; only some states license them elsewhere. The Tote (the company) is state-owned; at the time of writing, plans to sell it are on the shelf.

Bibliography

Books

Eclipse and O'Kelly

Anon., *The Genuine Memoirs of Dennis O'Kelly, Esq: Commonly Called Count O'Kelly* (C. Stalker, 1788)

Blyth, Henry, *The High Tide of Pleasure: Seven English Rakes* (Weidenfeld & Nicolson, 1970)

Church, Michael, *Eclipse: The Horse, the Race, the Awards* (Thoroughbred Advertising, 2000)

Clark, Bracy, *A Short History of the Celebrated Race-horse Eclipse* (London, 1835)

Cook, Theodore Andrea, *Eclipse and O'Kelly* (William Heinemann, 1907)

Hall, Sherwin, 'The Story of a Skeleton: Eclipse' in *Guardians of the Horse: Past, Present and Future* (British Equine Veterinary Association, 1999)

Sainbel, Charles Vial de, *Elements of Veterinary Art: Containing an Essay on the Proportions of the Celebrated Eclipse* (London, 1791)

Trew, Cecil G., *From 'Dawn' to 'Eclipse'* (Methuen, 1939)

Racing and General

Allison, W., *The British Thoroughbred Horse* (Grant Richards, 1901)

Anon., *A General and Particular Account of the Annular Eclipse of the Sun* (London, 1764)

—— *Historical Memoirs of His Late Royal Highness William-Augustus, Duke of Cumberland* (London, 1767)

—— *A List of the Sporting Ladies* (London, 1775)

—— *The Minor Jockey Club: Or a Sketch of the Manners of the Greeks* (R. Farnham, 1792)

Archenholz, Johann Wilhelm von, *A Picture of England* (P. Byrne, 1791)

Bayles, F. H., *Atlas and Review of British Race-Courses* (Equitable Publishing Syndicate, 1911)

Black, Robert, *The Jockey Club and Its Founders* (Smith, Elder & Co., 1891)

Blake, Robin, *George Stubbs and the Wide Creation* (Pimlico, 2006)

Bloch, Iwan, *Sexual Life in England* (Francis Aldor, 1938)

British Sporting Painting 1650–1850 (Arts Council, 1974)

Brown, Roger Lee, *A History of the Fleet Prison, London* (Edwin Mellen Press, 1996)

Buss, Frances Mary, *The North London Collegiate School 1850–1950* (Oxford University Press, 1950)

Cain, Glenye, *The Home Run Horse* (DRF Press, 2004)

Chinn, Carl, *Better Betting with a Decent Feller* (Harvester Wheatsheaf, 1991)

Church, Michael, *The Derby Stakes* (Racing Post, 2006)

—— *Three Generations of Leading Sires* (Racing Post, 1987)

Clayton, Tim, *The British Museum Hogarth* (British Museum Press, 2007)

Coaten, Arthur, 'The Evolution of Racing' in *Flat Racing* (Seeley Service & Co., 1940)

Conley, Kevin, *Stud* (Bloomsbury, 2002)

Curling, B. W. R., *British Racecourses* (Witherby, 1951)

Derby Day 200 (Royal Academy, 1979)

Egan, Pierce, *Anecdotes of the Turf, the Chase, the Ring, and the Stage* (London, 1827)

—— *Book of Sports* (London, 1832)

—— *Boxiana* (London, 1812)

—— *Sporting Anecdotes* (Thomas Hurst, J. Harris, J. Wheble, 1804)

Egerton, Judy, *British Sporting and Animal Paintings 1655–1867* (Tate Gallery, 1978)

—— *George Stubbs, Painter. Catalogue Raisonné* (Yale, 2007)

Ellis, Markman, *The Coffee House: A Cultural History* (Weidenfeld & Nicolson, 2004)

FitzGerald, Arthur, *Royal Thoroughbreds* (Sidgwick & Jackson, 1990)

—— *Thoroughbreds of the Crown* (Genesis Publications, 1999)

Fitzgerald, George, *An Appeal to the Jockey Club* (London, 1775)

Fitzpatrick, W. J., *Secret Service Under Pitt* (Longman, 1892)

Fountain, Robert, *William Wildman and George Stubbs* (British Sporting Arts Trust, 2004)

Fraser, Kevin J., *William Stukely and the Gout* (University of Melbourne, 1992)

Gatrell, Vic, *City of Laughter* (Atlantic Books, 2006)

Gill, James, *Racecourses of Great Britain* (Barrie & Jenkins, 1975)

Grego, Joseph, *Rowlandson the Caricaturist* (Chatto & Windus, 1880)

Grosley, Pierre Jean, *A Tour to London* (London, 1772)

Harcourt, Seymour, *The Gaming Calendar and Annals of Gaming* (London, 1820)

Harding, Samuel, *An Elegy on the Famous Old Horse Marsk* (London, 1780)

Hayes, John, *Rowlandson Watercolours and Drawings* (Phaidon, 1972)

Henderson, Andrew, *The Life of William Augustus, Duke of Cumberland* (J. Ridley, 1766)

Henderson, Tony, *Disorderly Women in 18th Century London* (Longman, 1999)

Hickey, William, *Memoirs* (ed. Peter Quennell, Hutchinson, 1960)

Hillenbrand, Laura, *Seabiscuit* (Fourth Estate, 2001)

Hitchcock, Tim, *Down and Out in Eighteenth-Century London* (Hambledon Continuum, 2004)

Holcroft, Thomas, *Memoirs of the Late Thomas Holcroft* (London, 1816)

Hone, William, *The Table Book* (Tegg & Co., 1827)

Hore, J. P., *History of Newmarket and Annals of the Turf* (Hore, 1885)

Jerdein, Charles and F. R. Kaye, *British Blood Lines* (J. A. Allen, 1955)

Kelly, Bernard W., *The Conqueror of Culloden* (R. & T. Washbourne, 1902)

Kiste, John Van der, *King George II and Queen Caroline* (Sutton, 1997)

Lane, Charles, *British Racing Prints* (Sportsman's Press, 1990)

Lawrence, John, *The History and Delineation of the Horse* (Albion Press, 1809)

—— *A Philosophical and Practical Treatise on Horses* (H. D. Symonds, 1802)

—— and John Scott, *The Sportsman's Repository* (London, 1820)

Leicester, Charles, *Bloodstock Breeding* (Odhams Press, 1957)

Lennox, Muriel, *Northern Dancer* (Mainstream, 1999)

Lillywhite, Bryant, *London Coffee Houses* (Allen & Unwin, 1963)

Longrigg, Roger, *The History of Horse Racing* (Macmillan, 1972)

Lyle, R. C., *Royal Newmarket* (Putnam, 1940)

Lysons, Daniel, *The Environs of London* (London, 1792–96)

Magee, Sean, *Ascot: The History* (Methuen, 2002)

Markham, Gervase, *How to Choose, Ride, Train and Diet, Both Hunting-Horses and Running Horses* (James Roberts, 1599)

Morris, Tony, *Thoroughbred Stallions* (Crowood, 1990)

Mortimer, Roger, *The History of the Derby Stakes* (Michael Joseph, 1973)

—— *The Jockey Club* (Cassell, 1958)

—— Richard Onslow and Peter Willett, *Biographical Encyclopaedia of British Flat Racing* (Macdonald, 1978)

Muir, J. B., *W. T. Frampton and the Dragon* (Sporting Fine Art Gallery, 1895)

Noakes, Aubrey, *Sportsmen in a Landscape* (Bodley Head, 1954)

O'Brien, Jacqueline and Ivor Herbert, *Vincent O'Brien: The Official Biography* (Bantam Press, 2005)

Orchard, Vincent, *Tattersalls* (Hutchinson, 1953)

Orton, John, *Turf Annals of York and Doncaster* (York, 1844)

Osbaldiston, William Augustus, *The British Sportsman* (London, 1792)

Oxford Dictionary of National Biography (Oxford University Press, 2004)

Pagones, Rachel, *Dubai Millennium* (Highdown, 2007)

Parsons, Philip, *Newmarket: Or an Essay on the Turf* (London, 1775)

Percivall, William, *Twelve Lectures on the Form and Action of the Horse* (London, 1850)

Picard, Liza, *Dr Johnson's London* (Weidenfeld & Nicolson, 2000)

Pick, William, *The Turf Register and Sportsman and Breeder's Stud Book* (York, 1803)

Piggott, Lester and Sean Magee, *Lester's Derbys* (Methuen, 2004)

Pigott, Charles, *The Jockey Club: Or a Sketch of the Manners of the Age* (H. D. Symonds, 1792)

Porter, Roy, *English Society in the 18th Century* (Pelican, 1982)

—— *London: A Social History* (Hamish Hamilton, 1994)

Prior, C. M., *Early Records of the Thoroughbred* (The Sportsman Office, 1924)

Randall, John and Tony Morris, *A Century of Champions* (Portway Press, 1999)

—— *Guinness Horse Racing: The Records* (Guinness, 1985)

Rede, Leman Thomas, *Anecdotes and Biography* (London, 1799)

Rice, James, *The History of the British Turf* (Sampson Low, 1879)

Robertson, J. B., 'The Origin of the Thoroughbred' in *Flat Racing* (Seeley Service & Co., 1940)

Robinson, Edward Forbes, *The Early History of the Coffee House in England* (Dolphin Press, 1972)

Seth-Smith, Michael, *Bred for the Purple* (Frewin, 1969)

Shoemaker, Robert, *The London Mob* (Hambledon Continuum, 2004)

Siltzer, Frank, *Newmarket* (Cassell, 1923)

Steinmetz, Andrew, *The Gaming Table, Its Votaries and Victims* (Tinsley Brothers, 1870)

Taplin, William, *The Gentleman's Stable Directory* (J. & J. Robinson and C. & G. Kearsley, 1791)

Taunton, Theophilus, *Famous Horses* (Sampson Low, 1901)

Taunton, Thomas Henry, *Portraits of Celebrated Race Horses of Past and Present Centuries* (Sampson Low, 1887)

Thompson, Jon, *Mark Wallinger* (Ikon Gallery, 1995)

Thompson, Laura, *Newmarket: From James I to the Present Day* (Virgin, 2000)

Thormanby, *Sporting Stories* (Mills & Boon, 1909)

Tyrrel, John, *Running Racing* (Quiller, 1997)

Ulbrich, Richard, *The Great Stallion Book* (Libra, 1986)

Waller, Maureen, *1700: Scenes from London Life* (Hodder & Stoughton, 2000)

Watson, Rev. John Selby, *The Reasoning Power in Animals* (London, 1867)

Waugh, Auberon, *Will This Do?* (Century, 1991)

Weinreb, Ben and Christopher Hibbert (eds), *The London Encyclopaedia* (Macmillan, 1983)

Wentworth, Lady, *Thoroughbred Racing Stock* (Allen & Unwin, 1960)

West, William, *Tavern Anecdotes* (London, 1825)

Whyte, James Christie, *History of the British Turf* (Henry Colburn, 1840)

Willett, Peter, *The Classic Racehorse* (Stanley Paul, 1981)

────── *A History of the General Stud Book* (Weatherbys, 1991)

────── *The Story of Tattersalls* (Stanley Paul, 1987)

Williams, J. D., *History of the Name O'Kelly* (Mercier, 1977)

Williams, Richard, *Egham Eclipses* (Egham-by-Runnymede Historical Society, 1999)

Williams, Sheridan, *UK Solar Eclipses from Year 1* (Clock Tower Press, 1996)

Yuill, Alan, *Thoroughbred Studs of Great Britain* (Weidenfeld & Nicolson, 1991)

Charlotte Hayes

Anon., *Nocturnal Revels* (M. Goadby, 1779)

Burford, E. J., *Royal St James's* (Robert Hale, 1988)

────── *Wits, Wenchers and Wantons* (Robert Hale, 1986)

────── and Joy Wotton, *Private Vices – Public Virtues* (Robert Hale, 1995)

Linnane, Fergus, *Madams, Bawds and Brothel-Keepers of London* (Sutton, 2005)

'OMIAH: An Ode Addressed to Charlotte Hayes', *The New Foundling Hospital for Wit* (London, 1784)

Rubenhold, Hallie, *The Covent Garden Ladies* (Sutton, 2005)
—— *Harris's List of Covent Garden Ladies* (Sutton, 2005)
Thompson, Edward, *The Courtesan* (J. Harrison, 1770)
—— *The Meretriciad* (C. Moran, 1761, 1770)

Epsom

Andrews, James, *Reminiscences of Epsom* (L. W. Andrews & Son, 1904)
Bawtree, Harold, *A Few Notes on Banstead Downs with Some Remarks on Epsom Races* (William Pile, 1928)
Dorling, E. E., *Epsom and the Dorlings* (Stanley Paul, 1939)
Dorling, W., *Some Particulars Relating to the History of Epsom* (Epsom, 1825)
Epsom Common (Epsom Common Association, 1981)
Harte, Jeremy, *Epsom: A History and Celebration* (Francis Frith Collection, 2005)
Home, Gordon, *Epsom: Its History and Surroundings* (Homeland Association, 1901)
Hunn, David, *Epsom Racecourse* (Davis-Poynter, 1973)
Pownall, H., *Some Particulars Relating to the History of Epsom* (Epsom, 1825)
Salter, Brian J., *Epsom Town Downs and Common* (Living History, 1976)
White, Reginald, *Ancient Epsom* (William Pile, 1928)

Racing Records

Cheny, John, *An Historical List of All Horse Matches Run, and of All Plates and Prizes Run for in England* (London, various years)
Duke of Ancaster's Stud Book (1772–78)
The General Stud Book (Weatherbys, 2006)
Heber, Reginald, *An Historical List of Horse Matches Run; and of Plates and Prizes Run for in Great Britain and Ireland* (London, various years)
Newmarket Match Book (1754)
Pick, William, *An Authentic Historical Racing Calendar* (York, 1785)
Pond, John, *Sporting Kalendar* (London, various years)
The Racing Calendar (Weatherbys, 1773–)
Towers, William Sydney, *An Introduction to a General Stud Book* (Weatherbys, 1791)
Tuting, William and Thomas Fawconer, *The Sporting Calendar: Containing an Account of the Plates, Matches, and Sweepstakes Run for in Great Britain* (London, various years)

Walker, B., *An Historical List of Horse-Matches, Plates and Prizes, Run for in Great Britain and Ireland* (London, 1769, 1770)

Newspapers and Journals

Annual Register (various years)

The British Racehorse (George Rathbone, 'Reconstruction of Eclipse', November 1963)

The Burlington Magazine (David Mannings, 'Reynolds and the Shaftos: Three Letters and a Deposition', November 1997)

The Field (December 1920; June 1937)

Gentleman's Magazine (November 1765; 1787 supplement; October 1802)

Guardian (Sean Magee, 'The Day When Arkle Became the Greatest', November 2005)

Independent on Sunday (Fiammetta Rocco, 'Ma'am Darling: The Princess Driven by Loyalty and Duty', February 1998)

Lloyd's Evening Post (1764, 1765)

London Chronicle (1764, 1765)

London Evening Post (1764, 1765)

The London Magazine (1772)

Monthly Review (1788)

Morning Post (1775)

The Newgate Calendar (exclassics.com)

Observer (Clare Balding, 'The Sheikh Is Unstirred', October 2005)

Pacemaker (Tony Morris, 'Sorting Fact from Fiction', October 2007)

Racing Post Bloodstock Review 2007

St James's Chronicle (1765)

The Sporting Magazine (various issues)

The Tatler (July 1927)

The Thoroughbred Record (September 1920; June 1924)

The Times (digital archive)

Town & Country (1769, 1770)

The Veterinary Record (March 1991)

Whitehall Evening Post (1788, 1789)

World Fashionable Advertiser (1788)

York Courant (1770)

Websites

Ascot.co.uk
Australian Government Culture and Recreation website/ Melbourne Cup
Bloodlines.net
British Horseracing Authority website
Coolmore.com
The Cox Library website
Epsom Salt Council website
Horsesonly.com (Mariana Haun, 'The X Factor')
HotBoxingNews.com
The Jockey Club website
Measuring Worth website
National Museum of Australia website
North London Collegiate School website
Pedigreequery.com
Royal Veterinary College website
SportingChronicle.com
TBHeritage.com
Traceyclann.com
Victorian-cinema.net
Weatherbys website

Archives

Canons records, North London Collegiate School
Clay Hill papers, Surrey History Centre
Fitzwilliam/Langdale papers, Public Record Office, Northern Ireland
Fleet prison debtors' schedules, London Metropolitan Archives
Fleet records, National Archives
Noble Collection, Guildhall Library
Papers of Colonel Andrew Dennis O'Kelly, Brynmor Jones Library, University of Hull
Plumer papers, London Metropolitan Archives
St Lawrence, Little Stanmore, burial records, London Metropolitan Archives
Wills of Dennis O'Kelly, Andrew Dennis O'Kelly and Charles Andrew O'Kelly, National Archives

Acknowledgements

Timothy Cox has been extraordinarily hospitable and helpful, allowing me to work at the Cox Library and hunting down information that I would never have discovered on my own. He has also offered many useful suggestions about the text. Any surviving errors are mine.

I got the idea to write this book when I read the passage on Eclipse and Dennis O'Kelly in Glenye Cain's excellent *The Home Run Horse*. She has been very generous in her encouragement. Sean Magee, another writer with far better qualifications than mine for this venture, has given me kind assistance. Michael Church, author of the splendid *Eclipse: The Horse, The Race, The Awards*, also selflessly welcomed me as I stepped on to his territory. I am grateful, too, for the help of the racing writers Tony Morris and Rachel Pagones, and of Martin Stevens of *Pacemaker*.

Caroline Baldock and Gerald Goodman of the Epsom Equestrian Conservation Group took me on a tour of Dennis O'Kelly's and Eclipse's haunts in Epsom. The trainer Philip Mitchell showed me the old stable block at Downs House, home to the O'Kelly racers. I thank John and Rebecca Morton of Thirty Acre Stables, and Jeremy Harte of Bourne Hall Museum.

David Oldrey answered my questions about the O'Kellys, the Jockey Club and the *Review of the Turf*. Dr Renate Weller made time to see me to discuss the Royal Veterinary College's work on Eclipse's skeleton; and I thank her colleagues Professor Matthew Binns and Elspeth Keith. Dr Mim Bower, of the McDonald Institute for Archaeological Research at the University of Cambridge, patiently explained her genetic research.

I thank Judy Burg and Helen Roberts at the archives in the Brynmor

Jones Library, University of Hull; Karen Morgan and the library staff at the North London Collegiate School for Girls; Anne Craig of the Public Record Office, Northern Ireland; Jane Lewis of the Surrey History Centre; Graham Snelling and Alun Grundy of the National Horseracing Museum; Diane Bellis of Waddesdon Manor; Kathryn Jones of The Royal Collection Trust; Wes Proudlock of the Australian Institute of Genealogical Studies; Dermot Mulligan of Carlow County Museum; and the staff at the British Library, National Archives at Kew, London Metropolitan Archives, Westminster City Archives, and Guildhall Library.

I also wish to thank Robin Blake, author of *George Stubbs and the Wide Creation*; Peter Mackenzie and Lindsay Ankers of Mainstream Publishing; John Sharp of Weatherbys; Adam Caplin; and Marion Regan.

My editor, Selina Walker, has been a constant guide, never allowing my knowledge of her faith in the book to settle into the complacent assumption that I could not make it better. I thank Sheila Lee for her expert and resourceful work on the illustrations; and everyone at my friendly, collegiate publisher, Transworld. And I thank my agent, Ros Edwards, a friend and support as always.

Picture Acknowledgements

151 The Oaks, Surrey, anonymous engraving.
156 'The Derby – At Lunch' from *London: a Pilgrimage* by Gustave Doré, 1872.
174 A view, in Indian ink, of Cannons, in the parish of Little Stanmore, or Whitchurch, near Edgeware, the seat of D. O'Kelly, Esq., c. 1790–1810: by permission of the British Library, Maps K Top 30.25.c.
202 *George IV at Ascot*, drawing by John Doyle: © The Trustees of the British Museum, Department of Prints and Drawings.
207 *How to Escape Winning* satire by Thomas Rowlandson, 1791: © The Trustees of the British Museum, Department of Prints and Drawings.
217 Dorsal view of the muscle structure of a progressively dissected horse, study No 7 from 'The Anatomy of the Horse', 1766 by George Stubbs: Royal Academy of Arts, London/The Bridgeman Art Library.
237 Anonymous portrait of Lord George William Cavendish Bentinck, pen and ink, nineteenth century: private collection/The Bridgeman Art Library.
268 *Elements of the veterinary art, containing An essay on the proportions of the celebrated Eclipse . . .*, by Charles Vial de Sainbel, 1791: The Huntington Library, San Marino, California, RB 614264.

Colour sections

First Section

Eclipse, by George Stubbs, 1770: private collection/The Bridgeman Art Library.

View of the Piazza, Covent Garden, coloured engraving after Thomas Sandby, 1770: Guildhall Library Print Room © Corporation of London; *Vauxhall Gardens*, aquatint after Thomas Rowlandson and A. C. Pugin, 1808: © Mary Evans Picture Library/Alamy; *The King's Place*, watercolour by Thomas Rowlandson: © Atkinson Art Gallery, Southport, Lancs./The Bridgeman Art Library; *A St James's Beauty*, coloured engraving, 1784: © The Trustees of the British Museum, Department of Prints and Drawings.

Marske aged 20, oil painting by George Stubbs, 1770: courtesy of Sotheby's Picture Library; *Eclipse with John Oakley Up*, oil painting by John Nost

Sartorius, 1771: © Christie's Images Ltd; *A Riding Party in a Country Landscape*, oil painting by Judith Lewis, c. 1755; detail of *Eclipse with Mr Wildman and his Sons*, after an oil painting by George Stubbs, c. 1770: © Mary Evans Picture Library/Alamy; *The Eclipse Macarony*, coloured etching by R. St G. Mansergh, 1773: National Portrait Gallery, London.

A Hint for an Escape at the next Spring Meeting, engraved satire after Isaac Cruikshank, 1792: © The Trustees of the British Museum, Department of Prints and Drawings; *The Jockey Club or Newmarket Meeting*, coloured engraving after Thomas Rowlandson, 1811: Jockey Club Estates; *Sir Charles Bunbury with Cox, his trainer, and a Stable-Lad*, painting by Benjamin Marshall, ?1801, a study for *Surprise and Eleanor*: © Tate, London, 2008.

Eclipse, coloured illustration from *Cassell's Book of the Horse*, 1890, after a painting by George Garrard: © Mary Evans Picture Library/ Alamy.

Second Section

Detail of *Hambletonian*, oil painting by George Stubbs, c. 1800: Mount Stewart, The Londonderry Collection (The National Trust) © The National Trust.

A Bookmaker and his client outside the Ram Inn, Newmarket, pen and water-colour, by Thomas Rowlandson: Paul Mellon Collection/The Bridgeman Art Library; *Dennis O'Kelly with Others, at Newmarket*, ink and watercolour, by Thomas Rowlandson: The Halifax Collection; *The Race Meeting*, ink and watercolour, by Thomas Rowlandson: courtesy of Sotheby's Picture Library; *The Betting Post*, watercolour by Thomas Rowlandson, 1789: copyright © V&A Images.

Tattersall's Horse Repository, coloured aquatint after A. C. Pugin and Thomas Rowlandson, from *Ackerman's Microcosm of London*, 1808: © Historical Picture Archive/Corbis; *The Subscription Club Room*, pen and watercolour by Thomas Rowlandson: private collection/© Agnew's, London, UK/The Bridgeman Art Library; *Richard Tattersall with Highflyer in the background* oil painting by Thomas Beach: private collection/The Bridgeman Art Library.

The Derby Jig, ink and watercolour, by George Moutard Woodward, 1797:

courtesy of Sotheby's Picture Library; *Fête Champêtre at The Oaks, near Epsom: the Supper Room*, oil painting by Antonio Zucchi (1726–95): © The Right Hon. Earl of Derby/The Bridgeman Art Library; *Derby Sweepstake*, oil painting by J. Francis Sartorius, 1791–2: Epsom Library, Surrey/The Bridgeman Art Library; *Derby Day,* poster by Vera Willoughby, 1932: © Transport for London; Derby Day, 1928, coloured photo by Francis Frith: Francis Frith Collection/akg-images.

Eclipse relics: Jockey Club Estates; Eclipse skeleton: Royal Veterinary College.

Index